Assisted Suicide: The Liberal, Humanist Case against Legalization

Assisted Suicide: The Liberal, Humanist Case Against Legalization

Kevin Yuill
University of Sunderland, UK

First published in hardcover 2013
Published in paperback 2015 by
PALGRAVE MACMILLAN

Palgrave Macmillan in the UK is an imprint of Macmillan Publishers Limited, registered in England, company number 785998, of Houndmills, Basingstoke, Hampshire RG21 6XS.

Palgrave Macmillan in the US is a division of St Martin's Press LLC, 175 Fifth Avenue, New York, NY 10010.

Palgrave Macmillan is the global academic imprint of the above companies and has companies and representatives throughout the world.

Palgrave® and Macmillan® are registered trademarks in the United States, the United Kingdom, Europe and other countries.

ISBN 978–1–137–28629–1   hardback
ISBN 978–1–137–48746–9   paperback

This book is printed on paper suitable for recycling and made from fully managed and sustained forest sources. Logging, pulping and manufacturing processes are expected to conform to the environmental regulations of the country of origin.

A catalogue record for this book is available from the British Library.

A catalog record for this book is available from the Library of Congress.

Typeset by MPS Limited, Chennai, India.

For Bridget, Bessie and Ellie

Contents

Foreword

If there is one issue that could do with some cool-headed rethinking, it is assisted suicide. In this moral conundrum more than any other, people have a tendency to take an intellectual position based less on reasoned, thoughtful consideration, and more on the pack mentality of their particular side in the modern-day culture wars. They take what they believe to be the 'expected position' of their social, cultural set.

So those who profess to be liberal, secular and humanist take a pro-assisted-suicide stance, imagining that this demonstrates their hostility to the exercise of medical or political authority over the sovereignty of the individual. And those of a religious persuasion, particularly amongst groups described as the Christian right, take a resolutely anti-assisted-suicide position, in the hope of proving their belief in the sanctity of human life and in the authority of God over the creation and ending of human existence.

Because these thinkers and activists tend to be driven by political expediency rather than by a genuinely open-minded engagement with the issue at hand, by a desire to say something about themselves and their characters rather than about the likely impact on society of legalizing assisted suicide, they end up tying themselves in all sorts of moral knots. They take a position on assisted suicide that actually runs counter to many of the fundamental tenets of their own professed moral outlook.

So we now have so-called humanists supporting what seems quite clearly to be a profoundly anti-human, misanthropic ideal: that is, that society should give an official green light to the snuffing out of lives that are considered by some to be worthless or 'too difficult', whether that be as a result of sickness, disability or mental malaise. And we now have Christians insisting that any hurrying of an imminent death is wrong, any private, love-driven assistance of the ending of a life is a sin, despite the fact that this practice has existed for as long as human beings have, and that without it, there would undoubtedly be an increase in human suffering – something that modern-day Christians, at least, claim to be against.

Into this theatrical and shallow moral punch-up comes Kevin Yuill's most welcome contribution. In forensically picking apart the idea of assisted dying, right down to interrogating the terminology that is now used to describe what in the past would have been known as 'voluntary euthanasia', Yuill very usefully reminds us that there is still a huge amount to excavate and pore over in this moral issue that has been treated in a largely superficial fashion by too many of those who have addressed it.

And more importantly, in critiquing the idea of assisted suicide from a liberal, humanist perspective rather than a religious one, Yuill demonstrates that careful and humane analysis is a better guide to morality than the instinct to obediently line up with one's own culture-war pack against Them, the other side. This book reminds us that if the essence of humanism is always to ask, 'Will this course of action benefit humankind or not benefit humankind?', then humanists ought seriously to rethink their position on the legalization of assisted suicide, and oppose it.

The humanist mistake

Amongst those who might broadly be described as secular, liberal and cosmopolitan, support for the legalization of assisted suicide is high. It is this section of the cultural elite that produces essays, newspaper articles and campaign literature on how important it is for people to have a 'good death' – for the very sick to be allowed to opt out of life towards the end, and for all of us to have a guarantee, in law, that if we become frail and useless in the future, then we too will be permitted to call upon our loved ones to 'assist' our suicide.

This thinking often gets packaged up as the 'right to die', as if what is driving this humanist-led campaign is the ideal of moral autonomy, of individual control over our bodies and our destinies. Indeed, it can often seem that the right to die is the only freedom that fires up and enthuses some sections of the cultural elite. They have little time for the right to free speech or the right of unfettered freedom of movement for migrants, to give just two examples. But the right to die? The right to end one's own existence and, with it, one's autonomy? That is a right they feel passionate about.

What we have here is the dressing-up of a downbeat, misanthropic political position in the language of freedom and autonomy. Recognizing that the old idea of euthanasia, of seeking to solve social and cultural problems through recourse to the killing of 'problematic' human beings, is for very good reason held in low esteem in the twenty-first century, these humanists have instead adopted the more acceptable language of rights for their promotion of assisted suicide. Strip this language away, however, and it soon becomes clear that the humanist drive for assisted suicide is actually underpinned by an anti-humanist outlook that is not a million miles away from the outlook of the euthanasia lobbies of old.

Very old, very sick and very incapacitated people who have a short period of time left to live must be given the freedom to kill themselves and to have someone assist them in this task, claim supporters of assisted dying. In short, this is all about individual freedom of choice, the exercise of personal sovereignty against legal and medical establishments that would force these unfortunate people to carry on living against their will. However, very often supporters of assisted dying reveal, sometimes unwittingly, that they are motivated fundamentally by social concerns, particularly by the social concern that we can no longer cope with the growing numbers of elderly, frail people, rather than by a passionate attachment to the ideal of individual autonomy.

Consider one of the most popular pro-assisted suicide newspaper commentaries of recent times. Written by Melanie Reid, a journalist who became a paraplegic following a horse-riding accident, and published in *The Times*, Britain's newspaper of record, the piece made the case for granting the very ill and the very incapacitated the right to die. It was hailed by assisted-suicide campaigners and by secularist thinkers as the 'unanswerable case for the right to die', the final word, surely, on this hotly contested liberty to end our lives in periods of extreme physical ailment.

However, amidst its pleas for choice and autonomy for the sick, Reid's piece contained the following, extraordinarily revealing sentence: 'It is ridiculous that an educated society, facing an unaffordable explosion in dementia and age-related illness, is still prevaricating over [assisted suicide].'

What is extraordinary about that sentence is, firstly, that it very clearly expresses an old-style euthanistic outlook; it expresses the idea that allowing sick and old people to kill themselves is important because there are *too many of them*, too many elderly folk with dementia, and they are 'unaffordable'. The second striking thing is that this idea seems to have been readily accepted by the numerous campaigners and journalists who praised Reid's piece. Certainly in their effusive promotion of the article, none of them sought to distance themselves from that sentence, suggesting either that they agree with it or that they do not consider the promotion of voluntary euthanasia on the basis that society cannot afford to look after certain people (in this case the old and mentally ill) to be remarkable or noteworthy.

The conflation of claims to individual autonomy with the depiction of death as a solution to alleged social problems is a recurring theme in pro-assisted-suicide campaigning. So the British peer and esteemed philosopher Baroness Mary Warnock, one of the best-known intellectual agitators for the right to die, has argued that some elderly people should consider their possible 'duty to die' if they feel that they are a 'burden on the state'. 'If you are demented...you are wasting the resources of the National Health Service,' she argued in 2008.

Likewise, in 2011, in a very influential piece in the *New York Times*, columnist David Brooks drew a link between the current economic crisis and the failure of society to grant people the right to die. Under the headline 'Death and Budgets', Brooks declared: 'The fiscal crisis is about many things, but one of them is our inability to face death – our willingness to spend our nation into bankruptcy to extend life for a few more sickly months.' In other words, not allowing the very ill to die sooner than nature intends is having a detrimental impact on society and the economy, since these sick people cost a great deal to look after.

Time and again, thinkers and activists who claim only to support the exercise of individual autonomy at the end of life talk openly about the fact that letting people die will save society money and resources. Indeed, this has become one of the key implicit arguments for assisted suicide, since, in Melanie Reid's words, it is 'ridiculous' that a society in crisis, a society filled with more old, demented people than have ever existed before, has failed to legalize the ending of sick people's lives.

Here, with this promotion of the death of ill people as a way of easing economic and social problems, the apparently humanist side in the debate about assisted suicide echoes the arguments of some of the most anti-humanist movements in history. In the nineteenth and twentieth centuries, amongst political movements that were regressive and racist, euthanasia became a popular cause. Bereft of humanist ideals, and possessed of the belief that all social ills were caused by the continued existence of undesirable and mentally or physically incapable people, these movements promoted euthanasia as a balm for an at-sea society.

Most notoriously, the Nazis pushed the idea that the old, sick and infirm were an 'unaffordable' burden, and thus society would benefit from their removal. For example, in justifying its euthanizing of disabled people, the Nazi regime said: 'They represent a spatial and economic burden...damaging the demands of those fit for life through the heavy expenditure which they occasion.'

Of course, modern-day campaigners are not remotely Nazi-like; absolutely no one is proposing the *forced* euthanizing of sick or disabled people. However, there is an uncomfortably uncanny resemblance between the modern description of certain people as an economic 'burden on the state' and the old euthanasia lobby's handwringing over the 'heavy expenditure' that infirm people occasion, which both suggests a link between euthanasia then and assisted suicide now and which calls into question the humanist pretensions of many of today's agitators for the 'right to die'.

How have some twenty-first-century humanists ended up campaigning for something as historically coloured as the promotion of dying as a solution to social dilemmas? It is in large part down to the return and rehabilitation of Malthusian thinking and the crisis of humanist ideals in the twenty-first century.

Ours is an era in which we find it increasingly difficult to assign value and meaning to human life. Human existence is today more likely to be discussed as something toxic (to the environment) and burdensome (to the economy) rather than as something potentially fruitful and beneficial in its own right. From the environmentalist idea of the 'human footprint', where mankind's impact on the planet is measured in terms of its alleged destructiveness rather than in terms of the vast progress it has achieved, to the idea of a 'grey tsunami', where the medical advances that allow people to live for longer than ever before are said to have unleashed a crisis of 'too many' old, sick people, we can see a relentless depiction of certain forms of human life as dangerous, destructive or just plain pointless.

This represents a return, in new language, of the ideology of the original population scaremonger, the eighteenth-century anti-humanist thinker Thomas Malthus. His belief that nature could sustain only a certain number of people is being rehabilitated under the guise of environmentalism. And his prejudice that certain kinds of human life were less useful and precious than others – in his view, reproduction amongst the poor and ill-educated was particularly problematic – is being rehabilitated in the modern idea that the very old and very ill, particularly those who lack the means to sustain themselves independently, are little more than a 'burden on the state', and are in fact one of the causes of the fiscal crisis, in David Brooks' argument.

Indeed, so uncomfortable have we become with the creation and exercise of human life that some thinkers now elevate non-existence as preferable to existence. For example, British population theorist David Nicholson-Lord has argued that because a 'non-existent person has no environmental impact', meaning that 'the emissions saving is instant and total', it is possible to say that *not* existing is more moral than existing.

Once, the arena of ethics and morality concerned itself with the question of the 'good life', of how humans might live fruitfully and happily; now, we are more likely to hear philosophical talk about the 'good death' and ruminations on the superior morality of human non-existence, where the most ethical life is that which leaves the smallest footprint, the least impact on its surroundings or on future generations, the tiniest 'burden', whether on nature or the economy.

This all points to a profound crisis in humanist thinking. It seems clear that today's renewed interest in euthanasia – or assisted suicide, as we must now call it – springs from this crisis, from the redefinition of human existence as toxic and from the dearth of belief in mankind's ability to find social, progressive solutions to social dilemmas such as our ageing population, the fiscal crisis, the problem of pollution, and so on. In such a climate, with true humanism in retreat and in the absence of any properly social-based discussion of the problems facing mankind, it makes sense that the idea of problematizing and possibly even removing individuals who are judged to be useless and burdensome should make such a comeback.

One of the most valuable contributions made by Yuill's book is its disentanglement of the ideals of traditional humanism from the current campaigning for legalized assisted suicide. For, as he recognizes, the reorientation of those who profess to be humanist around an issue underpinned by rehabilitated anti-humanist ideals actually speaks to the hollowing-out of humanism as we once knew it.

The new attack on autonomy

Yuill is also right to raise fundamental questions about the use of the term 'autonomy' in discussions about the right to die. Moral autonomy, the right of the individual to exercise dominion over his life and affairs, is the value most often claimed by supporters of assisted suicide. Presenting themselves as implacable critics of both political intransigence on the matter of end-of-life choice and the medical establishment's belief that it knows best when an individual should be permitted to die, the thinkers and activists of the assisted-suicide lobby claim to be fighting for the right of true individual autonomy.

However, this is disingenuous. Because in truth, the assisted-suicide lobby's insertion of social and economic criteria into very ill and very infirm people's end-of-life decisions also represents a powerful diminution of those people's moral autonomy. The injection of abstract, external concerns into the discussion about how sick individuals choose to live and die – concerns such as the need to ease the fiscal crisis by saving on healthcare for the elderly and the idea that the ageing popu-lation is 'unaffordable' – has the inexorable effect of polluting sick and elderly people's exercise of autonomy.

Supporters of assisted suicide most frequently use the word 'choice': all of us, when old enough and sick enough to fulfil the criteria set down by future legislation on assisted suicide, should have the choice to end our lives, if necessary with the assistance of another.

However, there is a great deal of implicit moral pressure in the dis-cussion and promotion of assisted suicide. The idea that certain groups of people are a 'burden on the state', and therefore that it would be a *good* thing for society to grant them the ability to end their lives, has the effect of, if not quite negating choice, then certainly demean-ing it by making it subject to external economic pressures and political prejudices.

This is particularly the case with elderly people. The economic cri-sis has heightened the modern generational hostility towards the old. In many of the public discussions about the economy, the recession is depicted as a product of generational ineptitude and selfishness on the part of the baby boomers – those born between 1946 and 1964 – rather than being understood as a social phenomenon driven by the structural decay of modern capitalism. It is now commonplace to hear members of older generations being described as 'bed blockers', for daring to live in three-bedroom houses on their own, and as having 'stolen the family silver', for daring to live comfortable lives in comparison with elderly people in the past. And as we have seen, the elderly are now also fre-quently discussed as a burden on society's resources, particularly in the arena of healthcare.

Into this anti-elderly hostility comes the idea that it would be good to grant infirm old people the 'right to die' – or at least that it is 'ridicu-lous' that recession-hit Western societies are still prevaricating over the establishment of this 'right'. One is compelled to ask: when sick old people are continually presented as a 'burden', even as the destroyers of the economic prospects of younger generations, are they really being given a clear, undiluted choice in the assisted-suicide discussion? Or are they being given something closer to an ultimatum: pursue your 'duty to die', as Baroness Warnock described it, and free up your bed and the health service for the benefit of young and middle-aged people who are still capable of contributing to society?

Under the cover of promoting moral autonomy for the very sick against those sections of society that would compel them to continue living, supporters of assisted suicide are in fact undermining autonomy

by institutionalizing an intellectual logic which would compel people to die; which implicitly promotes the idea of a 'duty to die', in
fact, and which infects end-of-life decision-making with highly dubi-
ous and often offensive ideas about sick people's unaffordable costs and
burdensome existence.

The so-called humanist side in this discussion profoundly misinter-
prets where the assault on autonomy is coming from today. It is not
coming from a state that callously forces even the suicidal to continue
living; after all, as Yuill points out, committing suicide is no longer
a crime in Britain and it is widely recognized that, in hospitals, care
homes and in the family home, very discreet, very measured 'assisted
suicides' are carried out. There is no one who, either by his own hand or
through the assistance of a loved one or a trusted doctor, could not find
a way to autonomously end his life without the authorities knowing (or
caring).

No, the undermining of moral autonomy is in fact being carried out,
ironically, by those who support assisted suicide. It is their misanthropic
morality, their intoxication of the discussion about the end of life with
their own moralistic take on the economy, society and the future, which
restricts the exercise of individuals' own moral autonomy. Indeed, today,
to insist on the right to continue living despite the economic or environmental cost of one's life, despite the 'uselessness' of one's life in
comparison with the lives of other, more able-bodied individuals, is
surely regarded as immoral – after all, it sins against the new moralities
of environmental awareness and generational responsibility.

The promoters of assisted suicide, in unthinkingly adopting many of
the anti-humanist sentiments of our age, have contributed to a situation
where sick and infirm people are implicitly encouraged to feel bad for
wanting to live, for doing that most human of things: struggling on,
continuing to exist because one sees profound moral worth in one's life
and relationships.

Religious opportunism

Criticizing the side that supports assisted suicide is not to imply that
the side that most vocally opposes it – mainly the Christian lobby – is
blemish-free and worthy of intellectual support. On the contrary, what
is most striking about the religious opposition to assisted suicide is how
much it is also driven by a crisis of values and legitimacy and by a need
to discover an issue through which Christianity might reassert itself in
our increasingly secularized, values-lite era.

This is where I might part company to a certain extent with Yuill. I think I am far more sceptical about the religious lobby's attachment to an anti-euthanasia outlook. It seems to me to be driven less by first principles and careful thought than by a quite desperate scrabble for an issue through which increasingly hollowed-out religious institutions might make a public performance of their continued relevance.

In Britain and other Western societies, these are hard times indeed for traditional religious institutions. The rise of moral relativism and the increasing intellectual hostility to big, overarching systems of faith and belief make it difficult for religious groups to justify or promote their traditions. They are under great pressure to accommodate to these morally relativistic times by jettisoning what would once have been considered key tenets of their faith.

Established religious institutions in particular, such as the Church of England, have rid themselves of what are today considered to be problematically absolutist ideas – such as the belief that Christianity is the only true faith or that hell awaits those who fail to repent for their sins. (The CofE gave a serious rethink to the idea of hell a few years ago, and decided that it was just an 'extended period of non-being'.) In the Catholic Church, too, a combination of an internal crisis of legitimacy and external pressure to embrace the outlook of relativism over certainty have led to the voluntaristic undermining of what would once have been considered some of their indispensable articles of faith.

It is in this climate that religious institutions have become so animated by issues of 'life' – particularly by abortion and assisted suicide. The Catholic Church's obsession with abortion is instructive here. This obsession is directly proportional to the crisis in the Catholic Church – the more the Catholic Church feels incapable of firmly and unabashedly stating its old beliefs on good, evil, God, heaven, hell and so on, the more it clings to the issue of abortion as the one area in which it might demonstrate principle and resoluteness.

The Bible says precisely nothing about abortion. It didn't feature in the discussions of church officials for centuries (despite being practised, illegally and often unsafely, throughout this time). It is only over the past three or four decades that Catholicism has concerned itself so myopically with the issue of abortion. Many believe this Catholic fury with abortion corresponds naturally and neatly with the legalization of abortion in many Western countries; it is better understood as corresponding with the post-1960s, post-Vatican II crises of legitimacy and direction within Catholicism, which compelled it to devise a platform upon which its faith in the authority of God over life might still be proclaimed.

Recently, assisted suicide has joined abortion as a largely performative issue for religious institutions in a state of moral disarray. In essence, having given up on everything that occurs between birth and death – that is, the fundamental questions about the good life, about sin, about the sanctity of marriage and the family, about the need for everyone to accept God's will and dominion – Christians have restricted themselves to dealing primarily with birth and death themselves, with the conception of human life and the extinguishing of it. This reorientation around 'life' issues speaks to the weakness rather than strength of religious bodies today; it reveals the extent to which they have abandoned the field of real life itself, and the question of how it should be lived, in favour of concerning themselves myopically with how life comes into existence and how it ends.

But such an opportunistic adoption of a so-called pro-life orientation towards end-of-life matters is also deeply problematic. It is an attempt on the part of religious institutions to discover one absolute – namely that helping someone to die is always a sin – in today's sea of relativistic thinking. But the end of their life is no time for absolutes. What one person considers to be a bearable terminal illness might be considered by another to be unbearable. That is why, throughout history, discreetly and without fanfare, both men of medicine and family members have helped people in extreme physical distress to die. It is not a sin to do this; it can in fact be a very humane thing to do.

Where the pro-assisted-suicide lobby makes life worse for those who want to live, by demanding that society give a green light to the suicide of people who are now offensively described a 'burden', the anti-assisted-suicide lobby makes life worse for those who want to die, by demonizing a human practice that has existed for centuries: the private, unspoken ushering to an end of a very frail, terminally ill, hopeless life.

Supporters of assisted suicide are driven by an astonishingly cavalier attitude towards the moral worth of human lives, and of human existence itself, while opponents of assisted suicide seek to import moral absolutes into end-of-life debates, primarily for PR purposes, to demonstrate that they still have something religiously coherent to say. Both sides are motivated by a powerful anti-humanist outlook.

New moral questions

Into this infuriating clash, it must be possible to volunteer a properly humanist take on the 'right to die'. Yuill's book suggests that it is. In challenging some of the unquestioned ideas and prejudices behind the drive for legalizing assisted suicide, Yuill both illuminates the issue as it currently exists and also points the way to a new understanding of it – not to a Third Way, as such, since that would imply a flaccid, compromising take on a divisive issue, but certainly to a radical rethink of matters of life, death and morality in the twenty-first century.

It strikes me that the humanist position on assisted suicide should be to oppose implacably the campaign to legalize it, for two reasons. Firstly because this campaign is underpinned by some very regressive views on the value of human life and is shot through with much of the Malthusian thinking that passes for radicalism today, both from the sphere of environmentalism and from the sphere of understanding the recession as a product of the avarice and ignorance of earlier generations.

The discussion of assisted suicide takes these trends to their dangerously logical conclusion, through promoting the idea that human life has little intrinsic value, and is a more destructive than positive phenomenon, and by venturing the notion that certain sections of society might have become so burdensome that they have a 'duty to die'. The fashion for backing assisted suicide is best understood as the endpoint of twenty-first-century radical misanthropy.

And the second reason the campaign for assisted suicide should be opposed is because in inviting the state to rule on end-of-life matters, it actually makes that area of life more difficult for those experiencing it, rather than less difficult. Institutionalizing rules and regulations about who might legitimately commit suicide, possibly even bringing in end-of-life panels at which one would endeavour to convince experts that one should be permitted to die, would make infinitely harder a part of the human experience that is hard enough already. In fact, it would diminish an individual's last opportunity to exercise autonomy, by putting the final decision about his life in the hands of the state and the courts.

It would replace love with law, zapping the private and familial goodwill that has normally attended such end-of-life matters and replacing them with the death sanction of the state. This would be bad for the individual who wants to die, bureaucratizing his final moments of life, and it would be bad for those who want to live, too, since it would add up to the state saying: 'Some lives are worth less than others and thus may legitimately be extinguished.'

But humanists should surely critique the religious side in this debate, too, for also making dying people's lives harder by introducing moral absolutes about life and death when they are least appropriate and unwanted. The religious lobby, and humanists in fact, have an important role to play in challenging the broader denigration of the value of human life today, but through an intellectual challenge to retrograde trends such as rehabilitated Malthusianism and anti-elderly hostility rather than by branding anyone who opts discreetly to die as a sinner.

A humane society should recognize that sometimes some people, with the help of loved ones, will end very painful lives. But it should not sanction or applaud such action; it should instead turn a blind eye to it. It should tolerate it but not make a virtue of it. Today, the transformation of the desire to die into a virtue, even a right that the state should legislate for, represents one of the most backward arguments of our time.

Brendan O'Neill

Brendan O'Neill is the editor of online magazine *Spiked* and is a columnist for the *Big Issue* in London and *The Australian* in Sydney.

His journalism has been published widely on both sides of the Atlantic, including in *The Spectator*, the *New Statesman*, *The Guardian*, the *Sunday Times*, *Slate*, *Salon*, *Reason* and the *American Conservative*.

He is described by the *Daily Telegraph* as 'one of Britain's sharpest social commentators'. His satire on environmentalism, *Can I Recycle My Granny and 39 Other Eco-Dilemmas*, is published by Hodder & Stoughton.

Acknowledgements

Many people have helped me throughout the years that I have investigated this issue. I have benefited from debating such excellent opponents as Raymond Tallis, Debbie Purdy, and former MP Bill Etherington. Thanks also to Iain Brassington who provided cogent questions regarding the chapter on suicide. I owe a debt of gratitude to the British Humanist Association, the Battle of Ideas, Nurses Opposed to Euthanasia, the University of Sunderland Research Conference and various others in front of whom I have debated these issues. I benefited greatly from a grant made possible by the Research Beacon of the Faculty of Education and Society at the University of Sunderland. Editorial help and criticism of my articles came from Brendan O'Neill, Rob Lyons and Mick Hume of *Spiked-online*, Stuart Derbyshire of the *Journal of Cancer Pain and Symptom Palliation*, Stuart Reid of *The Spectator* and John Wilkins of *The Tablet*. I have also had superb criticism and encouragement from Helen Reece, William Sutcliffe, Gren Yuill, James Harris and my colleagues at the University of Sunderland. As my opponents will no doubt readily agree, what is written here is my responsibility alone.

Finally, thanks to my family for putting up with too many mealtime conversations about what I'm sure all will agree can be a fairly depressing topic.

Introduction

Assisted suicide, also known as assisted dying, is seldom out of the news. Three cases, arising in three different countries, both reflect widespread interest in the subject and spell out some of the dilemmas involved. On the face of it, all three are compelling reasons to legalize assisted suicide. In Britain, the plight of the late Tony Nicklinson, a 58-year old man with 'locked in syndrome', unable to speak and paralyzed from the neck down after a stroke in 2005, has attracted huge attention. Nicklinson who, before being disabled, enjoyed an active life, playing rugby and parachuting, was a man, by all indications intelligent and competent, who consistently expressed the wish to die. As Nicklinson explained, by moving his eyelids to communicate through a computer, he felt his life is 'dull, miserable, demeaning, undignified and intolerable'. In 2012 the High Court gave him permission to proceed with a full hearing on his case. Nicklinson contended that a 'common law defence of necessity' could be used to protect his loved ones or doctors from prosecution if they helped him end his life. However, on 12 August, the court refused Nicklinson's request to die with assistance, saying that it was a matter for Parliament. Upon hearing the judgment, Nicklinson cried with frustration and disappointment, using one of the few expressions he was still able to express. According to his wife, he refused food after the judgment and on 22 August Tony Nicklinson died of pneumonia.

Nicklinson wanted the existing law on assisted dying to change so that, on a case-by-case basis, a court can decide that a doctor will be immune from prosecution. At present, if a doctor assists a suicide, he or she is liable to 14 years' jail. If a doctor gives a competent and willing individual a lethal injection, at that person's request, the crime is murder and the punishment is life. The British newspaper, the *Observer*, in a piece published shortly before Nicklinson's death, stated in an editorial

1

that it 'believes it is important that Tony has the option of death, at a time of his choosing. Such knowledge provides comfort; it confers power and promises control'.[1]

In June, 2012, a terminally ill Canadian woman, Gloria Taylor of West Kelowna, British Columbia, won the right to die after a judge in British Columbia struck down parts of Canada's law banning the practice. Justice Lynn Smith ruled that Canada's ban on doctor-assisted suicide infringes on the rights of the disabled. A 63-year-old divorced mother of two, Taylor suffers from Amyotrophic lateral sclerosis (ALS), also referred to as motor neurone disease. She said a few days after the decision: 'I'm so grateful to know that if I choose to do so I will be allowed to seek a doctor's help to a peaceful and dignified death. This brings me great solace and comfort.'[2]

The judge gave a year to give the Canadian Parliament time to amend the law, while granting an exemption for Taylor. In August, the highest court in British Columbia rejected the government's petition to prevent Taylor from having an assisted suicide before Parliament ruled on the issue. The judge insisted that Taylor would 'suffer the loss of the peace of mind and solace now available to her as a result of the exemption were a stay to be granted'.[3]

On the other side of the world, Professor Sean Davison, a 50-year-old microbiologist based in South Africa, faced a lengthy trial for a crime he admitted. Davison was last year charged in New Zealand with attempting to murder his terminally ill mother Patricia Elizabeth Davison, 85, a former medical practitioner, in 2006. His mother had summoned Davison back to New Zealand when she learned she had very little time left. She was diagnosed with cancer in 2004 and he gave her a lethal dose of morphine in 2006 when she could no longer move unaided. Davison pleaded guilty to a charge of procuring and inciting attempted suicide and was given a suspended sentence. The saga has re-ignited the assisted suicide and euthanasia debate in New Zealand and may prompt further political action.[4]

Certainly, there is no lack of heart-rending stories appearing on the websites of organizations working for legalization like *Compassion and Choices* in the United States and *Dignity in Dying* in the UK. Nearly all readers will sympathize with those who face an agonizing end and seek a way to avoid the last few unpleasant weeks of life when faced with a painful illness. Who would deny them what they want? It appears such sympathies are encouraging the public to support a change in the law. More New Zealanders thought assisted suicide should be legalized than not, as did more than two-thirds of Americans, between two-thirds and three quarters of Canadians and around 80 per cent of Britons and Australians.[5]

If we are to believe advocates of legal change, the only barrier to providing these people with the relief they want appears to be a small group of conservative religious zealots determined to impose their values upon those who do not share them. The question becomes, why not? Proponents of legalized assisted suicide bring up as many tragic cases as they possibly can because they know the immediate gut reaction benefits them.

Of course, there are determined opponents to legalization. Most point to the potential for elderly people to be pushed into an assisted death by hospitals anxious to reduce the financial outlay for the final months of life, or relatives either waiting for inheritances or simply tired of a drawn-out dying process. Disabled groups point out that to allow assisted suicide for those with physical conditions cheapens their lives. But religious-affiliated groups provide the mainstay of opposition, pointing to the sanctity of human life. Many also believe that it is up to God to either give or take away life.

The issue is far more complex than that. Take these three cases. They deal with very different actions, only one of them would be legal in the US states of Oregon and Washington or, if current legislative proposals are adopted, in the UK, Australia and the states within the United States where legalization is currently being proposed, and anywhere outside of Switzerland. Gloria Taylor's death would be a physician-assisted suicide; Sean Davison's action was a mercy killing and Tony Nicklinson's inability to self-administer (though there may be a technological fix available) made his proposed death difficult to define. Nicklinson's request would only have been legal in Switzerland (current British proposals would prevent someone who is not terminally ill from an assisted death). Davison's action is illegal everywhere on earth and there are currently no concrete proposals anywhere to make such an action legal.

Also, how necessary is legislation to these proposed or actuated killings? Had these individuals wished to keep their wishes quiet, there is little doubt they might accomplish them with little chance of prosecution. Taylor, with a little planning and determination, might have secured the drugs necessary to end her life. All three of the patients, if they were determined to die, could legally refuse food and drink and ensure their own deaths (Davison's mother apparently tried to do this but failed). Even if Nicklinson had had assistance to end his life, current guidelines issued by the Director of Public Prosecutions would almost

certainly ensure that no one was prosecuted. His sad demise also indicates the possibility, even for those totally incapacitated, of escape from
a life no longer wanted (sensibly, the police have declined to investigate
any further into his death). In Davison's case, he was not prosecuted
until he admitted what he had done in an unpublished manuscript that
was anonymously sent to a New Zealand newspaper. Looking behind
the emotional stories, there are clearly intricate and difficult issues.[6]

The purpose of this book is to complexify what initially appears to be a
simple question of reason versus dogma, to reframe the debate in different terms – in short, to muddy the waters. By analysing the issues behind
this deceptively simple problem, I make a liberal and humanist case
against legalization. Opposition to legalizing assisted suicide, I show, is
consonant with support for abortion rights, stem-cell research and even
tolerance of suicide and euthanasia in certain circumstances. Moreover,
my opposition is not to assisted suicide *per se* but to its legalization and
what I call the institutionalization of assisted suicide. This book provides
information, insight and analysis into the issues surrounding assisted
suicide and is the first to put forward an explicitly humanist and liberal
case against a change in the law.

For whom is this book intended?

This book is primarily written for people who share my secular humanist
perspective (by which I mean an outlook espousing reason, ethics and
justice above religious or supernatural dogma. For the record, I am an
atheist), who, like myself, consider themselves to have a generally liberal
and enlightened outlook on life, who wish to emancipate the individual as much as possible from unnecessary restrictions upon freedom.
Indeed, I find myself more in agreement with proponents of legalized
assisted suicide than many of those opposed on nearly every other subject. I support abortion rights for women (actively, having marched in
support of them in the 1980s and 1990s), acknowledge that an absolutist prohibition on taking lives is wrong, that withdrawal of treatment
and even euthanasia in particular circumstances are correct and appropriate actions, and that suicide is not always wrong and should remain
legal. I agreed with the Florida courts rather than with George Bush on
the Terri Schiavo case.

This book is not the first to put forward secular reasons to keep assisted
suicide illegal. In an enlightening exchange between two legal heavy-
weights, Yale Kamisar responded to Glanville Williams's defence of the
morality of voluntary euthanasia some 50 years ago, entitling his article

'Some Non-Religious Views against Proposed "Mercy Killing" Legislation'. However, this book is the first to put forward arguments showing that those with fairly libertarian perspectives, who support autonomy and freedom, should be opposed to legalization.[7]

Having debated the subject over a number of years, I find there are three categories: 1) convinced and often actively arguing for a change in the law; 2) decidedly opposed to a change in the law; and 3) those who have not given the issue a lot of thought but probably just support a change in the law because they have a secular, liberal outlook. This book is for them.

However, it is also for those who are convinced proponents of a change in the law. I have no illusions that this book will convince those who actively pursue a change in the law (though I live in hope) but, in my experience, a good book will inspire thought not only those who agree with its premise but those who disagree. That is, at least, my aim. I intend it as part of an ongoing debate and hope that my opponents, some of whom I have great respect and admiration for and have learned much from, will respond to the challenges and questions I outline below.

It will also give those convinced opponents of legalizing assisted suicide, I hope, additional weapons in their armoury as well as arguments and ways of framing the question that lead to rejection of legalization. There will no doubt be a wide gulf between us on questions like abortion but I hope they will welcome a contribution from another angle that pushes the debate forward.

Because I am a historian by trade, I have aspired to write this in a careful and academic tone but not one, I hope, that puts off the intelligent general reader. The approach is necessary analytical; we must look dispassionately at the implications of what are on the surface emotive, political and straightforward issues. Because assisted suicide involves so many issues – ethical, philosophical, theological, historical and sociological – this book cannot be restricted to one or even two disciplines. The heart of the matter, I feel, is philosophical and the deep and difficult discussions about meaning cannot be avoided. In showing how complex the matter is, I hope I have kept it simple and clear enough for the general reader.

Though I bring in European examples and discuss the Benelux countries and Switzerland, the focus is on the English-speaking world. Most legislative proposals in the United States, in the UK, Canada, Australia and New Zealand use the Oregon model, where patients ingest a poison prescribed by a doctor, rather than the Dutch model, where doctors are allowed to carry out voluntary euthanasia. Of course, the many European models are germane; it is simply that none of the serious proposals for legalization in the United States, UK, Canada or the Antipodes calls for the legalization of euthanasia (as in the Netherlands) or the assistance of any suicide with no restrictions (as in Switzerland).

Themes

There are essentially two arguments the book makes. First, the case for a change in the law is deeply flawed. Second, if it were to become institutionalized, it would be harmful, not so much for 'vulnerable' individuals but for its less tangible effect of undermining of our common moral assumptions and responsibilities.

One point of agreement I have with the pro-assisted-suicide camp is that very few take up the option where it is legal; it appears to be something everyone thinks they need but no one actually uses. Suicide is legal just about everywhere and no one currently languishes in jail because they assisted someone to die out of mercy; in England and Wales, very few cases have even been prosecuted under the Suicide Act of 1961 in its 53-year history.[8] Most of the sentiment pushing a change in law forward is, as pioneering author on death and dying, Elizabeth Kübler Ross, pointed out, projection of fears and anxieties of the living onto the dying.[9]

But assisted suicide, if it becomes accepted practice, will be damaging. The focus here is not on the individuals caught in terrible circumstances or on those allegedly 'vulnerable' people who will, in the imagination of some opponents, be forced into early departures (here, I also agree with proponents of a change in the law that the dangers have been exaggerated). Instead, it is on those left behind, upon our moral connections, our assumptions and accepted meanings upon which we base our relationships with others and understand ourselves in the world. That may sound very vague at this stage but by the end of the book I hope it will be clear.

One of the first tasks is to distinguish the various terms and proposals. The term 'euthanasia' is preferred by opponents of a change in the law, as it implies that legalizing assisted suicide would only be the start of a process that ended in euthanasia; proponents prefer 'assisted dying', a compendium of assisted suicide and voluntary euthanasia. The term 'assisted suicide' is used here because in both existing legislation in Oregon and Washington and proposed legislation in England and Wales, Scotland, Canada, Australia and New Zealand, assisted suicide is what is proposed, not voluntary euthanasia. It is disingenuous to use terms other than assisted suicide when that is what is proposed. Moreover, as the book shows, our attitudes towards suicide – whether we should pre-approve suicides in certain circumstances – is at the heart of the issue at hand.

It is also important to distinguish the terms because it is possible to approve of euthanasia in certain circumstances, to strongly support the right to refuse medical treatment – as I do – and even to approve of suicide after the fact while strongly opposing *legalization* of assisted suicide. I also believe that an attitude of tolerance – the way we have traditionally and, in most places, continue to view euthanasia and assisted suicide – is correct.

This book is not about individual decisions and actions. It would be arrogant to pronounce from afar just what those in desperate situations should or should not do, so the book uses individual examples only to clarify various points. I will stress that the whole issue is not political or legal but moral and that every individual case must be understood and judged within its own parameters. A law that says suicide may be pre-approved denies the value of all lives that meet the criteria under which suicide is approved. However, looking at a case of suicide *after the fact*, we might excuse the act or even accord it heroic status.

The arguments for the legalization of assisted suicide, I show, look solid only because of the weakness of the arguments against. They begin unravelling upon closer inspection. The main difficulty faced by proponents is in deciding the basis upon which we allow assisted suicide. If it is autonomy, we must allow all who feel they are suffering unbearably assisted suicides, or patronizingly tell those who do not fit the criteria that they are not really suffering. If it is compassion, how can we legislate acts of kindness? Surely, euthanasia or mercy killings would be more appropriate? Assisted suicide seems to be a halfway house, using both justifications but satisfying neither. Compassion may only be meted out individually; doctors, if legalization takes place, will not act from compassion but will be carrying out a professional duty. If, as studies show, pain is not the reason why individuals request assisted suicides, what possible justification can there be for restricting assisted suicides to those with six or 12 months to live? Why are they less valuable (and therefore allowed to kill themselves) than anyone else? This central contradiction between autonomy and compassion forms a fatal schism in the arguments of the pro-assisted-suicide camp.

Because of this fairly random restriction of assisted suicides to those with six or 12 months left to live, we set up an expansion of the categories that might avail themselves of an assisted suicide. Someone with a condition such as that of Tony Nicklinson will argue that those in his situation should be allowed to die. And why not? Someone whose life has been ruined in another way may argue that the suffering they feel is just as real as that of terminally ill people. By allowing assisted suicide for some, we patronizingly tell others that their suffering is not as valid.

But there are also more tangible harms whereby individuals are denied what I argue is an extremely important freedom – the right to refuse medical treatment. By blurring the line between dying by refusing medical treatment and dying through the actions of a doctor, pro-assisted-suicide campaigners (aided and abetted by some anti-assisted-suicide campaigners) undermine this freedom. If we deny suicides to those with more than six months to live on the basis that their lives are too valuable, why wouldn't we, on the same basis, deny those with more than six months to live the right to refuse treatment? The privacy of individuals and of the deathbed scene is also in jeopardy, I will show. Thus, the damage done by institutionalizing assisted suicide is tangible as well as destructive to moral assumptions.

Part of the project here is to reconstruct the development of the discussion and to understand, as well as criticize, the campaigns both for and against the legalization of assisted suicide, to understand the historian's favourite question: why is this happening at this particular juncture of history? In understanding it within its historical context, we can untangle the skein of motivations of what I conclude is a postmodern movement.

Chapters

The first chapter investigates definitions, indicating that even at this basic level, disagreements and disputes arise. In particular, the assisted dying/assisted suicide discussion is examined, as is why the term assisted suicide has been rejected only twenty years after it replaced 'voluntary euthanasia'. We will also look at existing laws around the world, current and past opinion on assisted suicide and how it is changing.

Chapter 2 outlines and criticizes the main arguments both of the anti-assisted-suicide camp and those who favour a change in the law. Whereas the former tend to rely on what might be a secular argument – the slippery slope – and the sacredness of human life, the latter are united only in their criticisms of the sacredness argument. When dissected, the pro-arguments tend to be contradictory and do not stand up to scrutiny.

Chapter 3 critiques one of the key assumptions underlying both sides – the idea that medical technology has provoked discussion by extending life but not quality of life, that the employment of 'halfway technologies' has created a crisis. Using historical examples, I show that it is not technological innovation but a growing suspicion of technology that has inspired the growth of the assisted-suicide movement.

Chapter 4 discusses suicide, the heart of the entire discussion on assisted suicide. Though suicide is sometimes right and occasionally noble, it remains an entirely individual act. It is a moral, not political or legal, issue. I argue that it is best seen within the context of Hannah Arendt's theory of action. Pre-judging a suicide as good or bad is impossible, I show. Yet we must judge it after the fact; assisted suicide seeks to remove it from the moral sphere, removing its individual nature and making it a medical treatment. But humanity is rightly passionate in its judgment about whether or not an individual voluntarily leaving our midst was right or wrong. To take a neutral stance on suicide is to blunt that passion.

There are many parallels drawn by both sides of the debate between the issues of abortion and assisted suicide. Chapter 5 defends abortion rights and shows that, though there are similarities, the essential difference is that the need for women's equality ultimately determines that we allow doctors to perform abortions. There is no composite societal interest in providing suicides. The pro-life and the right-to-die movements also have more in common than those within the movements care to admit.

In the final chapter, I show that the devil is in the detail. Real freedoms are threatened by institutionalizing assisted suicide, including the important freedom to refuse medical treatment. By bringing suicide within a program of legal regulation, the privacy of the deathbed scene is breached, as is the private contemplation necessary to make such a serious choice. Doctors take on a religious role in providing death as medical treatment; it is they who gain the right over whether individuals live or die.

1
Defining the Terms

Such is the cultural divide on the issue that neither side will even agree on the terms used. In fact, the words themselves have become a key battleground for the two sides of the debate. The way the language evolves over time indicates a shift in meaning behind the words rather than just increasing use of marketing ploys or politically correct terms. It also gives an important indication of where the debate is headed. Therefore, it is worth analysing in depth the words used by both sides.

However, pinning down such moveable targets is difficult. There has been a shift in the language of assisted suicide over the years, particularly from the campaign for voluntary euthanasia, associated with eugenics, medical efficiency and Malthusian perspectives in the inter-war years, to an emphasis on autonomy and the 'right to die' in the 1970s and 1980s, to a new concentration on embedding suicide as a treatment choice. Much as there are some false distinctions made within the literature, there are also many real distinctions cloaked by terminology.

Whereas some of the terms cannot easily be pinned down, others are unknowable. On some levels, the term 'death' seems obvious; the animate becomes inanimate, human beings cease being human, subjects come to be objects. We recognize death when we see it. But what does death mean for the individual, for the self? Is it the end of the individual or can an individual's interests exist after death? Do we 'experience' death or is it the end of all experience? Is death a negative to life or simply nothingness? How should we understand our own individual non-existence? It is impossible to avoid these philosophical questions when asking what appears to be a simple question. Within the contested meaning of terms exists what is ultimately behind the entire discussion of assisted suicide – a crisis of human meaning, a confusion of past, present and future, and a misunderstanding of human life.

Before launching into such deep waters, it is worth attempting to clarify as much as possible the basic terms that provide common grounds for the debate. Even this task is complicated; the terminology used often reflects the attitude expressed towards the issue of legalization.

Definitions

There are several definitions of the terms involved. Nearly twenty years ago, Ezekiel Emanuel usefully provided a basic, working definition of some of the terms current in the early 1990s:

> *Voluntary active euthanasia*: Intentionally administering medications or other interventions to cause the patient's death at the patient's explicit request and with full informed consent.
>
> *Involuntary active euthanasia*: Intentionally administering medications or other interventions to cause a patient's death when the patient was competent but without the patient's explicit request and/or full informed consent (e.g. patient was not asked).
>
> *Nonvoluntary active euthanasia*: Intentionally administering medications or other interventions to cause a patient's death when the patient was incompetent and mentally incapable of explicitly requesting it (e.g. patient is in a coma).
>
> *Terminating life-sustaining treatments* (passive euthanasia): Withholding or withdrawing life-sustaining medical treatments from the patient to let him or her die.
>
> *Indirect euthanasia*: Administering narcotics or other medications to relieve pain with incidental consequence of causing sufficient respiratory depression to result in a patient's death.
>
> *Physician-assisted suicide*: A physician providing medications or other interventions to a patient with understanding that the patient intends to use them to commit suicide.[1]

Publishing late last year in the UK, the Commission on Assisted Dying used these terms:

> *assisted suicide*: providing someone with the means to end his or her own life
>
> *voluntary euthanasia*: ending another person's life at his or her own request

non-voluntary euthanasia: ending another person's life when the individual is incompetent to consent to or refuse euthanasia and has
made no prior decision

assisted dying: a compendium that can refer to voluntary euthanasia
and/or assisted suicide.[2]

We might also add another accepted definition:

mercy killing: a compassionate act taken to end the life of a patient by
someone who is not a doctor.

There are also recent neologisms like 'directed death', 'hastened
death', or 'self-directed death' or 'self-deliverance'. Some are simply
euphemisms. Those who oppose the legalization of assisted suicide,
however, often prefer the catch-all term 'euthanasia'. Like the discussion in general, the language used by both opponents and proponents
has changed over the years, giving an indication of shifting meanings
as well as indicating which side of the debate the person using the term
occupies.

Euthanasia, the term favoured by all sides up until the 1940s, simply means, from the Greek *eu*, meaning good, and *thanatos*, meaning
death, a good death. So far, there is little controversy (few would wish
for bad death). However, it has come to mean that doctors under certain
circumstances be allowed to ensure an easy death not just by acting to
quell pain but to actively kill the patient in order to prevent needless
suffering. Peter Singer defined euthanasia as 'the killing of those who
are incurably ill and in great pain or distress, for the sake of those killed,
and in order to spare them further suffering or distress'.[3]

Voluntary euthanasia implies that those who are killed are in agreement with their killing and have made a request for it. Involuntary
euthanasia is when someone is killed who either did not request or
actively opposed being killed. It may be that others think a death is good
though the subject does not agree. Non-voluntary euthanasia refers to
those situations where the person killed is not able to assent to the
death and has made no prior consent. Confusingly, in the Netherlands
and Belgium, where euthanasia is legal, the term implies voluntary
euthanasia.

Just as bewilderingly, the terms distinguish between 'active' and 'passive' euthanasia. Passive euthanasia is sometimes used by both sides of
the discussion to refer to the removal of life-saving or life-sustaining
equipment and thus causing a death. Active euthanasia means to take

deliberate action to end a patient's life, such as administering poison or smothering the patient. But surely passive euthanasia – letting someone die, usually of a disease – must be in a different category, given the essential moral difference, although sometimes small, between letting something happen and making it happen. The latter is action (we will discuss a theory of action through which we can characterize suicide in Chapter 4).

Euthanasia generally implies an agreement amongst at least several people that the patient would be better off dead. Prior to the Second World War, euthanasia implied that the patient no longer wished to live – usually meaning forgoing the final weeks or months of a painful and debilitating disease – but also was used to signify the 'help' given to those whose existence, it was deemed, did not benefit wider society. In the United States especially, euthanasia and eugenics were closely associated and supporters of euthanasia, like Nobel Prize-winner Alexis Carrel, declared that sentimental prejudice should not obstruct the quiet and painless disposition of 'incurables, criminals, and hopeless lunatics'. Peter Singer goes further than most recent advocates in admitting that approval of voluntary euthanasia includes some involuntary euthanasia in a few very extreme cases.[4]

Whereas the proposed legislation in the UK is the 'Assisted Dying' Bill and 'death with dignity' is the preferred term in the US states of Oregon and Washington, where assisted suicide is legal, and by the organization *Compassion and Choices*, these terms hardly specify what is being sought. What exactly is 'dignity' and who defines it? The concept of death with dignity begs the question: are other deaths necessarily without dignity? Historically, the term 'death with dignity' was used by Representative Dr Walter W. Sackett, Jr., who introduced proposals using the term during the 1960s and 1970s in the Florida Legislature. Dr Sackett acclaimed his legislation as being a means of allowing the severely retarded in Florida's institutions to 'die with dignity' simply by refusing to treat infections and pneumonia.[5] Such slippery terms mirror the slipperiness of the debate.

It is only relatively recently that campaigners have called for voluntary euthanasia or assisted suicide only and not euthanasia in general. After all, it makes sense, if the aim is to alleviate suffering, to extend the power to end suffering not just to the individual involved but to doctors and, perhaps, to those nearest and dearest to the patient. The patient may not, in some instances, be able to act in his best interests. Perhaps the patient made clear her wishes but lacks the function to give final assent to the act. Up until 1970 (and, to a lesser extent, today) campaigners for a change in the law sought the legalization of both euthanasia and assisted suicide. Since then the emphasis has shifted to autonomy.

The evolution of terminology

By the 1950s euthanasia advocates advised changing the terminology in order to distance themselves from Nazi eugenics programs and well-documented and horrific medical experimentation during the Third Reich. In the *New Republic*, a euthanasia proponent called for new expressions: 'If we call these situations "assisted suicide" rather than "mercy killing", the moral content would be considerably changed ... The term "murder" implies anger: it is not the word to use for a courageous act of compassion.'[6]

We can see in outline a fundamental problem besetting those in favour of legalization: how does one legitimate acts of mercy at the same time as what was called even in the 1930s 'the right to die'? A mercy killing is clearly not a suicide unless one argues that the 'killer' acts on behalf of the patient and follows either wishes expressed by the patient or concludes from a range of evidence that death would be what the patient wanted in that specific situation if she was able to express her wishes.

The term euthanasia, while it remains in the title of many groups, has decidedly fallen out of favour amongst activists if not opponents. In the United States the *Euthanasia Society* changed its name in 1974 to the *Society for the Right to Die* (SRD), reflecting the new emphasis on autonomy and civil rights. As prominent member of the SRD, newspaper columnist Abigail 'Dear Abby' Van Buren, noted in 1974, 'a bill with the word "euthanasia" in it will never get passed'.[7] In 1977 the Euthanasia Educational Council changed its name to *Concern for Dying* (CFD).

Euthanasia remains the favoured term for opponents because it emphasizes a key point they wish to make; if assisted dying or assisted suicide is allowed, it will soon extend to voluntary euthanasia and to involuntary euthanasia (this is the 'slippery slope' theory that will be discussed in the next chapter).

Assisted suicide vs assisted dying

More recently, and particularly after 9/11, the word 'suicide' has fallen out of favour. One of the major themes in this book is that the apparent coherence behind the case for legalization quickly dissolves when looked at closely. The term 'assisted dying' is now the term of choice but is not simply the product of the search for more politic terms since the term 'suicide bombers' entered the news. Instead, it appears to denote a shift away from the emphasis on autonomy and self-determination towards a demand that death become a medical choice. We need to ask whether there are any real differences and, if so, what are they?

Some proponents now consider suicide to be pejorative; many activists would like to deny the association of suicide with, to use yet another favoured phrase, 'aid in dying'. Language evolves, proponents of a change in the law note, and to label aid in dying at the end of life as suicide is 'inaccurate, biased, and pejorative'. 'Just as terms like "retarded" and "handicapped" have gone by the way, so should the term suicide.' Advocates argue that it is in fact the disease that kills; they simply call for the individual's freedom to exercise choice in how they die.[8]

Using the term suicide is 'hurtful' to those in the invidious situation where they must make such a choice. Charlene Andrews, the patient-plaintiff in *Gonzales v. Oregon*, pleaded with reporters: 'Please do not call it suicide; that is an insult to my fight against cancer.' *Compassion and Choices* states '[I]t's inaccurate to call it suicide when a dying patient chooses to ingest medication to bring about a peaceful death. Labeling that "suicide" is politicized language that implies a value judgment and carries with it a social stigma.' The California campaign manager for *Compassion and Choices*, Steve Hopcraft, adds: 'The word "suicide" is completely pejorative. It's really insulting to people...who are facing a very grim and painful death — to call their desire to end their own suffering suicide. These people are dying from their disease, they're not committing suicide.'[9] Whereas language undoubtedly does evolve and no one would wish to insult people in terrible circumstances, the language of the campaigners is evasive rather than clarifying. In the United Kingdom, *Dignity in Dying* gives an indication of the differences between assisted dying and assisted suicide: 'Assisted dying is different to euthanasia and assisted suicide. Euthanasia is a term often used to describe life-ending medication being administered by a third party. Assisted suicide refers to providing assistance to die to someone who is not dying.'[10]

Shall we accept the term 'assisted dying' over 'assisted suicide'? After all, there may be the need for a term covering the different elements of voluntary euthanasia, where the patient agrees to be killed but someone else does the killing, and assisted suicide, where the patient takes the action aided by someone else, usually a doctor. Given that, if we view the needs of the patient as paramount, the effects of both actions are the same, shall we not use the broader term? There are reasons to reject 'assisted dying' as a useful term.

First, the vagueness of 'assisted dying' creates more questions than it answers. Presumably, capital punishment is a form of assisted dying. Or is it assisted dying only in cases where the prisoner agrees with his punishment? Or perhaps we should accept the idea that the difference pointed out by *Dignity in Dying* between 'the dying' and everyone else; assisted dying is helping the dying to die whereas assisted suicide is assisting someone who is not dying to die. But this in turn begs questions. Who is not progressing steadily towards death? How are we to define 'the dying' and by which criteria? And *who* defines it? And why should 'the dying' be a separate moral category?

'Assisted dying' means different things to different people. In the way it is defined by *Compassion and Choices* and *Dignity in Dying*, the use of 'assisted dying' also implicitly condemns suicide. To *Dignity in Dying* it means assisted suicide so long as someone is dying of a terminal illness – there is no time limit given on the site. The term assisted suicide has been surgically removed from their language. Doubtless most people have a negative connotation of suicide but there are noble suicides and, as I argue in Chapter 4, each suicide must be judged individually. In distancing themselves from suicide, these assisted suicide advocates are condemning all unofficial suicides, all suicides taken without express approval. This is despite the fact that suicide is illegal almost nowhere (India is one of the last countries where suicide remains a crime) and despite the argument often employed by pro-legalization forces (like Gloria Taylor's lawyers) that laws against assisted suicide are discriminatory because disabled people should have the right to suicide.

The compendium version of the definition of assisted dying, used by the *Commission on Assisted Dying*, whereby assisted dying refers both to assisted suicide and voluntary euthanasia, might seem the most reasonable. But, so used, it becomes useless in terms of framing legislation. It would be difficult to legalize all acts, whether taken by the subject, a doctor, or a friend or family member. Most legislation involves only the subject self-administering drugs.

Assisted dying is suicide affirmed by lawyers and physicians

Second, and much more importantly, the only real difference between assisted dying and assisted suicide is that the former has been officially sanctioned by doctors and by legality. Someone in Oregon with, according to two doctors, five months left to live who ingests poison is, according to *Compassion and Choices*, *Dignity in Dying*, other proponents of a change in the law and, since 2006, the Oregon Department of Human Services, an assisted death. Someone who is dying but has seven months to live who ingests the same poison is, according to the same sources, an assisted suicide.

The change in terminology, then, is not simply political correctness but an indication of a new role that proponents envisage for doctors. Importantly, the rejection of the term 'suicide' implies that the moral taint of suicide in particular circumstances that are determined by officials, lawmakers and doctors is to be removed. The action of taking one's life is no different in the two scenarios. But the former is given official imprimatur and is therefore an assisted death (good) instead of a suicide (bad).

Such a change has important implications. The obvious one is that, as priests and other religious officials have departed the deathbed scene, their place has been filled by doctors. For it would be difficult to deny that, in the scenarios outlined in the Introduction to this volume, doctors play a spiritual role only. As we shall explore in later chapters, suicide may be accomplished without the aid of official medicine so doctors play only an officiating role whereby they dispense deadly drugs that the patient might have bought herself, like a priest placing wafers on the tongues of his flock. The fact that the doctor dispenses the poison ritualizes the action within a set of bureaucratic guidelines.

The implication for the patient, similarly, is validation of their suffering. In the past, religious figures comforted the dying by rationalizing suffering as part of God's plan. Now, should assisted suicide be institutionalized, physicians will provide an end to depression and mental suffering (as we shall see, physical suffering plays very little role in requests for assisted suicide) by offering death as a medical treatment.

The change in terminology reflects an important shift away from moral responsibility for the act. Whereas the right to die, self-determination and assisted suicide all imply that the individual involved takes full responsibility for the act, assignation of moral responsibility for 'assisted dying' is more diffuse.

Importantly, such an apparently facile change lumps together very different things in moral terms – killing another person and suicide. Suppose I make a pact with my friend that, should I ever support a soccer team other than Arsenal, he should kill me and, twenty years later, I arrive to meet him with a Tottenham Hotspur shirt and he kills me. Alternately, suppose I agreed, upon meeting him with the offending

shirt, that I should be killed for my lack of loyalty and for now supporting such a ridiculous football team. Suppose I then asked him for his
gun and shot myself. These two very different acts might be construed
as assisted dying (to satisfy *Dignity in Dying* criteria, let us also say that,
at the time, I had fewer than six months to live), though, in a court
of law, the former would be murder and the latter suicide. Though the
effect would be the same for me (and, being dead, the question of my
responsibility moot) and though my friend might bear some responsibility even if I pulled the trigger, the two acts are profoundly different
for him. Yet the concept of assisted dying essentially equates these two
different acts.

In fact, as we shall discuss in Chapter 6, negating moral responsibility means that courts, where individuals are tried to determine the
degree of their responsibility for a crime, are less appropriate than professional regulatory tribunals, where the question becomes whether or
not a set of regulations has been followed properly. Rather than being
self-determining actors who choose our own fates, we become points
on an increasingly complex flow chart, requiring a huge apparatus of
bureaucratic experts.

If we accept *Dignity in Dying*'s suggestion that assisted dying involves
only those who are considered to be dying, an essentially philosophical question is determined by a professional regulatory body. There is
little agreement on this issue even between advocates. Oregon's and
Washington's legislation (and proposed UK legislation) define the dying
as those with a terminal illness and six months to live whereas the UK
Commission on Assisted Dying recommended that the subject be terminally ill and have 12 months or fewer to live. If the phrase 'suffering
unbearably' is employed as it was in the proposed UK legislation, how
will that be determined? Again, there is little clarity and great scope for
regulations at every step of the process.[11]

The assisted-suicide legislation and proposed legislation has created
a new identity in the 'dying'. But the division between 'the dying' –
whether they have six or 12 months to live – and the rest of us is false.
Who is not dying one day at a time? We are all 'terminal', and the worth
of our lives should not be crudely measured by the time we have left. Nor
is dying a medical act; long before any medical intervention occurred,
people were dying without any intervention at all. As Daniel Callahan
has noted, there is now a tendency to view death as something that is
done to us rather than something that occurs, 'as if death were now
our fault, the result of human choices, not the independent workings of
nature'. As the old joke has it, life itself is a sexually transmitted disease

that is always fatal. The difference between someone with fewer than six months to live and someone with many years is quantitative rather than qualitative. The 'dying' as a category are, in actuality, those who have little time left or, more controversially, as we shall explore in the next chapter, the elderly.[12]

Such a term also obscures the historically different motivations behind the campaign. Autonomy, in the classical sense, implies the freedom to terminate one's own life with no intrusion by the state or anyone else. Compassion might (mistakenly) motivate people to support a campaign for the dying to be put out of their misery. As expressed in the example above, if we support legalization of assisted dying, either we support selective suicides or selective killings. As we shall see in the next chapter, the movement for assisted dying builds upon distrust of medical personnel; none of the campaigns in the English-speaking world call for more power for doctors. As Professor Ray Tallis, prominent patron of the English proponent for a change in the law, *Dignity in Dying*, notes: 'It is one of the fundamental principles of medicine that you should be allowed to determine what is in your own best interest when you are of sound mind. Nobody else's views should be able to over-ride this right.'[13] Yet the voices of doctors, should assisted suicide be institutionalized, will, as we will see in Chapter 6, be the loudest in these decisions.

Criticisms of this re-branding of suicide are not all from the anti-assisted-suicide side. Such seasoned advocates of assisted suicide/dying as Derek Humphry have also questioned it. Reacting to news that the Oregon Department of Human Services chose in 2006 to replace references to 'assisted suicide' with 'assisted dying', Humphrey noted: 'To wrap up our support for physician-assisted suicide in fancy language invites our critics to say that we are trying to change the law covertly and that we are ashamed of being frank about what we really want, neither of which is true.' The Commission on Dying also refused to jettison the term 'assisted suicide', referring to 'assisted dying' as both assisted suicide and voluntary euthanasia.[14]

The real issue at the heart of the debate – one which is obscured by the term assisted dying – is suicide, not dying. The question at the heart of this debate is whether we wish to pre-approve suicide in certain circumstances. To call what happens in Oregon and Washington – where the physician prescribes a deadly drug to a patient fitting all the criteria of the Death with Dignity Act (DWDA) and the person ingests that drug without the physician present – anything other than suicide is patently ridiculous. Even in the Netherlands, where euthanasia is legal, 'the word has a more limited meaning; it only refers to the deliberate termination of the life of a person on his request by another person (i.e., active, voluntary euthanasia)'. In all cases, the patient must make the request. If death occurs entirely because of the purposeful action of the patient, is it reasonable to call it anything other than suicide?[15]

Moral responsibility for the death in the case of a suicide lies with the suicide himself. But part of the project of legalization is to fudge moral responsibility so that no one person takes responsibility for the action. If a doctor purposefully kills a patient, it is most likely to be an act of kindness but it may also be murder. Our judgment of such an act would not reflect our assessment of the worth of the life that has been taken. The proposal by assisted dying advocates is that those who are terminally ill (medically defined) with less than six months to live (the prognosis to be determined by two doctors) are absolved of moral responsibility on the basis of a medical prognosis. But neither is the doctor responsible for the act.

In fact, should assisted suicide be institutionalized, we are asked not simply to tolerate the actions of a few unfortunate individuals but to affirm them. This is what legalization means. It institutionalizes assisted suicide as a medical procedure, beyond moral judgement. The very different motivations for wishing to voluntarily depart the world are lost and we are asked to accept the decision of the individual concerned. They are beyond right and wrong.

So, even in what might initially appear to be a trite discussion about terminology, there are deep implications. It is not merely the words but the meaning behind them that is being challenged. In the attempt to replace the religious meaning of life and death with a medical one, by re-imagining death as therapy, assisted-suicide advocates effectively remove its moral meaning.

For these reasons, the terminology preferred in this book is assisted suicide rather than assisted dying. The former term recognizes that the real issue at the heart of the discussion is suicide.

Present opinion

In general, the public supports legalizing assisted suicide for those with a terminal illness but for no one else. A Populus poll for *The Times* in July 2009 found that 74 per cent of those in the UK surveyed thought that the law should be changed to allow doctor-assisted suicide in 'cases where an individual is of sound mind and has made unambiguously clear that they want to die and want or need help to do so'; 60 per cent supported the legalization of non-doctor (friends, relatives)-assisted suicide. But when asked about whether those with an incurable physical disability should have the right to die, less than half in a recent British poll answered yes. The same poll revealed that only 13 per cent believed that assisted suicide should be legal 'without restriction' and 85 per cent thought assisted suicide should be legal 'only in certain specific circumstances'.[16]

Americans have similar, if perhaps more changeable, perspectives on the issue. In a 2005 poll asking Americans whether an individual has the moral right to die, the percentage agreeing to suicide because of an incurable disease stood at 53, whereas the percentage agreeing with the morality of suicide because life was burdensome was 33. Other polls confirm that whereas most people agree with changing the law regarding assisted suicide, the majority also oppose allowing suicide with no restrictions.[17]

Broken down into groups, religious people, not surprisingly, tended to support legalization less than those who identified themselves as non-religious, but nevertheless a majority of some 71 per cent support legalization for some cases, according to the 2010 British Social Attitudes survey. The elderly, though recent polls suggest they are broadly supportive of assisted suicide, tend not to be as keen as younger groups. The July 2009 *Times* Populus Survey, which provided its results broken down by age group, found that 77 per cent of people aged 55–64 and 70 per cent of people aged 65-plus felt that the law should be changed to allow doctor-assisted suicide along the lines of what is practised in Switzerland. Disabled people were also more likely to be suspicious of assisted suicide; though a majority support legalization of assisted suicide, no fewer than 70 per cent worry that legalization may have a deleterious effect on the lives of disabled people.[18]

But it is probably true of most places that most people have no hard and fast attitudes on the issue. Besides the activists on either side, as, James Davison Hunter has observed, 'most Americans occupy a vast middle ground between the polarizing impulses'. As Ian Dowbiggin observes, there is unlikely to be a clear winner between the two opposed camps. In the United States there has been no *Roe v. Wade* (the Supreme Court decision in 1973 that effectively legalized abortion) paving the way for assisted suicide but nor is the pro-life camp likely to be victorious.[19]

Those who are involved or have experience of the dying process tend to oppose assisted suicide. The hospice movement has been one of the most important voices raised against legalization. Taken as a whole, 64 per cent of all doctors disagreed while 34 per cent agreed with legalization. Doctors who worked in palliative medicine were more likely to be opposed to assisted dying.[20]

Law

Where assisted suicide is legal, there are very different rules involved. A spectrum between Switzerland, where assisting any suicide is legal as long as there is a good reason (that is, not financial), to what might be called 'low country' legalization in the Netherlands, Belgium and Luxembourg, where euthanasia and physician-assisted suicide are legal but aiding a suicide is banned for non-medical persons, and Oregon, where euthanasia is illegal but physicians write deadly prescriptions for terminally ill patients to ingest at home.

At present in most states of the USA, the UK, Canada, Australia and New Zealand, assisting, aiding or abetting a suicide is illegal. As we go to press, Massachusetts' 2012 ballot initiative to allow assisted suicides was narrowly defeated, 51 to 49 per cent. Many European countries have no specific laws against assisting a suicide but can and do prosecute such cases under other legislation such as that governing manslaughter (Sweden) or failure to assist a person in danger (France). In Oregon, Washington and, it appears, in Montana,[21] assisted suicide is legal and in Oregon, where the law has operated for over 14 years, a few dozen people per year take up this option. A smaller percentage takes up the option in Washington (about .01 per cent of all deaths each year opt for an assisted death).[22] Assisting a suicide is not specifically mentioned in the laws of North Carolina, Utah and Wyoming. In the other 44 states, assisting a suicide constitutes a crime. In Switzerland, suicide and physician and non-physician assisted suicide is legal, as long as the motivations for the assistance are honourable. However, euthanasia is illegal. Since 2002, Belgium allows 'euthanasia' but only when it meets strict criteria; all euthanasia, like in the Netherlands, must be requested voluntarily by the patient. In the Netherlands voluntary euthanasia and physician-assisted suicide have been lawful since April 2002 for reasons of 'hopeless and unbearable' suffering, but tacitly permitted by the courts since 1984. Luxembourg has allowed physician-assisted suicide for terminally ill patients since 2008.

The law in the United Kingdom (except Scotland, where assisted suicide is also illegal) is the Suicide Act of 1961 (Canada, Australia and New Zealand have similar statutes). Although it decriminalized suicide, it stated that a 'person who aids, abets, counsels or procures the suicide of another, or an attempt by another to commit suicide, shall be liable on conviction on indictment to imprisonment for a term not exceeding fourteen years',[23] signalling continued disapproval of suicide. Campaigners generally wish to change this law to make assisting a suicide in specific circumstances legal (though not all wish to restrict the act of assisting a suicide to particular circumstances, all favour liberalizing the law). Though many favour the right to die and it has been the subject of a Supreme Court case, few proponents elaborate the meaning of this right or its considerable implications.[24]

The continuing campaign for a change in the law

Beyond this specific goal – changing the law – there is little focus either to the pro-campaign or to uniting opponents. Few campaigners *for* reform of the law wish to follow the Swiss model by calling for permission to assist all suicides (though, as will be discussed, Ludwig Minelli's *Dignitas* clinic in Switzerland allows suicide by those with no terminal illness or disability, reflecting Switzerland's law) and few campaigners *against* a change in the law wish to see existing law ruthlessly applied to cases whereby a doctor, motivated only by mercy, has terminated the life of a very ill and imminently dying patient to prevent further suffering. Most campaigners for assisted suicide approve of the hospice movement and wish to see more pain control in patients, and most opponents will admit that there are situations whereby keeping someone alive serves no purpose and may cause suffering.

In fact, it is not simply a change in the law but what I call institutionalization – the acceptance of assisted suicide as the moral norm – that motivates many proponents of assisted suicide. Here again, it is worth examining areas where the law has been liberalized and where, one might reasonably expect, the response of advocacy organizations to liberalized laws would be to stand down or disband.

For these campaigners at least, the purpose of their continued advocacy is twofold. First, they promote moral acceptance of the act of assisting a suicide. But second, confirming some of the fears of opponents about the slippery slope, there is evidence that advocates wish to extend the categories to larger groups of people. The Netherlands, where the practice has been tolerated since the 1970s, is the most important source of information here. After the practice was declared legal in 2002, 'right to die' organizations remain active. Aims such as those of the *Nederlandse Vereniging Voor Een Vrijwillig Levenseinde* (NVVE), an organization that claims 135,000 members, imply that this is not simply a movement that automatically disappears once the legislation is in place:

> The advancement of an as broad as possible use and social acceptance of the existing legal possibilities towards a free choice for the ending of life.

The advancement of the social acceptance and the legal regulation of a free choice for ending of life in situations which are not within the scope of the existing legal possibilities.

Striving towards the recognition of a free choice for the ending of life and assistance with it as a human right.[25]

The implication is that the Swiss model – where all suicides may be assisted – is the end result that these Dutch advocates seek. But perhaps more interesting is the more recent Dutch initiative to provide assisted suicides to all Dutch people over 70 who feel tired of life. This is the demand of a citizens' initiative in the Netherlands called Uit Vrije Wil (Out of Free Will) and supported by the relatively mainstream NVVE, the Dutch Green and D66 parties, former government ministers, artists, doctors, and legal scholars. According to its website, the initiative attracted 117,000 letters of support from Dutch people between January and May 2010. This group refers to that moment as the time 'life is completed, when lack of purpose befalls elderly people, when their family, friends and acquaintances have all passed away, and when they feel left behind and unable to escape an empty existence'. Such an initiative is not necessarily new – Dutch legal scholar Huib Drion proposed providing the old with an 'acceptable means to end their lives at a moment they see fit' as early as 1991 – but the fact that those behind the initiative now feel confident to canvass the public is surely significant.[26]

The legal scholar Eugène Sutorius said he considered the right a cultural matter, and that he was looking for freedom to face death 'in a stoic manner', without fear of a legal system that branded assisted suicide as criminal. The group wants to draw a line at age 70. Helping young people commit suicide 'cannot be justified', Sutorius said. When a younger person kills himself, it is always 'a disaster', he claimed. 'An older person can understand more, has more perspective.' The group admits the age of 70 was a somewhat arbitrary cut-off point. 'Whether it should be 65 or 90 is a good question. We think that once someone has reached old age, he has proved his ability to live. He can then choose to leave this life in a procedural, medically supervised manner,' Sutorius said. The initiative ultimately failed in the Dutch parliament but continues as a possibility.[27]

Such campaigners are not restricted to the Netherlands. Baroness Mary Warnock, a celebrated British philosopher known for her humanist views, advocated a 'duty to die' for the elderly and those suffering from dementia. 'If you're demented, you're wasting people's lives – your family's lives – and you're wasting the resources of the National Health Service. ...I feel there's a wider argument that if somebody absolutely, desperately wants to die because they're a burden to their family, or the state, then I think they too should be allowed to die.'[28]

It would be naïve not to locate the assisted suicide discussion within a broader anxiety about the 'greying' of the population and the resulting pressure on health services.[29] A main concern is that with the retirement of the baby boomers, the number of people of a working, taxable age will shrink or become stagnant. This could result in gaps in the jobs market, with businesses and public services lacking the workforce required. With the elderly being the fastest growing age group throughout the English-speaking world, increasing pressure is being put on healthcare and social services. Warnock's opinion may be more forthright, as most discussants are unwilling to discuss pressure on resources and assisted suicide in the same breath, but Dr Michael Irwin, a vocal supporter (and an admitted practitioner) of assisted suicides, has launched a new initiative called the Society for Old Age Rational Suicide (SOARS) which, like its Dutch sister campaign, recommends that all elderly people have the right to an assisted suicide.[30]

As an American author observes:

> The economic incentives for individuals to choose physician-assisted death are quite high...In a medical climate that is characterized by skyrocketing costs for advanced technological treatments and an aging population with prolonged years of disability and illness on one hand and strong incentives for physicians to save on medical expenditures on the other, assisted suicide and euthanasia would be the ultimate cost-saving tools.[31]

Of course, there are many advocates outside of Oregon, Washington and the Benelux countries who simply want a change in the law to allow for those very few cases of terminally ill patients who want to die. But for at least a few, changing the law for these few cases represents a first step, a moral beachhead, in a campaign to change the way we view the value of life past 70.

The main implication of such sentiments is the devaluation of age and experience. Elderly people have a 'lack of purpose' and clearly waste young people's time and medical resources. Unlike the 'disaster' of the suicides of young people, suicides of the elderly are to be welcomed. At first glance, it is odd that such campaigns emerge at a time when those over 70 lead longer and better lives than ever before.

Of course, Warnock, SOARS, Uit Vrije Wil and others carry on a tradition of attempts to deny medical treatment to various groups deemed pointless, as Chapter 3 notes. However, there was little suggestion by eugenics groups outside of Germany that the elderly (as opposed to various racial and ability groups, for instance) were nothing but useless consumers. It is difficult to resist the idea that age and experience are uniquely devalued today and that an important impetus behind the campaign is the idea that the elderly waste resources.

Clearly, there is a bigger agenda than simply legislation. These advocates call for increased social acceptance of assisted suicide as well as assisted suicide as a human right. The motivations of these organizations are not as straightforward as the discussion might initially imply. Here, if not in the way it is usually presented, is evidence for the 'slippery slope' that we will discuss in the next chapter.

Who does it?

The extraordinary fact – one pointing to the chimerical nature of the whole discussion – is that though a majority would like the right to die, no one will use it. The numbers going through with an assisted suicide are extraordinarily low. In Oregon, the excellent *Death with Dignity* reports give an indication of how few actually opt for such a contentious 'right'.

As the 2010 report notes:

> Of the 96 patients for whom prescriptions were written during 2010, 59 died from ingesting the medications. In addition, six patients with prescriptions written during previous years ingested the medications and died during 2010 for a total of 65 known 2010 DWDA deaths at the time of this report. This corresponds to 20.9 DWDA deaths per 10,000 total deaths.

In other words, about 0.2 per cent of all deaths in Oregon are assisted suicides, comprising less than one per cent of those who request information about an assisted death. Nor was there a rush towards assisted suicides in Washington, a state nearly twice as populous as Oregon, after legalization; 70 people died in 2011 after ingesting poison under the DWDA Act. In the Netherlands in 2005, a total of 2410 deaths by euthanasia or PAS were reported, representing 1.7 per cent of all deaths in the Netherlands. The estimated equivalent for the UK if either the Oregon model was adopted would be 986 persons per year. If the Dutch model was adopted, Britain could expect 8385 deaths per year as a result of euthanasia – voluntary and involuntary. To put it in context, the total number of deaths in the UK in 2010 was 493,242. The numbers of suicides in the UK and Ireland is around six thousand per year.[32]

Where euthanasia is legal, the numbers are dropping, largely because doctors now prefer terminal sedation (where the patient lives but does not recover consciousness). The numbers projected in the UK range from 650 to 1000 should it be legalized. The message is that, even if everyone wants to have such a 'right', very few will use it.[33]

The fact that very few people take advantage of such a 'right' is not in itself a reason why it should not be legalized; after all, why should anyone suffer needlessly? But it tells us about the nature of sentiment behind legalization – advocates want it more as a failsafe against their nightmares about medical technology. The need for legalization is chimerical; surely our present tolerant attitude towards suicide and euthanasia where genuine mercy motivates it can cope with the small numbers. The fact that few take advantage of legalized assisted suicide, as we will see in Chapter 5, indicates a basic difference from abortion.

Euthanasia and assisted suicide – part of the same trend?

Much as proponents of assisted suicide promote euphemisms that remove the taint of suicide, opponents tend to conflate assisted suicide and euthanasia. Like their opponents, they neglect the different moral connotations for those left behind of assisting a suicide and of killing itself. There is a clear attempt to identify the enemy as contemptuous of human life and casual in its attitude towards killing. 'Though an analytical distinction exists between assisted suicide and euthanasia, there is a great deal they share in common, and those who support legalizing one tend to support legalizing the other for the same or similar reasons,' notes Neil M. Gorsuch. John Keown asked: 'What, for example, is the supposed difference between a doctor handing a lethal pill to a patient; placing the pill on the patient's tongue; and dropping it down the patient's throat?'[34]

The differences Keown alludes to are stark in the context of this study. Euthanasia has been, at least up until relatively recently, a fairly common necessity for doctors based on a medical assessment of a patient's condition at the very end of life. Only the final hours or perhaps days of life are affected and the point of the doctor's action is to alleviate needless suffering, based on the doctor's experience with the progression of a particular disease or condition as well as her relationship with an individual patient; there is no manual instructing doctors exactly when is the right time to hasten the end of life. It is, above all, a humane action taken because the doctor is in a privileged position to end suffering, and not part of their professional duties. It is akin to the soldier who is begged by his comrade, who has just had his legs and lower torso blown off, to shoot him. We all hope we would be brave enough to take this action in those circumstances. Putting it bluntly, doctors are often in such circumstances, as relatively frequent witnesses to death. In a minority of situations, continued living means only extended suffering. The purpose of an action like this is nearly always to prevent needless suffering by speeding the process of dying. In many cases the patient has already, for all intents and purposes, left the land of the living.

There is no legal framework able to accommodate such actions. They are, above all, private actions that only come to light rarely, either because of an unlikely disagreement between those at the deathbed scene or because the doctor or carer tells those outside the deathbed scene that she did it. The latter is often is an indication of either attention-seeking or of campaigning individuals with axes to grind. No good can come of shoving these sad decisions into the public domain unless there is doubt as to whether the action taken was correct. In rare situations, the law on murder and manslaughter or assisted suicide can apply.

If we regard the issue at the heart of the issue of assisted suicide as moral – a central argument in this book – there is a wide gulf between Keown's three situations. To the suicide, it is immaterial if the pill is handed to him, placed on his tongue or put down his throat. But this is not the case for those left behind. There are varying degrees of responsibility that can be assigned to the doctor's action. By shoving the pill down the patient's throat, the doctor assumes full responsibility for her action; by handing the patient the pill, the doctor may intend only to give the patient reassurance and thus assumes only a small degree of responsibility should the patient immediately take the pill. The second scenario seems worst; the doctor clearly knows the intention but wishes to avoid the full responsibility of the third action – the equivalent of placing a gun to someone's head, putting his finger on the trigger but leaving the patient to pull it. If the death is desirable, surely shoving a pill down the patient's throat is the bravest and most desirable option.

We, as a society, currently tolerate actions by doctors in situations where most people are likely to agree that continued biological existence is not desirable. That is not to say that the law should be changed in order to allow euthanasia – each situation can only be judged individually and quality of life cannot be judged according to generic criteria. It is simply to recognize that in situations such as that of Terri Schiavo,[35] causing death, either passively or actively, might be the best course of action and that doctors are usually in the best position to judge.

Finally, there is evidence that the public understands that there is a major difference between euthanasia and assisted suicide. This was important, according to Howard Ball, in the success and failure of various voter initiatives which took place in the 1990s:

> One major difference between Oregon's successful Measure 16 and the defeated Washington initiative 119 and California's Proposition 161, was that the Oregon proposal explicitly prohibited euthanasia: it was a reasonable 'prescribing only' measure that barred any kind of lethal injection or other direct action on a dying patient by the physician. This difference was critical to the bill's success because it silenced the euthanasia threat to certain groups fostered by the opposition by exclusively endorsing the death-by-prescription model.[36]

Even before getting too deeply into the issues involved, definitions divide the pro- and anti-assisted-suicide camps. Rather than being a simple issue, the meanings of the terms involved are confounding. Both sides conspire to blur the distinction between suicide, euthanasia and 'passive' euthanasia. Such a distinction is important if we regard the issue as, at base, a moral problem. We shall return to these issues in the following chapters.

2
An Analysis of the Key Arguments on Both Sides

The real difficulty with the existing debate is that there is little recognition that, ultimately, the assisted suicide debate is philosophical and moral rather than religious, political, legal or sociological. In fact, there is a fundamental difference between the sides in that proponents tend to put forward political reasons for allowing assisted suicide whereas opponents stick to religious reasons for their opposition. Perhaps this is the reason why the discussion does not seem to move; both sides argue from utterly different cultural frameworks.

The discussion seems to consist of a gradual chipping away of the case against legalization amongst the huge, neutral group who are not intimately involved in the debate. Though it may appear counterintuitive to begin with the case against, it makes sense to examine the predicament of what is plainly the more beleaguered side of the argument. As Margaret Somerville has argued, 'The burden of proof has somehow shifted from those who promote legalization to those who oppose it . . . .'[1] The chief difficulty for many of those opposed to assisted suicide is that what has been in the past axiomatic is no longer unquestioned. Why is this so?

Reasons for opposition to assisted suicide: sanctity of life

The most important argument against legalizing assisted suicide is based upon the idea of the sanctity of life. All human life is sacred. It is wrong to take human life, whether my own or someone else's. Assisted suicide, euthanasia and, more arguably, abortion all involve taking a human life. Much as there are cases whereby taking a human life is the right thing to do (self-defence, the so-called 'policeman's dilemma'), legalizing assisted suicide would set a precedent.

The sanctity of life is sometimes expressed as the 'right to life'. Insisting on the right to life implies that every human being has the right to live, particularly in the sense of the right not to be killed by another human being. There is a certain amount of legal support for such a right. The Universal Declaration of Human Rights, adopted by the United Nations General Assembly in 1948, declared that 'everyone has the right to life, liberty, and security of person', echoing the United States Declaration of Independence's phrasing: 'life, liberty, and the pursuit of happiness.'

But a 'right to life' is as problematic as the 'right to die'. What sort of life do we mean? Do we really mean bare sentience, where a person exists only in a biological sense? How can someone exercise a 'right to life', particularly when faced with a deadly disease? And we must ask the question that appears throughout this book, what do we mean by 'life'? In fact, all the right to life really implies is a sanction against killing (we will expand upon this discussion in Chapter 5).

The absolute nature of the sanction against killing often undermines the arguments of opponents of assisted suicide. Of course, proponents rightly point out that the sanction against killing is not absolute; killing is sanctioned in particular circumstances such as war or self-defence. Why then, proponents ask, should it not be allowed when it is really a kindness and in the subject's best interests? Are opponents against doctors removing life support apparatus when further existence is futile? For many, as the case of Terri Schiavo showed, the answer is yes.[2]

There is a real basis to the sanctity of life, even for atheists, but it must be explicated rather than simply asserted. It is not always wrong to kill but, should someone kill, they must justify their action in a court of law. The sanctity of life argument is confused and unconvincing and often posed in absolutist terms. It should really be understood as a principle, a negative reflection of our equal valuation of human life that underwrites our laws against murder. Insisting on the sanctity of life is actually insistence on the equal valuation of all lives. One who murders an 89-year-old man is as culpable as one who murders a 24-year-old, just as the murder of a poor person horrifies us as much as that of a rich person. It is the presumed value of all human life that is being questioned; to argue on the basis of sanctity of life requires not that we simply insist upon it but that we expose the moral principle behind the prohibition against killing. Rather than insisting that life should never be taken, we need to argue against undermining the principle of the equal value of human persons reflected in existing law. In the present climate, where the campaign to legalize assisted suicide is by no means the only challenge to such a principle, such things must be explained anew.

Not only is such a stance problematic when discussing suicide or even those who sacrifice their lives for those of others (which is discussed in Chapter 4), the sanctity of life contention also is somewhat circular in modern secular terms. Life is sacred because we all think that it is sacred. Such logic lends itself to a constant questioning, and many point out the huge gap between such an abstract notion and examples of where life is not valued. Sustaining what in fact is a taboo in the face of relentless questioning is impossible.

The slippery slope

A second, related argument might be termed the 'slippery slope' argument (known as the 'wedge principle' in earlier debates). Favoured especially by secular opponents of legalization, it argues that if we allow the very few people who wish to have a legal assisted suicide to do so, more and more categories of people will be included in eligible groups. The pressure will mount upon people who feel they are a burden to their families or even to their healthcare providers. Assisted suicide will soon slide into euthanasia which may even become involuntary euthanasia. Of course, many, if not most, of those using the slippery slope argument take a much more limited approach. Still, this skein runs through most opposition arguments.

There is, again, a basis to the 'slippery slope' argument but the slippery slope is not a threat in the way that opponents normally pose the issue. It is demonstrably not an immediate practical problem. Set out as such, it can be demonstrated to be false using the material made available in the excellent Oregon Death with Dignity (DWDA) Reports. In Oregon, at least, there is no sign of increasing deaths or any good evidence that anyone has been euthanized against his or her will. Just as with the sanctity of life, there is a real basis to the slippery slope argument but it deals with intangibles rather than practical issues. Allowing assisted suicide might very well lead to a more casual perspective towards killing but it is difficult to marshall evidence to prove this. To such charges proponents can easily reply that it is unfair to posit such intangibles against the real suffering of real individuals. Moreover, the slippery slope view also contains a conservative core based on unforeseen risks, something that holds little appeal to mainly liberal proponents and, it seems, the majority of people in the UK, Canada, Australia, New Zealand and the United States.

Nearly all commentators opposed to assisted suicide return to these arguments. Nigel Biggar, opposing the right to die, admits that there is a difference, as proponents John Harris, Ronald Dworkin and others claim, between 'biographical' and mere 'biological' life (and I agree). Biggar, in an interesting claim, notes that the ability to be responsible is the key to biographical life; he worries that responsible patients may be manipulated. Pointedly, Biggar notes the difficulties in dividing biographical from biological life, though he admits that, if all are agreed that the biographical side is gone, it is permissible to euthanize a person, even if they have not agreed. Biggar also claims that biographical life is sacred and making euthanasia acceptable undermines esteem for human life.

Despite the sophistication of Biggar's arguments, they rest upon notions of the sanctity of (biographical if not biological) life and the slippery slope. As such, he can do little other than assert the sanctity of life. Moreover, Biggar's cogent argument about the diminution of respect for human life rests upon the slippery slope view – in this case, its contribution towards the acceptability of euthanasia. Proponents will simply reply that safeguards can prevent any descent into euthanasia.[3]

As in some other accounts, Arthur J. Dyck offers many arguments against assisted suicide, almost as if the sheer number of arguments might confound critics. He begins with the time-honoured tradition of using a personal perspective into the issue. His central plank is, again, that human life is sacred, though Dyck offers both religious and secular arguments as to why this is the case. Dyck concentrates on a common morality that he locates in Christian and Western philosophical thought. He makes an excellent point when he criticizes the idea that the value of human life can be measured in time left to live.

Despite his many challenging criticisms of arguments in favour of the right to die, Dyck's laudable arguments about the devaluation of human life implicit in legalization soon collapse into the slippery slope argument. Thus, his examples of the Serb sniper and of a veterinarian who became used to killing and increasingly casual about it can be easily countered by the safeguards argument. He argues for the right to life as a natural position but is somewhat circular when he attempts to explain why it exists. 'Current laws presuppose a shared moral outlook that characterizes life as sacred,' he notes, but fails to define the idea of the sacred satisfactorily or to support its continued existence.[4]

Neil Gorsuch provides a readable, lucid and effective attack on the proponents' arguments, leaning heavily on the sanctity of life argument. Sharing a characteristic of many on his side of the argument, he stumbles on the question of personhood, particularly its definition. His concept of the inviolability and the inherent value of human life as it is now constituted, though, as he rightly notes, is easily recognized by nearly everyone, but is somewhat mystical. Where, exactly, is the basis of our valuation of human life? Though Gorsuch avoids direct discussion of religious matters, the shadow of God can be seen throughout this thoughtful book. Gorsuch agrees with Ronald Dworkin, a powerful proponent of legalization, that there is an inherent value to human life. This may well be the case but to simply assert it raises the question of the origin of such a value. Does it exist outside of time and space rather like the monolith in *2001: A Space Odyssey*? The subtext of Gorsuch's efforts is that God injected mere biological matter with importance beyond the materials that constitute human beings. Like those of so many others, Gorsuch's arguments, while often cogent, ultimately rely on a mystery, rendering them less effective than they might have been had they been anchored to something more tangible.[5]

There *is* a secular conception of the sanctity of life, which is alluded to by Jonathan Glover. Glover speaks of an 'an absolute barrier, an absolute ban, not derived from a religious source, on the intentional taking of innocent human life', which he thinks is identical to the religious version. However, Glover does not elaborate fully. Many proponents also give credence to the principle of the sanctity of life, though they feel it is not as important as other considerations in the debate. As Lord Joffe stated to the Select Committee on the Assisted Dying for the Terminally Ill Bill: 'Autonomy trumps sanctity of life.'[6]

Margaret Somerville positively celebrates mystery in a Kierkegaardian sense, using arguments very unlikely to convince humanists and those who make it their goal to demystify life. She presents a similar perspective to Dyck, Biggar and Gorsuch, but discusses the sanctity of life in terms of the mystery of death. That which unites us, which makes us more than the sum of our material parts, remains mysterious. Somerville sharply points to the reductive individualism inherent in the campaign for legalization. The fact that many organizations promoting assisted suicide continue to be active in countries where legalization has occurred indicates that she is on the right track with her assertion that death talk reflects a fear of death and is manifested in the promotion of assisted suicide. Somerville's strengths lie in her discussion of why the whole discussion is appearing now and in her attack on autonomy.

However, she conflates assisted suicide (or, more accurately, physician-assisted suicide) with euthanasia. 'The term "physician-assisted suicide" is used to describe what is really euthanasia. The physician carries out the act that causes death. In physician assisted suicide...physicians would give patients the means to kill themselves with the intent that patients would so use them.'[7] This confusion (Somerville attacks the confusion sown by pro-assisted-suicide advocates) misidentifies the meaning of the pro-campaign. As we observed in the previous chapter (and as will be elaborated in Chapter 4), few campaign today for increased powers for physicians; it is the autonomy argument that now carries weight. The question is essentially about suicide rather than euthanasia.

Gorsuch identifies the slippery slope argument as existing from at least as far back as St Augustine of Hippo. Augustine argued against the Donatists, who took from the Apostle Paul's intimation of suicide in Corinthians – 'If I give my body to be burned' – that suicide was permissible. If death could be seen as a way to escape temporal troubles, why not allow suicide to avoid future sins and other degradations? But it is important to note that this is more rubicon than slippery slope. The latter concept implies a series of steps leading to a gradual lack of control and unintended descent. The former metaphor sees the initial step as the crucial one.[8]

The real basis of the modern slippery slope argument came after the publication of Leo Alexander's 'Medical Science under Dictatorship' in 1949, a rather horrifying article about medical abuses under the Nazis. Leaning heavily on Alexander, Thomas Martin argued against legalization of euthanasia in the United States: 'As a matter of fact, where euthanasia has been established by law in modern Western Civilization it has been extended to all who were considered socially unfit. [...] It started with the acceptance of the attitude, basic in the euthanasia movement, that there is such a thing as a life not worthy to be lived.'[9]

Even today, the Nazi association continues, particularly in some of the more more blunt attacks on assisted suicide, such as Wesley J. Smith's *Forced Exit: The Slippery Slope from Assisted Suicide to Legalized Murder*. But the slippery slope argument also forms the basis of more sober, considered and balanced discussions such as that contained in John Keown's book *Euthanasia, Ethics, and Public Policy: An Argument against Legalisation*. Keown argues that legalization of euthanasia yields a practice that cannot be controlled. Keown notes, in a common argument among those who oppose assisted suicide, that the example of abortion bolsters the case for the slippery slope on both an empirical and logical basis (see Chapter 5).[10]

Perhaps the most influential piece outlining slippery slope objections is *The New York State Task Force on Life in the Law*. An influential body formed in 1985 to 'develop public policy on a host of issues arising from medical advances', it introduced one of what Keown has referred to as empirical arguments for the slippery slope. The report above all focused on possible abuse resulting from legalzing assisted suicide, concluding: 'We believe that the practices would be profoundly dangerous for large segments of the population.' Later, the Task Force compared assisted suicide to capital punishment: 'Even our system for administering the death penalty, which includes the stringent safeguards of due process and years of judicial scrutiny, has not been freed of error or prejudice. For example, blacks who kill whites are sentenced to death at nearly 22 times the rate of blacks who kill blacks...'[11]

Whereas this position is well-argued in the report, it can be refuted effectively by recourse to the Oregon Death With Dignity Act (DWDA) reports issued annually since 1999. These reports indicate that the very few who make the choice of assisted suicide tend to be white, well-educated and on average younger than those who fit the criteria but die naturally. As Raymond Tallis noted: 'Contrary to expectation, those patients who receive assistance in dying tend to be "feisty", self-assertive characters from higher social classes, not the cowed, complicit, vulnerable, frail individual that opponents to liberalization worry about.' So there is little to support the worries expressed in the New York Task Force's 1994 report. Proponents can simply point to the evidence showing that the number of assisted suicides is fairly stable, that there is very little evidence of coercion or that the practice is becoming widespread.[12]

Bonnie Steinbock wrote her works after the DWDA reports became available but relies upon the fundamentally conservative argument that we cannot be sure that the vulnerable are safe. She is one of the very few opponents of the legalization of assisted suicide who supports abortion rights for women. Steinbock rejects the absolutist sanctity of life view that leads many to see abortion and assisted suicide as assaults on humanity. Instead, she bases her objections on the riskiness of allowing assisted suicide. Such an argument throws light upon the fruitless quest for absolute certainty about life and its limits that haunts those who wish to control their own deaths. In a sense, Steinbock presents a postmodern answer to what might be thought of as a postmodern question. Just as the assurance of the possibility of assisted suicide might be thought of as providing at least a certain answer to the prospect of suffering, so Steinbock argues that society can never be entirely sure that the vulnerable will not be swept up in the process.

After delivering some cogent criticisms of pro-assisted-suicide arguments, Steinbock reminds readers of the consequentialist arguments of Yale Kamisar, who confronted the liberal perspectives on euthanasia over fifty years ago. Steering clear of the difficult sanctity of life discussion, Steinbock develops the 'vulnerable' argument, asserting that inequalities in society will be reflected in patterns of legalized assisted suicide. 'Women might also be a vulnerable group, partly because of sexism which both devalues women and idealises women as self-sacrificing, and partly because studies have shown women to be at greater risk for inadequate pain relief and for depression.' We can never be sure that changing the legislation will not be harmful, she notes. Such an argument, as Glanville Williams, writing even earlier than Kamisar, noted, 'could be used to condemn any act whatever, because there is no human conduct from which evil may not be imagined to follow if it is persisted in when some of the circumstances are changed'.[13]

There are several problems with the slippery slope argument that are not overcome in the literature. Both the DWDA reports and those from the Netherlands allow pro-assisted-suicide campaigners to appear calm and rational and caricature their opponents as religious absolutists. Where is there any evidence for the slippery slope? Second, as Neil Levy has pointed out, the slippery slope argument effectively blocks all other argument, avoiding the real philosophical and moral debates about assisted suicide. It is by nature entirely conservative, despite Steinbock's liberal gloss; it is an argument against legalization of anything and, ultimately, any change that risks upsetting the status quo.

Third, it shares with pro-assisted-suicide arguments a concentration on fanciful situations and projections. 'What if...' frequently kicks off arguments on both sides. Proponents dream up terrible situations at the end of life, imagining themselves trapped in worn-out bodies. Every site set up by campaigners on both sides of the argument is replete with horrific stories. In response to the effect of proponents' examples, opponents, rather than questioning the value of extrapolating from these examples, come up with horror stories of their own, imagining that battalions of Mengeles will begin a process of eliminating useless eaters. The end-point of both arguments is careful legislation with safeguards rigorously applied, which is, after all, what nearly every proponent seeks.

There is a reality to the slippery slope argument but we need to accurately describe where the slope leads to rather than reciting fears about what might happen, if we are to employ the argument against legalization effectively. The complaints against assisted suicide – particularly physician-assisted suicide – made by disabled groups and their representatives merit attention. Disability rights activist Baroness Jane Campbell repeats the slippery slope fears when she notes: 'If they can make it legal for the life of a single person to be prematurely ended, they will then seek to broaden the criteria. Once early death becomes an "option", it will gain a respectability that will erode the resolve of many people experiencing personal difficulties.' We might see evidence for this broadening of categories in the recent guidelines issued by the Director of Public Prosecutions in England and Wales, Keir Starmer. Saimo Chahal, the lawyer for the British assisted-suicide advocate, Debbie Purdy, stated in respect to Starmer's guidelines: 'Significantly, the requirement that the victim have a terminal illness, a severe, incurable physical disability or severe degenerative physical condition, as a factor weighing against prosecution has been removed – and rightly so. [...] The absence of this requirement is clearly consistent with the right of any person to end their life, whether ill, disabled or otherwise.' We have also seen evidence of the expansion of categories considered eligible for assisted suicide in the previous chapter when we looked at the Dutch campaign to legalize assisted suicide for the over-70s.[14]

Opponents would do better to not concentrate narrowly on the effects of proposed changes but on the message transmitted by legalizing assisted suicide. Campbell and other disabled activists rightly note that allowing assisted suicide for *some* people in certain conditions cheapens the existence of *all* under those conditions. Saying that people who suffer from, say, Multiple Sclerosis (MS) should have the right to legal assisted suicide, implies that all sufferers of MS live fairly inferior and expendable lives. A similar case exists with those over 70 years old should the *Society for Old Age Rational Suicide* or the *Uit Vrije Wil* campaigns be successful. There is an inherent inequality between those free from disease (leading lives that should be preserved) and those with (leading lives that they might dispose of). The disability activist organization, *Not Dead Yet*, consistently opposes legalizing assisted suicide for this reason.[15]

Of course, the Oregon and Washington legislation pointedly does not allow assisted deaths for those with more than six months to live. However, more recent proposals, such as those put forward by the British Commission on Assisted Dying, call for those with fewer than twelve months to live to be allowed assisted suicide. Many others, such as the late Tony Nicklinson, have argued that those with permanent disabilities or conditions that are not terminal should have the right to an assisted suicide. The late Dr Jack Kevorkian included amongst his many patients some who showed no evidence of physical illness at all. In the Netherlands, voluntary euthanasia has been administered to those who are merely 'tired of life'.[16]

The importance of the 'slippery slope' is not that it is a danger to individual patients; the DWDA reports indicate that doctors are particularly careful and err on the side of caution in these cases. Such objections can also easily be met with safeguards. Instead, the danger of the slippery slope is the expansion of categories of people for whom suicide is pre-approved and, therefore, who are deemed to be leading inferior lives.

Corrupting medicine

Another point made by those opposing assisted suicide is that it transforms the relationship between doctor and patient. Allowing doctors to kill patients invalidates the Hippocratic Oath, the defining document of medical practice for over two thousand years. Leon Kass has especially argued against legalizing assisted suicide because it would be harmful to the doctor–patient relationship: 'Abuses and conflicts aside, legalized mercy killing by doctors will almost certainly damage the doctor–patient relationship. The patient's trust in the doctor's wholehearted devotion to the patient's best interests will be hard to sustain once doctors are licensed to kill.'[17]

However, there are several replies to such an objection. First, Kass's predictions appear premature; as evidence emerges from areas where assisted suicide and euthanasia are permitted, there is no sign that doctor–patient relationships have suffered.[18] Second, Kass has no real argument as to why doctors should not include euthanizing practices within their remit; legalization would allow this widespread practice to be regulated. Third, the Hippocratic Oath has already been breached in that doctors provide abortions ('I will not give a woman a pessary to cause an abortion').

Perhaps one more of the arguments against assisted suicide deserves to be considered. Kathleen Foley and Herbert Hendin note hopefully that hospice care has improved over the past years so much that legalizing assisted suicide is not necessary. After all, as Foley, Hendin and others point out, the Oregon DWDA surveys indicate that pain is not the most important reason why people opt for assisted suicide. Their remaining lives (and, more importantly, the anxieties of those who are far from death but favour keeping the option of assisted suicide open) might be improved by the prospect of a hospice death.

The difficulty with this argument is that, like the slippery slope line of reasoning, it avoids any moral difficulties, hoping to put in place an alternative with which no one can disagree. Assisted suicide advocates no doubt also wish for hospice care but can rightly point out that the two are not completely incompatible. Hospices as an alternative to assisted suicides mistakes the underlying issue, assuming that any need for assisted suicide can be overcome with technology. But, as we will see, the underlying issue is the morality of suicide and the way we understand life and death. We need to consider whether suicide is or should be morally acceptable or not. Hospice care no doubt responds to the immediate crises of those facing the personal crises written about in a constant stream of individual examples. But it is not about individuals – it is about our attitudes towards life and death. We should not – nor do we need to – attempt to sidestep the issue. Foley and Hendin rely finally upon the consequentialist version of the 'slippery slope' argument. They set out their stall early on in the book: 'The conditions peculiar to our age have made those who are dying in our culture profoundly vulnerable.'[19] Vulnerability can be answered, as proponents rightly note, by increased regulation.

Like the other arguments against legalization, the charge that it changes the doctor–patient relationship has a basis in truth but the damage done is less tangible than what has been presented by opponents. Instead, as we mentioned in the last chapter,[20] if assisted suicide is institutionalized doctors will play a quasi-religious role in that they remove the moral taint from suicide as well as a counselling role in assisting with actions that a patient is able to accomplish herself.

The arguments of the pro-assisted-suicide camp

The strength of the pro-assisted-suicide arguments lies in the weakness of those arraigned against it. Both the apparent religiosity of the sanctity of life argument and the inherent conservative nature of the slippery slope argument have provided ample cover for pro-assisted-suicide arguments, hiding the fact that they have altered and continue to change and covering over the huge and basic flaw that ultimately undermines their case. The pro-camp becomes the questioning, rational and progressive side of the dispute simply by virtue of the crumbling nature of their opponents' edifices. As Peter Singer puts it: 'The best argument for the new commandment is the sheer absurdity of the old one.'[21]

So questioning of the pro-assisted-suicide case is itself the most effective part of those arguing against assisted suicide, despite the confused nature of the entire discussion. Below, we will see that, rather than simply listing the flaws in the arguments of the pro-assisted-suicide side, it is necessary to highlight the central contradiction between the two most important arguments of the pro-assisted-suicide camp.

Timothy Quill and Jane Greenlaw list three reasons given by proponents for legalizing assisted suicide – autonomy, mercy and nonabandonment. Margaret Pabst Battin, one of the most articulate of the philosophers arguing for legalization, lists the important arguments for a change in the law as autonomy and relief from pain and suffering. Such is implicit in the name of the largest pro-assisted-suicide US lobbying group, *Compassion and Choices*, an awkward binding of two very different and, as we shall see, fairly incompatible terms. Up until recently, the most important reason for proponents – especially for more academic proponents – is almost always autonomy. Today, autonomy, though it survives, is being supplanted by another contradictory concept – professionalization. Now autonomy is redefined, ironically, as enablement by various different agencies and professional helpers.[22]

Compassion: solipsism or cowardice?

Compassion emerges as one of the strongest arguments in favour of a change in the law. This is why nearly all arguments begin with powerfully emotive stories. How many people can argue against compassion? But, if we interrogate the compassion that is claimed by proponents, it is either a faux compassion – either a projection of the self onto the dying person or a pointless and emotive anger at suffering – or a compassion of the most cowardly variety that prefers to hand the gun to the suffering individual rather than take responsibility for the action itself. In the latter sense, true compassion does not suggest assisted suicide but euthanasia – a legal option nearly universally rejected by proponents.

The initial justification is simple, emotive and wrong. As *Compassion and Choices* notes on its website: 'Too many suffer needlessly. Too many endure unrelenting pain. Too many turn to violent means at the end of life.' We shall leave aside the no doubt interesting discussion about whether using violent means to terminate one's life is any worse than any other means. The immediate appeal of the compassion angle appears in the many stories of those who wish to avail themselves of assisted suicide but are prevented from doing so by archaic and cruel laws. Britain's *Dignity in Dying*, the biggest British organization campaigning for legalization, notes that, '[w]ithout a change in the law, terminally ill people will suffer against their wishes at the end of life...' Organizations in Australia, New Zealand, Canada and elsewhere dedicated to legalizing assisted suicide express similar reasoning.[23]

Compassion also figures in more academic arguments for legalization, though more as a backdrop to the autonomy argument. It is used to summon up passion or to lend pro-assisted-suicide arguments moral legitimacy. It is used to justify the position taken by the six prominent philosophers – Ronald Dworkin, Thomas Nagel, Robert Nozick, John Rawls, Judith Jarvis Thomson and Thomas Scanlon – who signed the *Philosophers' Brief* concerning the US Supreme Court cases of *Washington v. Glucksberg* and *Vacco v. Quill* in 1997. Ronald Dworkin, who drafted the *The Philosopher's Brief,* draws upon compassion when it uses phrases like 'so feeble or paralyzed that they cannot take pills themselves and who beg a doctor to inject a lethal drug into them' or 'patients who are not dying but face years of intolerable physical or emotional pain, or crippling paralysis or dependence'. Paul Badham argues that Christian compassion must allow people to seek assisted suicide in the (thankfully rare) cases where pain is still an issue.[24]

As Timothy Quill and Jane Greenlaw, who promote legalization of physician-assisted suicide, note, compassion or mercy underlines support for assisted suicide: 'If a patient's pain and suffering cannot be sufficiently relieved with state-of-the-art palliative care, then the physician has an obligation to do everything within his or her power to relieve that suffering, even to the point of hastening death if there are no realistic alternatives acceptable to the patient.' We might ask, must doctors alleviate psychic as well as physical pain? Should they alleviate suffering as a compassionate act or is it part of their professional duties? Shall we change the law to make killing a patient part of their medical obligations? In other words, should doctors as doctors kill patients or should compassion be somehow linked to the individual humanity of a person who has the power to end needless suffering?[25]

Other scholars quickly distance themselves from compassion in favour of autonomy, perhaps sensing the inherent problems with compassion. Sheila McLean appeals to the compassion argument: 'There are costs – even harms – caused to those who wish to be spared suffering when this is not available to them; indeed, there may be additional costs associated with living life knowing that an assisted dying will not be available, however much it is seen as a good option.' However, McLean, perhaps more than most proponents, sees autonomy as trumping compassion: '...autonomy is the driving principle where life-sustaining medical treatment is lawfully refused and could equally be applied to the choice for a directly-assisted death.'[26]

Most recently, the philosopher Baroness Mary Warnock rejected autonomy in favour of compassion:

Everybody knows that in a civilised country, subject to the rule of law, one can't always have autonomy. One has to give up some freedoms in order to obey the law ... I don't think the principle of patient autonomy is really a very strong ground [for assisted dying] ... It's more a principle of compassion that should motivate people who want to secure for other people the kind of good death that they want. [...] I think it should be possible to incorporate the concept of compassion within the law.[27]

We might detect a further contradiction between compassion and Warnock's other somewhat more calculating concern that the elderly are a drain on resources. But what sort of compassion are we talking about? Curiously, this compassion is a variation on a Christian theme of charity used by humanists to bludgeon Christians who oppose legalization. 'How can you deny these people what they really want: a peaceful death?' But the passion of the outrage expressed by campaigners reflects the way the question should really be expressed: 'How can you deny *me* what *I* think *I* would want if I were in this unfortunate person's position?' Much of what passes for compassion is simply reflected fear on the part of those with little prospect of death in the immediate future. There is a fiction to the stories usually told to convince the as-yet unconvinced that assisted suicide is necessary. Usually, we have a scenario where a dying patient cries out for relief, and sympathetic nurses wish they could help as the doctor shakes his head sadly before moving on. Such needless suffering occurs, of course, because a law that no longer makes sense in a secular age stops anyone from relieving this suffering. This scenario is, of course, entirely imaginary, though there are undoubtedly cases where continued life amounts to pointless suffering.

If we accept that the scenario is largely imaginary (and we must for, as we have seen from the numbers, very few people really wish to have assisted suicides), the compassion expressed is really self-centred fear for one's own prospects. Whereas it might be construed as a constant hazard implicit in compassion to mistake one's own feelings for the feelings of the object of pity, the impetus for assisted suicide is utterly self-centred rather than compassionate.

Attending a play involves an imaginary scenario and we feel compassion in relation to tragedy because it allows us to feel what others feel. Those who advocate allowing assisted suicide do so not out of compassion for the actual dying but out of fear that they might meet the same fate. As A. N. Wilson, philosopher and patron of *Dignity and Dying*, states: 'It is because we believe in the dignity and value of life that we hope for a good death. [...] To linger on against *my* will on a half-life is no life at all.' Or, as US talk show host Montel Williams, justifying his support for legalized assisted suicide, put it: '*I've* been on a journey now for the last ten years of my life trying to find everything *I* can to figure out ways to live better, to mitigate some of *my* pain, to make it so that *I* have a relatively normal life. But *I* can't ask anybody else to do that. And if it ever hits that time again for that "10" [on 1–10 pain scale] with me, *I* want that option; *I* want that option.'[28]

Underlying the falseness of the scenario is that pain, the spectre haunting Montel Williams, is generally controllable. Furthermore, it is not why people seek assisted suicides. The 2009 Oregon Death With Dignity Act Report stated: 'As in previous years, the most frequently mentioned end-of-life concerns were: loss of autonomy (93.8 per cent), decreasing ability to participate in activities that made life enjoyable (93.8 per cent), and loss of dignity (78.5 per cent).' Pain was not mentioned. Another study by Linda Ganzini et al. surveyed social workers who had received requests by hospice patients for assistance with suicide noted that 'the desire to control the circumstances of death, the wish to die at home, loss of independence or fear of such loss, and loss of dignity or fear of such loss were the most important reasons for requesting prescriptions for lethal medication'. The findings here are consistent with every major study of assisted suicide throughout the world. Moreover, the imaginary nature of the scenario where we are wracked with pain at the end of our days is reflected in those with the most experience of death and dying. The Hospice Movement and the major medical associations, as well as a majority of doctors in the United States, Canada, the UK, Australia and New Zealand, reject assisted suicide, contrasting with the general public.[29]

No one, of course, should suggest that the problem of pain at the end of life has entirely faded into the past. But the answer to the pain issue is improved pain control. Pain control continues to improve with technological advances being made. It is worth pausing to consider why such technological advances receive little attention compared to their supposed contribution to 'bad deaths' where patients, in the words of one assisted suicide advocate, 'consigned to living deaths hooked to tubes and machines, and medical science in its relentless drive for progress ignored the human well-being of dying patients in favour of prolonging merely biological life'.[30]

Moreover, if dealing with pain is the real motivation behind the campaign of legalized assisted suicide, so-called 'terminal sedation', also known as palliative sedation, whereby patients in pain are put into a deep sleep until they die naturally, might be posed as an excellent compromise, preventing the need for assisted suicide.

Projection of fears and anxieties onto the dying is what powers so-called compassion in these organizations. It is not feeling sorry for others but self-pity. Such sentiments are understandable. When we witness a relative dying, one of the most difficult aspects is when the dying occurs slowly and we witness gradual disintegration of the dying person. Many relatives and friends silently declare that they would wish to die much quicker than has the departed. But this is not compassion. As the pioneering writer on death, Elizabeth Kübler Ross, noted in describing why she opposed legalizing assisted suicide: assisting a suicide is 'projecting your own unfinished business' onto that person, cheating them of part of life.[31]

Self-pity motivates campaigners to call for a change in the law, and not for an increase in compassionate acts by caring individuals – the real meaning of compassion. By its very nature, mercy is a spontaneous and individual act, and institutionalizing it makes little sense and misunderstands the nature of compassion. Compassion, or pity as it used to be called, pre-exists political or legal structures and is simply beyond the realm of regulation. As Martha Nussbaum notes, 'compassion, in the philosophical tradition, is a central bridge between the individual and the community'. Compassion depends upon a generalized view of human flourishing that the compassionate individual contrasts with the situation of the person for whom she feels pity. Compassion is not the same as justice, though it may be a necessary step in the rendering of justice; the object of pity does not necessarily have the right to relief. Equally, justice may take place without pity. Calling for a law to change on the basis of compassion rather indicates its falseness.[32]

Of course, legislation may provide for compassionate responses to bad situations; assisted suicide advocates might well reply that all they are attempting to do is to remove punishment for compassionate responses in very particular situations. But law correctly generalizes against, say, larceny despite the fact that in very particular situations the law might side with the larcenist. An emotional response to a situation may not be the correct one. Just as acts inspired by anger or jealousy may be but are more usually not right in the eyes of the law, so acts inspired by pity and compassion are not necessarily just. The case of Frances Inglis in the UK illustrates the point. Inglis killed her severely disabled 22-year-old son with a massive injection of heroin. She was convicted of murder despite the claim – evidently believed by the court – that she did so out of love for her son, who had not spoken since an accident more than two years previously. 'I asked myself what I would want,' she told the court. 'I would want someone to love me enough to help me die.' However, the jury in her trial held that such a compassionately motivated act was murder. Good motives do not always lead to good actions.[33]

Cowardly compassion?

Another reason why mercy or compassion is not explored in the pro-assisted-suicide literature is that it leans towards euthanasia rather than assisted suicide, a point picked up by critics. What kind of compassionate person refuses to take the action herself and instead simply says to the suffering person: 'It's your choice'? An act of compassion is an action rather than waiting around to see what a suffering person wants. The compassion peddled by proponents lacks any real moral backbone. It is not secure enough to assume responsibility for the action. Again, such a perspective points to the self-regarding nature of such 'compassion'. Because it is essentially a projection of the fears and insecurities of the self, euthanasia might threaten the future self.

What are proponents' arguments against euthanasia? Many do not really oppose euthanasia but understand that their chances of successfully changing the law depend upon allaying the fears that legalizing assisted suicide will lead to euthanasia. Here, they make use of the slippery slope objections of opponents of legislation. In response to their criticism that voluntary euthanasia provides the doctor with too much power and increases 'the risk of error, coercion, or abuse', as Timothy Quill put it, none of the recent or proposed legislation includes a demand for legalized euthanasia. As Quill says, 'we have concluded that legalization of physician assisted suicide, but not voluntary euthanasia, is the policy option best able to and protect this vulnerable population'.[34]

Killing and allowing to die

A subsidiary to the compassion argument follows James Rachels' argument that there is no real moral difference between a doctor allowing a patient to die by removing machinery that keeps him alive and giving the patient a lethal injection that kills him. As proponents point out, the former is legal whereas the latter is not. From the point of view of the patient, or from the perspective of preventing suffering inherent in the compassion justification, there is no difference whatever between killing and letting die. Mary Warnock and Dr Elizabeth McDonald note: 'In conclusion, it can be said that assisted dying is effectively equivalent to withholding and withdrawing treatment.' Why shouldn't, in the interests of kindness, we acknowledge that killing a patient is sometimes the right thing to do and set up a legal framework whereby doctors are answerable for their actions?[35]

On a practical level, campaigners are correct that there are situations when killing rather than letting a disease take its course is the kindest action. Often missed by those who proclaim the sanctity of life is the fact that doctors have long done this kindness, not as part of their medical duties but because they are in the right place to do so. Lord Dawson admitted in parliament killing King Edward V in this way, noting that 'all good doctors did this'. Recent research indicates that doctors in the UK hasten death in thousands of cases per year. The question is really whether to create legal safeguards around these actions.[36]

As we have already discussed, the moral implications lie with the person assisting or accomplishing the killing, not with the person dying, for whom responsibility is no longer an issue. The question of whether death is by murder, suicide or natural causes is of no consequence for the deceased, except for their legacy. But on a legal basis the distinction is crucial and real. Certainly, courts must decide whether or not the law has been broken on the basis of this distinction. As the US Supreme Court said in the *Glucksberg* (1997) case: 'The decision to commit suicide with the assistance of another may be just as personal and profound as the decision to refuse unwanted medical treatment, but it has never enjoyed similar legal protection. Indeed, the two acts are widely and reasonably regarded as quite distinct.' In *Vacco* the Supreme Court's majority decision reported that '[t]he distinction between letting a patient die and making that patient die is important, logical, rational, and well established...'[37]

The question lies therefore with those who might provide assistance. The campaign for assisted suicide wishes to formalize the procedure so that the actions of doctors are transparent. First, this will make the doctors' task much more onerous. At present, in the rare cases where doctors hasten death, they seldom need to justify their actions; family and friends usually agree with the action and a sensitive doctor will normally (in my albeit limited experience) informally consult others with an interest in that person about the action.

Second, Rachels may be right that both killing and letting die in the specific scenario he mentions may be equally bad but one is clearly passive and the other active, at least creating separate moral categories wherein each must be evaluated separately. Also, the issue more concerns assisted suicide than euthanasia. In Rachels' example, the respective culprit's share of moral responsibility for the deaths is nearly equivalent; there is clearly an implied moral – if not legal – obligation to save people's lives when we can. However, there is a clear difference between assenting to a patient's wish to discontinue treatment to assenting to their request to assist a suicide. Again, if we step back from the immediate interests of the patient, the situation becomes clearer.

Whereas we need not honour a patient's wish to commit suicide, we must honour the patient's request to end treatment. Why? It is not, as David Orentlicher would have it, a 'distinction between a patient rejecting the burdensomeness of medical treatment and a patient rejecting the burdensomeness of life'. It is, as we detail in Chapter 6, because not honouring the latter's request would threaten an important basis of autonomy – the freedom from unwanted interference with our person. There are coercive elements to forcing treatment upon a patient against her will and there are no coercive implications in society refusing to honour a suicidal wish. It is in all of our interests that no competent person is subjected to treatment against his or her will. Any breach of that principle leaves everyone less free. However, if we refuse to honour a suicidal wish, no one's freedom – not even that of the would-be suicide – is diminished. In the refusal to act upon a suicidal wish, society refuses to become part of the suicide, to validate it and affirm it as correct. In honouring the wish of someone not to have medical treatment, society underlines the right of all individuals to make decisions about themselves. We will return to this distinction later.[38]

There is also an issue of moral responsibility. If I help a man who wishes to jump from a bridge to kill himself, I am partially responsible for his action. If he tells me he wishes to jump off the bridge, as he makes his way to the bridge, and I urge him to rethink his intended action and try and convince him not to do so, I have done all I can to stop him. I cannot legally prevent him from going on to the bridge (though I might morally justify physically preventing him – see Chapter 6) and, in the end, I know that if he is determined to do so, he will kill himself no matter what I do or say. I am not morally responsible for his action. When a patient refuses treatment, all concerned should make very clear the implications of withdrawing treatment to the patient but allow the patient to do so.[39]

Non-abandonment

A further subsidiary argument of compassion, non-abandonment, has been argued especially by Timothy Quill. He and others argue that the doctor should stay with the patient to the end and that any reasonable medical system ensures that doctors remain to care for the patient after all treatment has been stopped. 'Nonabandonment places the physician's open-ended, long-term, caring commitment to joint problem solving at the core of medical ethics and clinical medicine. There is a world of difference between facing an uncertain future alone and facing it with a committed, caring, knowledgeable partner who will not shy away from difficult decisions when the path is unclear.' Quill used his experiences with a cancer patient called Debbie to argue that assisting a suicide (Quill helped Debbie to die) was part of non-abandonment.[40]

At first glance, non-abandonment might seem a good idea. No one wishes to be abandoned in their hour of need and part of the job of physicians is to provide relief from pain. However, when we recall that pain does not feature as the most important reason for assisted suicides, it provokes the question: what kind of suffering is the doctor alleviating? Moreover, Quill's determination to be not simply a doctor but a 'committed, caring, knowledgeable partner' places the physician in a quasi-religious or therapeutic role, as a counsellor. Instead of, as in the past, the priest or religious figure refusing to abandon one of his flock in their hour of need, today it is the doctor. This is not what is currently expected of doctors nor is it what they signed up for (not surprisingly, the majority of qualified doctors in most polls reject the legalization of assisted suicide).

My objection to so-called non-abandonment as a reason for legalizing assisted suicide is that it actually expresses the very opposite (though this was not the case with 'Debbie'). In fact, assisted suicide is abandonment whereas the promise that the doctor will stay to the end and, if necessary, speed up the dying process would be non-abandonment. The doctor is in a unique position to make these decisions, knowing the prognosis and having perhaps witnessed patients with similar conditions. Real non-abandonment would entail the doctor quietly making that most brave and difficult of decisions (as Quill perhaps did in the case of Debbie) and taking responsibility for it, if not boasting about the action later.

If we are talking about a humane non-abandonment, we might also see it as determination to keep the patient in the land of the living for as long as possible, perhaps to argue passionately for continued existence, for that patient to continue to share our mutual bonds, to stress the value of her life. Otherwise, the doctor literally abandons the patient to a nonhuman status where the ordinary bonds and obligations of human society no longer apply, to dump her in some hinterland between life and death. Thus, non-abandonment, if it is to help the patient to kill herself, is precisely the opposite of what it claims to be.

Autonomy

Given the self-regarding nature of what passes for compassion in the arguments of proponents, it is not surprising that autonomy is actually at the core of the whole case for legalized assisted suicide. In fact, most discussions of euthanasia, as in the anti-assisted-suicide literature, tend to elide the autonomy and compassion arguments, causing the observer to wonder why the compassion argument is ever mentioned. H. Tristram Engelhardt, Jr. notes that '[e]uthanasia is, as such, the issue of assisted suicide, the universalization of a maxim that all persons should be free, *in extremis*, to decide with regard to the circumstances of their death'.[41]

Indeed, there is a contradiction between these two pillars of support for assisted suicide that is reflected in the debate about compassion. As Nussbaum notes of the arguments for and against pity:

> One sees the human being as both aspiring and vulnerable, both worthy and insecure; the other focuses on dignity alone, seeing in reason a boundless and indestructible worth. One sees a central task of community as the provision of support for basic needs; it brings human beings together through the thought of their common weakness and risk. The other sees a community as a kingdom of free responsible beings, held together by the awe they feel for the worth of reason in one another.

There has been a shift in the definition of autonomy from its classical definition by John Stuart Mill as freedom from the interference of others to what might be termed 'enabling autonomy', where choice is maximized by reliance on others. Assisted suicide belongs in the second category though the essential choice of the patient has not been jettisoned (as that would imply euthanasia) but remains in the background (this is explored in Chapter 6).[42] The fact that assisted suicide rather than euthanasia is called for today in the English-speaking world (it was not always the case – see Chapter 3) means that, ultimately, autonomy continues to be the most important reason to support a change in the law. It is control over one's own dying that animates the discussion. As all roads lead to Rome, so all arguments in favour of legalizing assisted suicide eventually rely upon the autonomy argument. Autonomy receives the most attention and is often wielded triumphantly as the argument that defines the entire discussion. But, as we shall see, it does not.

According to the autonomy viewpoint, it is the individual who should choose. Many see the assisted-suicide discussion as an extension of the discussion about whether others should constrain our personal choices because of their personal moral beliefs. Philosopher Margaret Battin resolutely sides with individual political rights over and above any collective moral sense. We may not, even if we consider suicide to be utterly immoral, prevent individuals from taking their own lives on the basis of our moral perspectives. The question thus becomes a *political* one based largely on autonomy. 'Autonomy, involving both freedom from restriction (liberty) and the capacity to act intentionally (agency) is the central value to which this argument appeals, and respect for a person's autonomous choice the social principle it entails.'[43]

The issue also might be thought of in terms of sovereignty. In an argument going back to John Locke, the individual is sovereign of his body and no one else should interfere with his decision so long as it affects only him. Assisted suicide advocates argue that, as the individual concerned is making the decision, laws that prevent him from asking for assistance are hangovers from the days when religious mores were imposed by clerics. Today, secular morality has no place for such laws. Who is it, they ask, that would prevent an individual in those invidious circumstances described above from seeking and gaining assistance from someone else in order to ensure a peaceful death. The British organization *Dignity in Dying* has as its byline, 'your life, your choice'.[44]

The cause of freedom as sovereignty is the most serious philosophical argument for the legalization of assisted suicide, from Battin and the philosophers who signed the *Philosophers' Brief* to Sheila McLean and Iain Brassington in the UK.[45]

Sheila McLean sees the question of assisted suicide in the light of Mill's *On Liberty*, which famously argued for toleration of the private affairs of others so long as they did no harm to us: McLean says: 'I start from the position that the legitimacy of state control over private choices is not to be taken for granted unless it can be shown that the failure of the state to intervene results in harm to others.' Later, she enlists Mill as an assisted suicide proponent: 'My discussion, therefore, starts from the assumption that Mill's approach is a legitimate way of addressing this issue.' Often, the apparent freedom to commit suicide is contrasted with the lack of freedom to choose to die in an assisted suicide.[46]

Mill looms large, especially in his warning against the 'tyranny of the majority', in the treatises of assisted suicide proponents. The *Philosophers' Brief* called for the freedom to make 'the most intimate and personal choices a person may make in a lifetime, choices central to personal dignity and autonomy'.[47] Ronald Dworkin, who wrote most of the text of the *Philosopher's Brief*, noted: 'The Constitution insists that people must be free to make these deeply personal decisions for themselves and must not be forced to end their lives in a way that appals them, just because that is what some majority thinks proper.'[48]

Peter Singer appealed directly to the Millian harm principle, whereby people may not be restricted in their actions unless these actions cause harm to others, when he asserts: 'Incurably ill people who ask their doctors to help them die at a time of their own choosing are not harming others.'[49] Proponents of assisted suicide tend to fly the autonomy flag whenever their determination to legalize it comes under question. You have the right to value your life as you see fit, they retort, but I will value my life as I see fit and I do not share your assessment of life as sacred in all instances.

The appeal to freedom and autonomy allows proponents to invoke the civil rights struggles of the past. The right to die is the 'ultimate civil right'. Leave aside for a minute the vaguely insulting notion that this lobby without a constituency applauds itself for continuing the struggle of African-Americans to be included in American life (during that struggle voluntary euthanasia campaigners called for eugenics programs, which many segregationists cheerfully supported) or upon the struggle of women for abortion rights (see Chapter 5). Such arguments appeal to libertarian free-thinkers and humanists, lending a false air of scientific respectability and objectivity to their cause. Such an image is maintained more by the religiosity of many of their opponents and by their vapid arguments about the 'right to life' than by any real scientific or humanistic case.

The inappropriateness of autonomy to assisted suicide

It is not that the autonomy argument is objectionable or that people should not have the freedom to choose their own fates; as I argue later, there should be more freedom, autonomy and true choices to make. It is simply that the autonomy argument or what John Harris and Sheila McLean, amongst others, have called the 'liberal view of euthanasia' is deceptive in the way it is discussed in pro-assisted-suicide arguments. What campaigners really seek is affirmation, not autonomy.

The central confusion comes because assisted-suicide proponents would treat what is fundamentally a moral and philosophical issue – whether we as a society should approve of individual suicides – in legal and political terms. To proclaim – often with great indignation – that people should be free to determine their own ends is simply one more self-deception, a way of avoiding the much more difficult moral question involved.[50]

The way one frames the question allows the deception of reducing the question of the moral rightness or wrongness of suicide, as well as its definition, to that of whether it is right for the state to prevent such action. David Benatar refers to the 'significant freedom' still not accorded to people even in liberal democracies 'to obtain assistance from others in taking one's own life or to be actively and voluntarily euthanized by those willing to help one'. But there is a large leap between freedom to take one's life and the freedom to 'obtain assistance' or be euthanized.[51]

There is a further discrepancy between conceptions of the state inherent with the new definition of autonomy. The Enlightenment, Lockean conception – one which powered the right-to-die movement in the 1970s and 1980s – has the state as night watchman. A more modern conception conceives of the state as an 'enabler' of individuals. The latter directly undermines the former by creating a dependence of individuals on the state for doing things which they are capable of accomplishing without state help. Whereas much of the assisted-suicide lobby sees itself as liberatory, ridding citizens of pointless laws based on outmoded moral systems that prevent individuals from doing what they wish, they in reality call for government assistance (for doctors are, even in the United States, representatives of the state) and further regulation of a sphere formerly administered privately.

It must be observed that the suicide herself is hardly encumbered by laws. We are already free to take our lives. There are few places left in the world where suicide remains a criminal offence but even there most of the onerous penalties have disappeared. Suicide was at one time a crime in common law and remains a crime in several US jurisdictions, although the relevance for law in the United States is generally only for insurance litigation in the few states where it remains on the statute books.[52] Moreover, suicide was always an option even when penalties were harsh; whatever the law, the successful suicide was soon beyond its reach. In the UK, suicide was decriminalized with the passage of the Suicide Bill of 1961. Even in areas where suicide is still illegal, such as India, few prosecutions take place. Nobody today could be hanged for attempting suicide, as was the case in the nineteenth century, nor would they be imprisoned for an unsuccessful attempt. The estates of suicides are no longer confiscated.

The historic reform of law against suicide, as argued in Chapter 4, reflects a trend towards the extrication of the state from issues of morality. It is, in general, no longer the business of the state to punish those who commit acts generally thought of as immoral but which do not harm others. This is a welcome development. It recognizes the ineffectual nature of any law proscribing suicide and the perversity of punishing those hurt most by the success of the suicide. It further recognizes that punishment of unsuccessful suicides is neither effective in resolving their situations nor capable of dissuading the most determined from succeeding later.

So far, so good, but the whole concept of the 'right to die', like the 'right to life', makes no sense. First, all have the right to die. Each of the so-called patients of Dr Jack Kevorkian, the assisted-suicide activist, were physically capable of bringing about their own deaths. Anyone, with a little forward planning and much determination, can kill themselves without fear that relatives or friends will be punished financially or needlessly shamed by their action. Even those with 'locked-in' syndrome, paralyzed entirely except for eye movements, have an option of refusing food and water as long as they can communicate their wishes.

The freedom to die is pre-political and pre-legal. Moreover, it is now easier to take one's life, thanks to technological innovation, than it was in the day of the Roman dramatist Seneca, who famously said to an old man complaining that he longed to be free of his troubles:

> Foolish man, what do you bemoan, and what do you fear? Wherever you look there is an end of evils. You see that yawning precipice? It leads to liberty. You see that flood, that river, that well? Liberty houses within them. You see that stunted, parched and sorry tree? From each branch liberty hangs. Your neck, your throat, your heart are all so many ways of escape from slavery... Do you enquire the road to freedom? You shall find it in every vein of your body.[53]

We have always been able to take our own lives without enlisting doctors in the cause and it is difficult to envisage a situation in which a competent and determined individual cannot do so. Suicide is one of those choices outside the province of law or political freedom. There is no need to enshrine the right to die within the law; nor is any law preventing suicide likely to be even a primary consideration of the prospective suicide, as we discuss in Chapter 4.

As discussed in Chapter 6, in the case of assisted suicide we find that freedom is actually curtailed for the individual rather than furthered. We may, under the plans of almost all proponents, not choose assistance to die if we do not fit the rigid criteria set down by, for instance, the law in Oregon or the propositions contained in the British Commission on Assisted Dying. The arbitrary nature of many of these criteria – like whether six or 12 months to live justifies assistance with suicide – threatens real freedom rather than bolstering it.

Rather obviously, if autonomy were the basis for the ability to obtain assistance to die, we should honour all requests to die from competent individuals. Either we approve of all acts of self-destruction on the basis of the who-are-we-to-judge principle, whether they be for reasons of religious belief, suffering in the throes of a failed love affair or because of the onset of a terminal illness, or we continue to judge individual suicides as good or bad. If the autonomy of the individual making the decision to die was really the prime consideration for the campaign for assisted dying, there could be no justification for honouring one request and not the other. As John Safranek states: 'Thus proponents of autonomy can restrict the right to assisted suicide only by implicitly or explicitly articulating normative claims, for example, that the young or the physically healthy should not be assisted in suicide because their lives are worthwhile or might later improve.'[54]

Assisted-suicide advocates leaning on the autonomy argument may truly honour autonomy only by approving of *all* suicides. They may not restrict assistance only to those requests of which they approve. Nor can they give any consideration to mercy if they are to uphold the autonomy of the individuals making the requests. Such suicides as those of Marshall Applewhite and 37 of his followers in the Heaven's Gate Cult, who killed themselves in order to avoid the recycling of planet earth, should be respected – if we privilege autonomy – as much as that of an elderly man suffering from terminal cancer. If 'autonomy, self-determination and personal control' are the most important reasons to support assisted suicide, we should also approve of the death of Bernd Juergen Brandes, who agreed to be eaten by the 'cannibal of Rotenburg', Armin Miewes. After all, Miewes surely respected Brandes' choice to be killed and eaten by providing assistance. To approve of assisted suicide on the basis of autonomy necessarily extends to all autonomously arrived-at decisions, including that of Brandes.

By restricting assisted suicide to the terminally ill and unbearably suffering, assisted-suicide advocates deny liberty and agency to those who do not fall within these categories, denying them autonomy. Very few proponents of legalization confront this issue; when they do, they tend to be evasive. Battin, for instance, fails to acknowledge that her two self-identified strongest reasons for legalizing assisted suicide – autonomy and mercy – are incompatible. Shall we afford assistance to those contemplating suicide on the basis that *we* feel pity for them in their awful situations or because *they* take an autonomous decision that they wish to die? Whose decision is it?

Sheila McLean admitted, in response to the question about the randomness of restricting suicide assistance to terminally ill patients: 'If it is the case that everyone, and not just those more obviously "in need", can lay claim to the same right to seek assisted dying, so be it.' But she leaves the argument at that, neglecting to draw out the implications of her admission.[55]

Iain Brassington, conversely, confronts the argument head-on in an interesting article. Though he bravely discusses the Miewe case, he side-steps the discussion after admitting the inadequacy of the terminal-illness criterion: 'So the terminal illness criterion, taken on its own, seems not to be defensible: this does not make it *impermissible*; it just means that, if there is a reason to include [the terminal illness criterion] in euthanasia or assisted dying legislation, it must be because it represents a component part of a wider concern.' What is, in fact, impermissible is the randomness of a law based on the terminal-illness criteria; random and unsupportable criteria for law are the basis of tyranny and inequality. Perhaps even more impermissible is the implication of the terminal illness criterion – to be explored in the next chapter – that those with less time to live lead less valuable lives than the rest of us.[56]

The case of Jim Jones and the 'People's Temple' suicide of 907 people in Jonestown, Guyana, in 1978 or that of Marshall Applewhite's Heaven's Gate cult serve as examples as to why autonomy is simply inappropriate to the debate. If assisted suicide is legalized on the basis of autonomy, presumably there would be no reason why these supporters of legalization would have refused any theoretical requests for assisting these suicides. There is enough evidence that all these deaths occurred with the consent of the dead even if not by the hand of the dead person. Assisted-suicide supporters may well regard the People's Temple and Heaven's Gate cults as delusory but, as long as the members freely entered into the decision to kill themselves, their suicides should, under the logic of autonomy, be legal and receive widespread approval.

Those who argue for legalized assisted suicide on the basis of autonomy must reckon with the fact that autonomy and any criterion that imposes conditions upon the autonomous decision by an individual are opposed in principle. Therefore, it is not possible to say that individuals may freely choose death if we state that they may only do so in these certain situations. That is not freely choosing death. It is asking authorities to pre-select criteria whereupon such wishes may be granted, and to submit a form proving that said citizen fulfils these criteria.

As with compassion, in the autonomy argument the whole issue of responsibility for an action and the judgment of that action is evaded. J. L. Lucas observed that 'I, and I alone, am ultimately responsible for the decisions I make, and am in that sense autonomous.'[57] Assisted-suicide advocates set random and unjustifiable restrictions upon the 'right' to seek assisted suicide, making the decision not ultimately that of the person concerned but rather of some ethics committee in a presumably un-smoke-filled back room. Any real commitment to autonomy demands that the individual is free to make her own choices, good or bad, no matter how much others disagree. The constrained, qualified and restricted choices available under every assisted suicide proposal put forward so far are not about autonomy.

Perhaps, though, proponents would argue that freedom for some is more desirable than freedom for none. As we shall discuss in Chapter 6, in this case freedom refers to freedom *of the doctor assisting the suicide, not of the suicide himself,* preventing doctors from facing a jury of their peers in a case brought forward under legislation to prohibit assisting a suicide or under murder/manslaughter legislation. Such is made very clear in the recent Report by the Commission on Assisted Dying.[58]

We have a situation now where real tolerance occurs. No one assisting a suicide for reasons of genuine mercy is likely to suffer unduly; under the current UK legislation, not one successful prosecution has taken place for assisting a suicide, despite many admitting that they have done so. Throughout the world, prosecutions are extremely rare and tend to follow noisy confessions by dedicated activists. So there is hardly a restriction of freedom for anyone involved with cases of assisted suicide.

The most important undermining factor of the autonomy argument for assisted suicide is inconsistency. Not one genuine justification for providing autonomy for some and not for others has or can be made. How can one call for legalization for assisted suicide for some categories and not for others? If assisted suicide was really a right, it should surely be accorded to all. If we reject laws against assisted suicide as paternalistic, we should also reject laws preventing assisted suicide for all as paternalistic.

Other reasons for supporting assisted suicide

There is one more category of reasons for supporting the legalization of assisted suicide – social pessimism about future shortages of resources. Unlike most of the other reasons, few proponents openly argue resources-related reasons for legalization and many, especially those of a liberal persuasion, would probably disagree with resources-based arguments. However, it is worth pointing out that at least some of the support for legalized assisted suicide rests on arguments about overpopulation or scarce resources.

Richard Lamm, the former governor of Colorado, spoke of the 'duty to die', pointing out that the elderly must make way for younger people. Philosopher John Hardwig agrees that there does exist a duty to die in the elderly, who take up too many resources in their last years of life. Daniel Callaghan, who is an opponent of legalized assisted suicide, suggested that health care for the elderly should be rationed. Such arguments are occasionally marshalled by proponents of assisted suicide.[59]

There is of course a moral duty to die in some situations, such as that of Hardwig's example of Captain Oates. There may be situations where one preserves something of oneself – for instance, one's honour – by suicide. But the underlying sentiment expressed by these discussions is that which is discussed in the next chapter – that technology creates a medical crisis by providing the means to keep someone – barely – alive at great expense to both that person and to society in general.

Conclusion: unravelling the case for legalization

The arguments at first glance appear simple. As Raymond Tallis argues, the case for assisted dying is 'easily stated' and 'unanswerable', but there is less clarity to the discussion than initially appears. In particular, translating what are often nobly motivated sentiments regarding the end of life into legislation is difficult. Much as many of the arguments made by opponents to a change in the law express mystical concepts, the perception of proponents as calm, cool rationalists resisting a tide of religious bigotry can likewise be challenged. In fact, there are more contradictions and confusions in the case for than the case against.

What we face, when examining the case in favour, are more questions than answers. Who defines 'unbearable suffering'? If we accept the definition of Lord Joffe (who proposed legislation legalizing assisted suicide in Britain's House of Lords) – that it is determined by the patient herself[60] – how can we justify denying an assisted suicide to someone who is suffering unbearably but has more than six months (or a year) to live? If we legalize euthanasia on the grounds of compassion, surely it is the doctor's *response* to the patient's situation that determines the action; the patient's actual wishes are beside the point. But if assisted suicide is justified on the grounds of (the patient's) autonomy, the doctor's perception of the situation is hardly relevant. Indeed, why is assisting a suicide necessary when an autonomous individual, with planning and determination, can bring about his own death?

The bizarre halfway house where we feel compassion only for *terminally ill* people who are suffering unbearably (or, as the proposed Scottish End of Life Bill substitutes, those who 'find life intolerable') and repeatedly request assistance in dying has not been justified nor can it be. It is not compassionate to restrict assisted suicides to those in situations, such as terminal illness or incapacity, where we can imagine we might feel life to be intolerable, nor does it honour autonomy.

In fact, rather than being a coherent case successfully convincing the public that legalizing assisted suicide is necessary, the case for legalization seems to reflect public opinion. Whereas two-thirds of the UK thought assisted suicide might be acceptable in some situations involving terminally ill people, only a third thought it was acceptable to assist the suicide of a non-terminally ill patient.[61] However, the drive behind the movement to legalize assisted suicide remains powerful, and will be discussed in the next two chapters.

3
The Origins of the Right-to-Die Movement

In a parallel to the point made earlier that the horrible scenario imagined by supporters of legalization ('If I ever become like that, I will want to die') is largely chimerical, as the actual numbers taking up the option where it is legal attest, so is the societal anxiety about technology that ostensibly created the demand for assisted suicide. Though it is no doubt true that medical technology keeps people alive longer than ever before, such an observation might have been made at nearly any point of the twentieth century. It is our attitude to medical technology, rather than innovation itself, that inspires interest in assisted suicide. This chapter indicates that the image of the runaway train of medical technology keeping people alive against their will is simply a modern nightmare.

The purpose of this chapter (which is for the most part historical) is to show the falsity of the idea that technological developments pointed towards the need for an assisted-suicide movement in the early 1970s. But I also discuss the growth of support for assisted suicide from a tiny movement forty years ago via its rise in the 1990s to its mass-appeal status today.

Several trends converged to create mass interest. Particularly in the United States, medicalization – a historical trend towards understanding moral, political or social issues as medical problems – in the postwar period forms the basis of the new right-to-die movement. Death became a medical rather than spiritual issue but by 1970, medical technology, the object of reverential faith in the earlier postwar period, faced suspicion and questioning of what were often exaggerated claims made on its behalf. The assisted-suicide movement reflected growing concern about dehumanized technological life-prolonging machinery and a pervasive feeling that medicine acted not in the interests of the patient but to further medicine's own goals.[1]

As Michael Fitzpatrick has argued, medicalization involves incorporating more and more categories within medicine: 'The expanding range of medical intervention characterised as the medicalisation of life involves two inter-related processes. On the one hand, there is a tendency to expand the definition of disease to include a wide range of social and biological phenomena...'[2]

It is important to see that assisted suicide is both an extension of and a reaction against medicalization in the sense that the subject wishes to take control away from the alleged depredations of medicine, which will fight to preserve her life at any cost, but enlist the help of medicine to do so. In particular, death is being made a medical rather than a spiritual, existential or philosophical issue. Within this medicalized perspective, suicide becomes a treatment option. Whereas it may wrest control from doctors, it depends upon physicians to back up such decisions to die.

Other important trends that emerged in the 1970s include a focus on the aged by modern-day Malthusians. One of the complaints heard is the 'greying of America' and that medical resources are spent pointlessly on the elderly and should instead be directed towards younger people. As I argue below, such a perspective makes less sense today than in the very hopeful years after the Second World War when resources were scarce and technology primitive relative to today. What has changed are attitudes to resources and technology rather than, as much of the literature has it, qualitative changes in resources or technology.

Why did assisted suicide emerge as an issue in the 1970s?

Interestingly, pro and con agree in their assessment of when and why assisted suicide became an issue. Essentially, both sides agree that the modern movement emerged around 1970. Moreover, they agree that the excesses and grand expectations of the 1960s contributed to the perceived need for assisted suicide. Observers on both sides of the issue see technological development as key. Opponents emphasize the displacement of religion by technology as the most important development fuelling the desire for the right to die. Proponents (and some opponents) point to the depersonalization of modern medical technology and the over-reliance on technology and technological solutions in the 1950s and 1960s as leading to situations where machines sustain life when it is no longer wanted. But both agree that this development occurred recently and that runaway technology is to blame.

George Pitcher, the UK newspaper columnist and Anglican priest who has recently published an argument against assisted suicide, blames 'the development of individualism; the Sixties hippy-hegemony of "self"; the assumption of consumerist "choice" which prospered in a neo-liberal economy' and other purported ills of our time. Pitcher puts forward here, in an otherwise fairly well-balanced book, a familiar-sounding litany of blame that can be heard elsewhere in conservative diatribes on moral slippage in the 1960s.[3]

In fact, Pitcher is not entirely wrong about the movement towards self and choice but gets the timing wrong. It was not the experimental 1960s but the retreat from progress in the 1970s when what might be reasonably called a technophobic attitude towards medical progress flourished. Today, the apparently self-evident idea that medical technology created the perceived need for assisted suicide infects nearly every account of it and underlies the bioethical perspectives that arose concomitantly with the assisted suicide movement.

The advent of modern interventions, of antibiotics, respirators, dialysis machines, has, for many, created ethical difficulties that require the corrective of the right to die. Machine medicine steams past the consideration of the individual in its mission to extend life longer and longer. As the bioethicist Ruth Macklin noted: 'These advances have been a mixed blessing. The use of medical technology in all its forms causes undesired side effects and untoward consequences... The other price – no doubt unforeseen – is the creation of ethical dilemmas rarely if ever confronted in the past.'[4]

Medical technology, according to most proponents, means that individuals must retake control of their deaths, away from 'machine medicine', as it has been called. *Compassion and Choices*, the largest and most mainstream United States organization campaigning for legalization of assisted suicide, looks at the history of the controversy in a passage that is worth citing at length because it sums up many contemporary attitudes within the pro-assisted-suicide camp. Citing the case of Karen Ann Quinlan, the brain-damaged girl whose parents' struggle to let her die reached the Supreme Court in 1976, *Compassion* claims:

> Karen was one of the first victims of medical technology, a confluence of doctors and science coming together to prolong a life that otherwise would be lost. [...] The dilemma that faced the Quinlans would not have occurred just fifty years earlier. At the beginning of the 20th century when someone sustained an injury or became ill they either recovered or they died. But with the 1950s a new era of medical

miracles was being ushered in with the seeming cry of 'the more medicine the better' (Porter, 1998). During this time period the first successful open-heart by-pass surgery took place, soon to be followed by the first organ transplant. Widespread use of penicillin was introduced to counter once-fatal infections, and a vaccine for polio was perfected. Technological inventions like the pacemaker, improved dialysis equipment and diagnostic scanners that could 'look' inside the body without invasive surgery were all hailed as medical breakthroughs. In the last fifty years these advances have been responsible, at least in part, for an increase in the average adult life expectancy, which has gone from 68.2 years in 1950 to its current 78 years (and climbing). As a result the very definition of what it meant to be 'elderly' was also changing.

But it was not all good news. With longer life spans came the emergence of degenerative age-related diseases such as Alzheimer's, stroke and arthritis, creating a need for hospitals and nursing homes where people were sent to die rather than be cured. As medicine and technology continued to advance, there came the haunting realization that futile prolongation of life was often going too far. Living longer was not always living better and the demand for the quality of life, versus quantity, was beginning.[5]

This, at least, represents an attempt to historically ground the debate. One may imagine that most of the academics who write on the subject might have a more solid historical understanding of the rise of sentiment in favour of legalization or at least refer readers to a body of scholarship that explicates this critique of technology. Unfortunately, this isn't the case. Most either fail to ask how the issue came to be or simply repeat the unwarranted assumption that the development of medical technology inevitably created the assisted-dying dilemma.

Mary Warnock and Elisabeth McDonald, who have presented an interesting case in favour of assisted suicide, note that 'in an age when medical technology is constantly becoming more sophisticated many people who die in hospital could be kept alive almost indefinitely on life support machines. For such people, death is not a matter of "nature taking its course", but a matter of deliberate decisions, not their own.' Such an observation elucidates a connection with the therapeutic ethos that will be discussed below. In the past death was an unfortunate but natural event. Today, however, we seem to allocate responsibility for death and the way we die to other people. This is what Daniel Callahan has called 'technical monism', the tendency to erase the difference between human action and independent, natural biological processes.[6]

Margaret Pabst Battin and David Mayo, supporters of legalizing assisted suicide, indicated in 1980 the reasons for the philosophic reconsideration of suicide: 'This has been due very largely to the development of sophisticated medical techniques, which make it possible to extend human life to limits which are sometimes not desired, and the recognition that voluntary euthanasia, over which there has been so much recent controversy, is, at root, a kind of suicide.' To be fair, Battin has elsewhere denoted other reasons why the controversy emerged, but the centrality of this canard comes through in many if not all of her discussions of assisted suicide.[7] More recently, philosopher Sheila McLean noted: 'Modern medicine raises the possibility – doubtless welcomed by some – of extending lifespan, with or without perceived quality. For others, these same capacities are perceived as a threat.'[8]

A powerful thinker like Ronald Dworkin also lightly glances over the question of origins when he notes that the 'increasing power of new medical technology has plainly increased people's interest in that way of controlling the time and manner of one's own death'. Elsewhere, he muses that 'Science also promises – or threatens – new medical and surgical techniques of increasing life expectancy, in some accounts to biblical magnitudes...'[9]

It does not logically follow that various wonderful medical advances should be greeted by pointing out their potential drawbacks. Though, as we have seen, many advocates cloak themselves in the mantle of reason and enlightened humanist thinking, championing free-thinking and liberal views, their conservative response to the emergence of technological innovations expose not only an untested assumption underlying attitudes towards assisted suicide but exposes them as the enemies of scientific progress and rationality. What they fail to note is that, rather than a problem created by technology, it is an issue (not, importantly, a problem) created by a new attitude towards technological authority.

In this sense, the right-to-die movement shares its origins with its religious enemies in a hostile reaction to scientific advancement. As will be seen in Chapter 5, the right-to-life movement of the 1970s arose in response to the moral 'permissiveness' of the 1960s, made possible by the wealth and technical prowess that rose to its height in that decade. Many saw the widespread availability of the birth control pill and the acceptance of abortion as heralding an age of no responsibilities.

Above all, conservatives shared with their ostensibly liberal counterparts the feeling that technological changes necessitated a rethink of morals and morality. Just as conservatives fretted about the pill and

the availability of abortion on the grounds that it undermined traditional morality, the pro-assisted-suicide camp worried over the negative
implications of life-saving technology rather than revelling in the freedom and improvements to life it created. This new moral framework
is summed up neatly by Peter Singer: 'Technology creates an imperative: "if we can do it, we will do it." Ethics asks: "We can do it, but
should we do it?"' The United Church of Christ, in its statement supporting the right to die in 1973, observed that medical science 'has made
tremendous progress in the last half century'. But 'these new-won technical abilities have out-stripped the categories of conventional medical
ethics'.[10]

Few delve deep into the question of why the interest started. However, Christel Manning, writing in 1991 at a high point in interest about
assisted suicide, dedicated an entire section to 'Why is Euthanasia an
Issue Today?' 'Initially emerging in the 1960s, the controversy intensi-
fied in the 1980s,' she noted. She lists several interrelated reasons. First,
the number of reported cases increased dramatically in the 1980s. This
reasoning is tautological; we must ask *why* cases became high-profile.
They make the news because there is interest in these cases rather than
the other way around. Besides listing the 'graying of America', Manning
sees 'a questionable medical technology that maintains life but does not
cure' as well as '[a]rtifical life support systems and "halfway technologies" such as kidney dialysis and artificial organs let people survive but
render them technology-dependent'. She lists the 'high costs of health
care' but also the emergence of an organized opposition in the 1980s.[11]

It is not that such reasons are inaccurate but they need further analysis. But as many pro-assisted-suicide pundits express profound suspicion
towards technological developments in medicine, so do opponents.
'We live in an age when scientific knowledge has provided human
beings with an unprecedented ability to manipulate life and death',
begins the preface to Arthur Dyck's *Life's Worth: The Case against Assisted
Suicide*.[12] Nigel Biggar refers to technological innovation as a 'mixed
blessing'. He asks:

> What has provoked such a challenge to the Western legal tradition
> and to the moral principles that have informed it? The most basic
> stimulus has come, ironically, from successes in developing medi-
> cal technology to as to make it possible to prolonging life to an
> unprecedented extent.[13]

Daniel Callahan, a pioneering bioethicist who opposes legalizing
assisted suicide, also sees technological change as important: 'Perhaps

the single most important reason for this [the complicated nature of modern decisions about the end of life] is the advances in medicine in recent years, and particularly the application of medical technology.'[14]

The falsity of the technology argument

The vagueness of this assumption gives a clue about it verity; very few subject the claim to any analysis. Superficially, of course, some points made about technology are true. Technology *has* extended life to an unprecedented extent. As Tom Kirkwood notes, over the course of the last half-century, life expectancy has continued to increase steadily by two years each decade.[15] Those over the age of 85 constitute the fastest growing demographic in the USA, Canada, Australia, New Zealand, the UK and many other European nations. There is no question that technology can extend lives artificially and that its ability to provide years of 'life' to someone in a coma is of questionable value. But most of the observations about technology might have been made at any point during the twentieth century. Importantly, few saw the negative aspects of medical technology earlier in the century.

The first artificial kidney was developed and used by Willem Kolff in Nazi-occupied Holland in the early 1940s. In 1960, continuous hemodialysis became possible with the invention of a vascular access device that permitted the repeated connection of the patient to the machine without recurring surgery. Later innovations reduced the volume of patients' blood in the 'extracorporeal environment', eliminated cooling and rewarming of blood, improved vascular access through the invention of alternative techniques, and increased the available membrane surface area while simultaneously reducing the size of the dialyzer. But no one at the time worried about technological dependence. Instead, as a *Science* magazine in 1952 expressed, only the possibilities counted:

> In any event, it improves one's perspective to remember that the artificial kidney is merely another of the multifarious products of an engineering that gives us artificial eyes, teeth, breasts, limbs, and brains. The prosthetists are busy even now polishing their artificial heart valves, and it is not so difficult (for those who are not biochemists) to envisage the day of the factitious liver.[16]

Even more consternation might have greeted the iron lung, a monstrous piece of technology straight out of Fritz Lang's *Metropolis*. As James

Maxwell observed, the 'iron lung has ... come to represent medical technology in its most palliative form, prolonging life but only at great cost in terms of the quality of life prolonged'. But no handwringing pessimism attended its development. After Philip Drinker and his associate Dr Louis Shaw developed the iron lung in 1928, only good news stories appeared, indicating how poliomyelitis victims lived for extended periods of time. Typical was a news story picturing a smiling youngster with his head protruding from an early iron lung who surmised that his survival of 101 days trumped that of others. Another story in the late 1930s told of a young man who travelled to China in an iron lung. The negative perception of the iron lung had to wait until 1971. Then, Louis Thomas condemned it as a prime example of 'halfway medical technology', a technical fix, inefficient and requiring the costly expansion of hospital resources with little societal benefit. Before Thomas's critique, the only complaint about the iron lung was that there were not enough of them.[17]

The history of voluntary euthanasia

There already exist several useful books on the history of the issue of assisted suicide in the United States and the history of the Voluntary Euthanasia Society (VES) in the United Kingdom is well known.[18] There is no need to restate the history of euthanasia here (some of the history of suicide is discussed below). The most important point for our purposes is that the rubicon between the euthanasia movement and the right-to-die movements was crossed around 1970. In the 1970s, Ian Dowbiggin notes, '[e]uthanasia ceased being defined as active mercy killing, with its disturbing overtones of coercion and social usefulness, and increasingly became viewed as personal freedom *from* unwanted interference in one's own life'. At this stage, a cranky group of euthanasia advocates found, for the first time, popular support for their message.[19]

Of course, the movement growing in the 1970s employed many of the same arguments as its precedents and continued the aim of legalizing assisted deaths. But the focus of this study is on the different motivations behind voluntary euthanasia and assisted-dying movements after 1970 – their essential redefinition in terms of autonomy, bodily control and dignity – rather than on the familiar arguments that characterized euthanasia and right-to-die discussions continuously since the 1930s. Tragic cases of mercy killings and voluntary euthanasia come to light every few years and have done so for nearly as long as they have occurred. The reception given to these arguments depends greatly on the historical context in which they take place.

Between the 1930s and 1960s, the chief aim of the VES in the UK and the *Euthanasia Society of America* (ESA), founded in 1935 and 1938 respectively, was to further medical control over society. As such, it represented an elite project of scientific control over problems in society, part of Weberian rationalization and related to 'scientific' race theories, birth control, 'mental hygiene' and eugenics. Euthanasia – rather than the right to die – was the focus for an elite group of supporters who often subscribed simultaneously to euthanasia, eugenics and population control. Thinking of themselves as liberals, they opposed Hitlerian persecution of the Jews but praised the forward thinking of the Third Reich in relation to eugenics.[20] A prominent proponent of voluntary euthanasia, Margaret Sanger, stated in 1932: 'Keep the doors of immigration closed to the entrance of certain aliens whose condition is known to be detrimental to the stamina of the race, such as feebleminded, idiots, morons, insane, syphilitic, epileptic, criminal, professional prostitutes, and others in this class barred by the immigration laws of 1924.'

In the same article, she called upon readers to 'Apply a stern and rigid policy of sterilization and segregation to that grade of population whose progeny is already tainted or whose inheritance is such that objectionable traits may be transmitted to offspring.' Sanger, who was a founding member of the ESA, wished to rid all Americans of what she termed 'biological slavery'. In her mind – and in those of many other Americans at the time – eugenics, birth control and euthanasia were all part of a progressive agenda dedicated to that project.[21]

However, despite the associations with racial eugenics, the motivations behind progressive reformers who made up the membership of the ESA included the noble concern to liberate humanity from disease, disability, suffering in old age and create a society organized along rational, modern lines, something that was lost in the individualism of the post-1970 right-to-die movement. Even eugenics, when divorced from Malthusianism and the spurious racial categories that nearly all observers – not simply Sanger and the ESA – took as fact in the interwar era, may yet have some progressive application.

Despite some knowledge of Nazi atrocities, the ESA created a committee in 1943 to draft a bill legalizing involuntary euthanasia for 'idiots, imbeciles, and congenital monstrosities'.[22] In some ways, the war might have driven sentiment towards legalizing voluntary euthanasia, especially given the wartime attitude towards state control. As ESA president Dr Robert Latour Dickinson told a CBS radio audience in 1946, the state 'already selects its healthiest citizens to expose to slaughter and life-long maiming to release others from greater ills. Why deny it the power to end life that is not worth living?'[23]

In the postwar period, however, as Nazi crimes in the name of eugenics and scientific knowledge emerged, euthanasia movements across the world lost support. Voluntary euthanasia survived but supporters had to scramble to distance themselves from the involuntary euthanasia practised in the Third Reich.

The ESA and others who wished to legalize assisted suicide faced issues that would change the whole nature of their cause. First, American and, to a lesser extent, other Western societies looked to science and *technological* solutions to what had previously been seen as political problems. In light of the Nazi experience, psychologists were enlisted to explain what appeared to leaders to be the bewildering motivations of men and women who became committed Nazis or Communists.[24]

Medicalizing society's problems

To understand why issues such as death became medicalized, it is necessary understand not only the huge technological strides of the postwar years but also the inability to defend traditional moral and political positions in the wake of the war. In a famous passage, Arthur Schlesinger, Jr. wrote:

> Western man in the middle of the twentieth century is tense, uncertain, adrift. [...] The grounds of our civilization, of our certitude, are breaking up under our feet, and familiar ideas and institutions vanish as we reach for them, like shadows in the falling dusk. Most of the world has reconciled itself to this half-light, to the reign of insecurity.

Looking back in 1970, Schlesinger noted that the book combined a 'certain operational optimism with philosophical pessimism', an accurate characterization of the dominant perspective of the postwar period in the United States and Western Europe. Building, perhaps, on the optimism of earlier philosophical trends like pragmatism, many reframed difficult moral and religious questions as technological and therefore, they then thought, resolvable problems.[25]

Margaret Somerville, who penned one of the more thoughtful attacks on legalization, characterized assisted suicide and euthanasia as a technical solution: 'Euthanasia converts the mystery of death to the problem of death, to which we then seek a technological solution. A lethal injection is a very efficient, fast solution to the problem of death – but it is antithetical to the mystery of death.'[26]

Whereas Somerville's emphasis on the 'mystery' of death reflects her religious standpoint, she notes correctly the technical nature of assisted dying. It is an imagined quick, medical fix for the nightmare of fear and uncertainty haunting those for whom death is still a far-off prospect.

It is worth highlighting the considerable investment that went into technology in the years after the Second World War. Technology became the answer to what had previously been political, social and moral issues. Whereas capitalism appeared politically and morally bankrupt, its growth in material terms encouraged what historian Robert Collins has termed 'growth liberalism' that buried social, moral, and political concerns of the past in dollars.[27]

Economic growth began to be seen not just in quantitative terms but as a solution to what had been seen as qualitative problems. The 'dog-eat-dog' problems of the 1930s, the battles between the 'haves' and 'have nots' that plagued history, all these might be overcome by distributing such a vast volume that exactly how it was distributed was not an urgent issue. Looked at another way, as long as everyone moved up constantly on the ladder of opportunity, people would not pay so much attention to which rung they were on. Godfrey Hodgson summed up the thinking at the time: 'The abundant society could short-circuit the two quintessential questions of politics, the question of justice and the question of priority: Who gets what? What must we do first?'[28]

Technology became the method of delivering this constantly expanding growth, particularly after the successful launch of the Soviet satellite *Sputnik* in 1957. This event spurred the West on to greater and greater emphasis on technology and the technological one-upmanship that characterized the ensuing space race: 'Sputnik triggered an abrupt discontinuity [that] transformed governments into self-conscious promoters, not just of technological change but of perpetual technological revolution.'[29]

Government and technological leaders became partners, with the latter wielding unprecedented authority. John F. Kennedy promised to put a man on the moon and British Prime Minister Harold Wilson promised to harness the 'white heat of technology', as he called it in 1963. John F. Kennedy noted in 1962: 'The fact of the matter is that most of the problems, or at least many of them that we now face, are technical problems, are administrative problems. They are very sophisticated judgements which do not lend themselves to the great work of "passionate movements" which have stirred this country so often in the past. Now they deal with questions that are beyond the understanding of most men.'[30]

Technologists were given leadership roles but every person was enlisted in the crusade for technological dominance, given its key role in combating communism. This was the age of experts. As their authority grew, so did their remit. Entire spheres of life became medicalized or subsumed under medicine's close relation, psychology, as scientists sought explanations for human behaviour in the absence of political explanations.[31]

The ascent of medicine

Huge hopes – not entirely unfounded – were invested in medicine after the Second World War. Moral issues faded into the background. Newspapers, magazines, journals and the new medium of television championed 'medical miracles', identifying them as offshoots of military research. Newfound techniques and machinery extended life: blood plasma, sulfa drugs, substitute bladders, dialysis machines, respirators, plastics, and stainless steel as well as the establishment of banks for human skin, eyes, organs and blood developed after the war. As David Serlin noted, 'Americans gravitated towards medicine as a tool of self-realization'. This was the era of medical miracles, of medicine as a panacea for all that ails. 'It will be possible to replace whole organs that are diseased', *Collier's* predicted in a 1950 article titled 'Can Humans Be Rebuilt?'; 'It will be possible, even, for a person with two diseased kidneys to have them replaced with sound ones. Or do you wish a new leg, or lung, or a whole eye? All of these will be theoretically possible if (medical) researches succeed.' Medical science epitomized the idea that life was getting better.[32]

Medical science enlisted, along with science in other fields, with the anti-communist crusade of the time not only in the United States but in most Western countries, closely tying its fortunes to the political establishment. Useful metaphors involving medicine emphasized the Cold War fears and insecurities at the time, highlighting the fact that technical solutions to political problems were employed because of perceived lack of political arguments against communism. Arch Cold Warrior and Federal Bureau of Investigation director J. Edgar Hoover wrote in the bulletin of the American Medical Association: 'Communist germs, spawned in the swamps of iniquity and terror, have blotted out...the sunshine of free thought, independent research, and unfettered inquiry. They have "sickened" many nations and literally killed countless persons. These germs are infectious and deadly, easily transmitted and often difficult to detect.'[33]

With the rising authority of medicine came great expectations. The image of a successful battle against invasive germs suited Hoover and others. Medical science had largely triumphed against communicable diseases; such diseases as poliomyelitis virtually disappeared during this period. The rise of the phrase 'mental illness' occurred at this time, along with the hope that it and other conditions might be cured by medical intervention. As Thomas Szasz, an early critic of medicalization, wrote in 1970:

> Instead of being born into sin, man is born into sickness. Instead of life being a vale of tears, it is a vale of diseases. And in his journey from the cradle to the grave man was formerly guided by the priest, so now he is guided by the physician. In short, whereas in the Age of Faith the ideology was Christian, the technology clerical, and the expert priestly; in the Age of Madness the ideology is medical, the technology clinical, and the expert psychiatric.[34]

Various kinds of behaviour that might have been condemned as immoral in the past became products of a 'sick' mind. An academic psychiatrist wrote in 1963: '[j]ust as the functions of the sick body and the healthy body proceed in accordance with the laws of physiology, so sick and healthy minds function in accordance with the laws of physiology.' Crime was understood not as a problem of law and morals but a problem of medicine and therapy. As will be discussed below, suicide, which had been understood in sociological or moral terms, became a medical problem.

The fall of technocracy

With such raised expectations, the failure of technological solutions to deliver victory against poverty and the Vietcong or to 'cure' white Americans of their racism provoked widespread questioning of the authority of technocrats. Rather than questioning the applicability of technical solutions to moral and political problems, however, the focus of criticism fetishized technology itself, imagining it as a Frankenstein.

The 'runaway train' of technology became a popular metaphor, impart-ing the idea that technology created its own purposes that ran counter to those of humans.

The spirit of the times emanating from this failure of technology to deliver its promises was a pervasive feeling of lack of control. Rather than questioning the political and moral wisdom of attempting to resolve so many social and political issues with technological solutions, the desirability of the goals themselves – extending life spans, creating more wealth, producing cheaper and more plentiful goods – came under fire. After such a hopeful consensus on the rapid progress of society fragmented, people looked to themselves for solutions, hardly trusting authorities or even doctors.

One of the main trends accompanyting the crisis was the destruc-tion of moral guides to human behaviour, of ethical assumptions that guided human actions during the postwar period. In the wake of the implosion of moral authority, many questioned whether any universal principles might be applied. Without them, each moral question became a moral dilemma. As Ezekiel Emanuel notes, 'within the last two decades or so, medical ethical *questions* have become irresolvable medical ethical *dilemmas'*.[35]

In the recent past, doctors simply assumed the authority to take action in what they thought were the best interests of the patient. What are commonly called 'end of life' issues today involved (and still involve) doctors dispatching patients where further treatment was deemed hope-less and continued existence of little value. No one objected or saw any need to discuss the matter further. But when such paternalism began to be questioned – not least by doctors themselves – people began to take responsibility for their own health decisions, including the question of when to end their lives.

There is an important difference with issues involving suicide, as most campaigners for a change in the law insist. Rather than the right to die by one's own hand, campaigners seek to assume the authority that doctors had in the past to decide when continued existence is futile. Deceptively called the right to die, what is sought is the right not to be forced to live, a scenario borne of a deep midnight of the mind – febrile imaginings, rather than experience.

Limits

The term 'limits' featured in many discussions occurring in the 1970s. It became important for end-of-life dilemmas in several ways. First, the conceptualization of limits undermined the image of ever-increasing technical capacity to resolve the difficulties facing society. Second, it mirrored limits on a societal level in the individual; death represents the outer limit of the life of an individual. Third, conceptualizing limits provided an economic justification for providing the right to die. A zero sum of beds available for hospitals and health trusts made useless treatment immoral, given that it potentially robbed a more deserving patient of a bed, rather than simply futile and wasteful.

Limits to Growth, a 1972 work questioning whether economic growth was possible or even desirable, began a trend of questioning what was possible throughout many spheres. Fred Hirsch rejected the thesis of physical limits in his book *Social Limits to Growth*, arguing that 'to see total economic advance as individual advance writ large is to set up expectations that cannot be fulfilled, ever'. Hirsch argued that satisfaction can really be measured not by absolute material wealth but by an individual's relative wealth.[36]

Perhaps most germane to this discussion is pioneering bioethicist Daniel Callahan's early discussions of limits. Callahan, who created the Hastings Center, perhaps the world's most pre-eminent centre for the study of bioethics, has consistently questioned the technocratic goals of medicine and emphasized the limits of medical technology. Callahan directly attacked the unbridled technological imagination that he felt raised unreal expectations: 'The question is not so much what should be done with technology, and what goods should be sought, but what boundaries should not be transgressed in the process.'[37]

In an article written in 1973, Callahan at once expressed a sensible 'refusal to believe that the answer to the derangements of society is technological' and the extremely conservative call for limits to expectations or 'even a sense of guilt for demanding too much'. His anti-technological or even anti-scientific sentiments can be seen in his demands for what might have been seen as 'totalitarian' only a decade before: 'A science of limits must, as a minimal demand, be able to establish the legitimacy of prohibitions, repressions and interdictions in the use of technology.'[38]

Despite his protestations to the contrary, Callahan's science of limits creates conditions of imagined scarcity and a survivalist ethos, not high expectations. In a zero-sum situation, distribution becomes imperative and one's fellows become competitors. As economist Herman Daly advised the incoming US administration in 1969:

> For several reasons the important issue of the stationary state will be distribution, not production. The problem of relative shares can no

longer be avoided by appeals to growth. The argument that everyone should be happy as long as his absolute share of wealth increases, regardless of his relative share, will no longer be available...The stationary state would make fewer demands on our environmental resources, but much greater demands on our moral resources.[39]

The problem of how resources are divided thus becomes increasingly moral rather than technical. The whole discipline of bioethics largely emerged to deal with questions of scarcity. Bioethics, the province of a 'small but influential group of philosophers and health care policy makers', emerged largely to deal with ethics in a post-scarcity age. Which groups should get resources and which should not? When should treatment be deemed inappropriate (and resources directed elsewhere)?

Euthanasia and death in general became an important metaphor for limits and the futility of technological solutions to problems. Though it asked a sensible question – why extend a patient's suffering through the needless use of technology? – its importance was really in its perfect expression of the feeling of terminus that stalked the land. There was no more need for euthanasia or assisted dying in 1970 than there had been in 1960 but the issue moved from the shadows into the public eye in the 1970s. The tragic case of Karen Ann Quinlan had many precedents but the fact that her plight became a public issue rather than a private tragedy reflected the timing of her situation.

Both sides of the assisted-suicide debate frame their arguments within an assumption of scarcity of resources. Those opposing assisted suicide frequently accuse those in favour of it of financial or resource-based reasons for advocating it. On the other side, advocates point to the disproportionate amount of healthcare spending dedicated to the last two years of individuals' lives. Does it not seem sensible in resource terms, they ask, to allow those who wish to opt out of expensive life-sustaining treatment in the last stages of life to do so? Underlying both sides is anxiety about how resources either are or will be distributed. As Callahan adroitly observed, 'scarcity becomes psychologically endemic, with every person so affected living under a constantly perceived threat of degradation or annihilation'. These twin fears power the debate forty years after Callahan made this observation.[40]

Of course, resources *are*, at any one time, limited. But resources dedicated to medical care are increasing every year. Despite the pessimistic and suspicious attitudes towards medical technology, much more is possible than when the first iron lungs allowed those with severe respiratory problems to extend their lives. As Tom Kirkwood noted, life expectancy is increasing by one minute for every five lived. That this is viewed as a problem rather than as a glorious triumph is due at least in part to the perception that elderly people will swallow up a large portion of resources and will leave others without.[41]

In the past, doctors made decisions within a hospital about which patients to prioritize, which patients should have their treatment withdrawn, which drugs should be provided and which should not, based on their own perception of prognoses and likely outcomes. People, in general, trusted doctors to take the right decision. But the erosion of the authority of medical practitioners created the need for bioethics. Formerly private decisions based on individual circumstances have become formalized. Whereas in the past, the fact that a hospital doctor prioritised a thirty-year-old man's life over a terminally ill septuagenarian's last few days caused little anxiety or questioning. Most accepted the authority of doctors to make these unfortunate decisions. But suspicion of medical authority led to a demand for transparency about and justification of any decisions like these.

Thus, bioethics was born. Bioethics provides moral guidance for certain decisions that, before the mid-1960s, would have been defaulted to technological authority or left to individuals in given situations. But it can never resolve those questions because many of the questions, by their very nature (such as how resources should be divided), can be endlessly contested. The existence of bioethics is testament to lack of a moral compass to guide everyday ethical decisions since the implosion of authority in the 1960s and 1970s.

The right to die becomes a mass movement

Prior to the 1970s, voluntary euthanasia was supported by a coalition of population eccentrics and eugenicists. Its members might be described as members of the elite cohort of a generation that matured in the 1920s and 1930s. By 1951, ESA members moaned that public interest in euthanasia was waning. By 1958 the ESA could no longer afford to keep its offices open between Monday and Friday. As medical historian Stanley Dreiser noted: 'Public and professional discussion of euthanasia continued to be sparse up to the mid-1960s.'[42]

Historians tend to see a continuation between the original VES in the UK, the ESA and their modern day counterparts. Partly, this is because the discussions taking place in 1958 are so familiar to later generations of discussants. In particular, an exchange between Yale Kamisar and Glanville Williams in the 1950s rehearses many of the arguments familiar to those examining the issues today. Moreover, the existence of ruminations about suicide dating back to classical times has led some to conclude that interest in assisted suicide is cyclical, related to economic factors that lead many to consider measures born of social Darwinism.[43]

However, the origin of the VES and the ESA was in the appliance of scientific knowledge to end human suffering. It was always conceived of as a tightly controlled collective process, which is how they thought euthanasia differed from suicide. The emphasis on autonomy and the right to die was absent from their arguments up until 1970.

As the authority of organized religion and medicine waned, movements to control one's own spiritual and medical destiny emerged. The alternative health movement and the assisted-suicide movement share a similar provenance. Feminism also contributed to popularizing the right to die by attacking the paternalistic attitude of doctors towards women patients and questioning whether the doctor did indeed know best. This new feminist approach to the body fed both into an alternative health movement and assisted suicide in the cause of self-determination. The preface to the 1973 edition of *Our Bodies, Ourselves* describes the original conference inspiring the book that took place in Boston in 1969:

> At one point [of the conference], we took part in a small discussion group on 'women and their bodies.' Not wanting the discussion to end, some of us decided to keep on meeting as a group after the conference. [...] In the beginning we called ourselves 'the doctors group.' We had all experienced similar feelings of frustration and anger toward specific doctors and the medical maze in general, and initially we wanted to do something about those doctors who were condescending, paternalistic, judgmental and noninformative.[44]

What these women indicated was growing suspicion of medical authority and alienation from physicians as authorities over the health of individuals. Women's bodies had become, in their eyes, objects to be operated upon with little reference to the individual. Barbara Ehrenreich, prominent left-wing feminist and author of *The American Health Empire: Power, Profits and Politics*, noted in 1975 that 'there has been an expansion of *jurisdiction* of medicine. More and more problems are considered to be medical problems: medicine impinges on people in more and more aspects of their lives. What we are seeing is the medicalization of everyday life.'[45]

Ehrenreich was correct in identifying the medicalization of everyday life as problematic. With heightened expectations of the possibilities of medical technology, death became a medical failure rather than the inevitable end of every living being. But rather than challenging the perception of moral, spiritual or even political problems as medical issues, health feminism sought an alternative source of authority. Just as the alternative health movement sought a return to more natural cures, the right-to-die movement sought a return to more natural death. But, importantly, the right-to-die movement did not challenge the idea of death as a medical problem rather than a natural occurrence. Whereas one of the criticisms from the right-to-die movement had been that doctors determined when life or death occurred; instead, they insisted, the individuals themselves should make the decision. Lost was the idea that God or nature in fact controlled when an individual died.

In this light, it is possible to understand the modern assisted-suicide movement's moral elision between killing and letting die. It depends upon the assignation of responsibility for death of any kind onto doctors. As Callahan notes, there is a link between the emphasis on lifestyle in relation to health and the apparent omnipotence of doctors in relation to death: 'It is nothing less than blaming the victim, as if death were now our fault, the result of human choices, not the independent workings of nature.' Death became a choice; the question was, should the doctor or the patient have it?[46]

So much is obvious from early discussions amongst feminists. As Carol Downer wrote at the 1975 Conference: 'When we started our Self-Help clinic, we did so because we were determined to gain control over our own bodies... We demanded increased use of paramedics, more preventative health care, less dangerous drugs and treatment, and more humanized treatment. We demanded these changes as a right.' Though the following passage is stilted and awkward, the importance of Downer's perspective on health to the future of the right-to-die movement is obvious: 'The indiscriminate use of surgery and drugs to deal with health problems that merely enable the individual to continue functioning in an unhealthy but adaptive manner with her status quo is using women as a status of social control rather than as a service to women.'[47]

By 1975 the health feminists increasingly identified themselves as their bodies, limited by biology. As *Our Bodies, Ourselves* noted: 'What are our bodies? First, they are us. We do not inhabit them – we are them (as well as mind).' Though feminists led the new emphasis on autonomy and bodily rights, this movement expressed what was rapidly becoming a majority sentiment. Well before *Quinlan*, Americans and others were reconsidering attitudes towards death and dying. By 1973, polls showed that 62 per cent of Americans believed that they ought to be able to tell their doctors to let them die rather than to extend life with no cure in sight.[48]

The ESA became attuned to these changes. The entrepreneurial Joseph Fletcher, who had argued earlier for the destruction of 'monstrosities at birth and mental defectives', moved away from arguments for the scientific control of the birth and death processes that had been the basis of support for the ESA in the past. As Harold Vanderpool noted: 'In 1968 Fletcher gave his still ardently held views a new cast – that euthanasia offers and escape from modern medicine's propensity "to prolong life (or, perhaps, to prolong death)".' Fletcher complained that 'Nowadays' people die 'sedated...betubed nasally, abdominally, and intravenously...more like manipulated objects than like moral subjects.' Fletcher then accused medicine of the errors he formerly attributed to Catholicism. It turned the 'bare sentience of biological life into an idol'.[49]

Euthanasia, while it remains in the title of many groups, has decidedly fallen out of favour amongst activists if not opponents. In the United States the Euthanasia Society changed its name in 1974 to the Society for the Right to Die (SRD), reflecting the new emphasis on autonomy and civil rights. As a prominent member of the SRD, newspaper columnist Abigail 'Dear Abby' Van Buren, noted in 1974, 'a bill with the word "euthanasia" in it will never get passed'.[50]

In 1977 the Euthanasia Educational Council changed its name to Concern for Dying (CFD). Following the success of his moving best-seller, *Jean's Way: A Love Story,* which told the story of his wife Jean's suicide after a long struggle with breast cancer, in 1978, Derek Humphry started the Hemlock Society in 1980, recalling ancient Greek society with its reference to the punishment meted out to Socrates. The Hemlock Society capitalized on more grass-roots support and forthright expression of its goals. In contrast, CFD and SRD expressed the interests of an older generation of social reformers and East Coast social elites.

The transformation between a eugenics-based rational death envisaged by a medical and social elite concentrating on mercy and the autonomous right-to-die embraced by a majority today took place between 1970 and 1988. As Albert Jonsen has observed:

The 'mercy' aspect of killing, which implied 'doing good' for 'Idiots, criminals and the worn-out senile' by eliminating their suffering and our burden, has disappeared. Many physicians, having accepted both the principle of respect for patient autonomy and the ethical probity of allowing to die, began to wonder whether any relevant moral distinction could be made between passive and active euthanasia. [...] So, the problem of active euthanasia slowly was subsumed into bioethics' favored principle, autonomy: The person competently requesting death alone defines benefit. The language of 'aid-in-dying' and 'assisted suicide' reflects this shift. The moral question is now, 'What reason can be given to exclude self-life ending (killing is not a politically correct word) from the repertoire of actions permitted to an autonomous person?'[51]

The emphasis shifted subtly from 'intractable pain', a feature of earlier pro-euthanasia advocacy, to the more subjective 'unbearable suffering'. In the Oregon legislation, no one needed to prove intractable pain but has the option if they have six months or less to live. Jonsen sees the shift to autonomy as the result of public fears about mental deterioration. The case of Nancy Cruzan, who had remained in a permanent vegetative state for seven years after a car accident, featured in a US Supreme Court ruling handed down in 1990. The Court ruled that all Americans had the right to have life-support withdrawn as long as there was clear and compelling evidence that this reflected their wishes.[52] In the wake of *Cruzan*, prominent Americans like Richard Nixon and Jacqueline Kennedy Onassis announced that they had written up living wills. The new nightmare imagined not so much pain as entrapment within an unrecognizable being, a half-life between life and death.

Dr Kevorkian

Dr Jack Kevorkian, the famous former Michigan pathologist, was perhaps the most successful campaigner for the right to die. A fascinating and fairly complex character, Kevorkian was subject of an HBO movie released in 2010 starring Al Pacino as the doctor, interestingly titled *You Don't Know Jack*. Kevorkian, who wrote and performed jazz music and created art using his own blood and with subjects including 'a child eating the flesh off a decomposing corpse', personified the right-to-die movement in the early 1990s. Despite his maverick ways and willingness to go to prison, Kevorkian was simply the best (and probably most committed) publicist of the right-to-die movement. His aim was never to alleviate pain but to publicize the plight of his 'patients' and, arguably, himself. He was the attention-seeking publicist that a movement based on recognition of the plight of the dying needed.

Many proponents disassociate themselves with Kevorkian, citing his illegal methods and pugnacious attitude as unhelpful to the cause of assisted suicide. However, Kevorkian probably did more than any other single figure to implant in the public's mind the fears that inspired his patients to seek his help. Kevorkian, who movie producer Steve Jones said 'walks in the footsteps of Martin Luther King and Nelson Mandela', not only copied the civil disobedience of King and others but tried to establish the dying as a bona fide civil rights group by raising their plight forcefully.

In June 1990, Kevorkian's 'thanatron', a suicide machine, was used for the first time by Janet Adkins, a 54-year-old teacher from Portland, Oregon, who was in the early stages of Alzheimer's disease. Kevorkian created the device and installed it in the back of a rusting VW van. He had tried to advertise it in a medical journal in 1999. When that failed, he peddled his story to a local newspaper and ended up on a nationally syndicated talk show. Adkins contacted Kevorkian after seeing the show.

Kevorkian hooked Adkins up to a heart monitor, slid an intravenous needle into her arm and started a harmless saline solution flowing through the tube. Then he sat back and watched the monitor as she pushed a big red button at the base of the machine. Immediately, the saline was replaced by a painkiller; one minute later came the poison potassium chloride. Within five minutes Janet Adkins was dead of heart stoppage.[53]

Kevorkian then called the police and told them what he had done. In the ensuing years, he assisted in the deaths of more than, according to his lawyer, 100 more 'patients' using the thanatron and, because his licence was revoked by the Michigan authorities and he could no longer get the substances needed for the thanatron, he developed a 'mercitron' that employed carbon monoxide. Juries failed to convict Kevorkian in five trials and a sixth was declared a mistrial. But on 17 September 1998 Kevorkian videotaped himself injecting Amyotrophic lateral sclerosis (ALS or Multiple Sclerosis) sufferer Thomas Youk with a lethal injection. Though Youk had agreed to the injection and was unable to inject himself, Kevorkian was convicted of second-degree homicide and sentenced to 10–25 years' prison.[54]

Conclusions

Rather than a real crisis facing modern humanity based on a new ability to extend life to biblical proportions, the modern assisted-suicide movement after the early 1970s might be thought of as the product of what Howard S. Becker called 'moral entrepreneurs' who exploited changes in public perception and attitudes. Rather than reacting to real changes in technological life-extension that present new challenges, the assisted-suicide movement feeds upon alienation from technology. However, as we have seen, the movement, rather than challenging the medicalization of society, medicalizes death, presenting it not as something that naturally occurs but as a treatment option, the result of choice rather than independent circumstances.

It is then not so surprising that the ostensibly rational assisted-suicide movement shares much with so-called New Age belief systems. Within the literature of the assisted-suicide movement are clues: 'self-deliverance' (to where?) or 'experiencing a peaceful death' (surely, death is the end of all experiences for the individual?). Borne of a spiritual rather than a technological crisis, the prospect of assisted suicide places our eventual fates in our own hands rather than, as past (Christian) generations were more likely to believe, into the arms of Jesus. Rather than reflecting upon what legacy we leave, on what our lives mean to present and future generations, the assisted-suicide movement concentrates on what death means to the self, surely a pointless exercise.

As Deborah Lupton has observed: 'In this secular age, focusing upon one's diet and other lifestyle choices has become an alternative to prayer and righteous living in providing a means of making sense of life and death. "Healthiness" has replaced "Godliness" as a yardstick of accomplishment and proper living.' Health became not simply the absence of disease but an idealized state that could only obtained through hard work (exercise) and sacrifice (abstaining from tobacco, excesses of alcohol and unhealthy food). And in the concept of a 'healthy death' perhaps we have the final irony.[55]

4
Considering Suicide

As we observed in other chapters, at the heart of the debate on assisted suicide and assisted dying is suicide. How should we look upon suicide in relation to question of whether to accept assisted suicide as medical treatment?

Suicide, of course, is an extremely difficult issue that can only be partially addressed in this chapter. In fact, we can really only begin to define it here, to etch out a few points in relation to our specific question. Accordingly, I define suicide as a moral (not a political or legal) issue. Suicide – though, importantly, not every suicide – is best viewed as a sin, as a breach of the moral norm, as having 'gone outside the universal', as philosopher Søren Kierkegaard put it. We might also employ Hannah Arendt's theory of action; suicide is a deliberate destruction of the norm in order to realize some goal. Whereas the decision to commit suicide must be the individual's decision, 'prepared within the silence of the heart', it becomes, by virtue of it being a deliberate, dramatic action of the highest import, something we must judge as either right or wrong.[1]

That most advocates of assisted suicide agree that suicide is a sin is demonstrated by the fact that they seek to draw a heavy line between the suicides of terminally ill people and those of others who are not deemed to have legitimate reasons to commit suicide. I argue that suicide in some situations is right and even noble, that assisting a noble or 'good' suicide is not wrong but that setting up preconditions where suicide is either always wrong or always permissible mistakes the individual nature of the act and the social nature of our recognition of the act. Legalizing assisted suicide is wrong because suicide should be an individual decision in order to assign responsibility, because it robs the purposeful ending of a life of its dramatic power and shields such an act from judgment, and because it renders the lives of those within the circumstances where suicide is allowed less worthy than others. Suicide should remain legal but generally disapproved of and we should not pretend that the act of taking one's life is anything but suicide.

Most suicides are wrong and hurtful to those left behind. But can suicide ever be right? Yes. A self-killing is usually bad but sometimes good, always shocking and awe-inspiring and must never be of no consequence to those left behind. Legalizing assisted suicide reduces suicide to a medical treatment choice. What should be profound and meaningful, the most human of actions, loses its meaning. The question of whether 'to be or not to be' becomes a medical rather than a moral question.

Of course, the suicide may prefer an easy medical treatment rather than a more difficult and potentially messy end. However, the focus here is upon those left behind, those who must live with the suicide. Suicides graphically illustrate the connection between all of us; even strangers are appalled that someone is despairing enough to take their own life and regret that they might have but did not help. Even the act of condemning or lauding such an action indicates that we care, that we are involved and have some relationship with the person. Assisted suicide renders the act neutral. Either we approve of the act of suicide on the basis that the individual's wishes automatically confer moral approval on the act, or we are neutral and the life and death of another individual means nothing to us. Legalizing assisted suicide in this way weakens the bonds between all of us.

G. K. Chesterton, the writer and inveterate Christian apologist, reacting to the (fictional) idea of suicide machines set up on various street corners, castigated suicide as worse than murder:

> Not only is suicide a sin, it is the sin. It is the ultimate and absolute evil, the refusal to take an interest in existence; the refusal to take the oath of loyalty to life. The man who kills a man, kills a man. The man who kills himself, kills all men; as far as he is concerned he wipes out the world. His act is worse (symbolically considered) than any rape or dynamite outrage. For it destroys all buildings: it insults all women. The thief is satisfied with diamonds; but the suicide is not: that is his crime. He cannot be bribed, even by the blazing stones of the Celestial City. The thief compliments the things he steals, if not the owner of them. But the suicide insults everything on earth by not stealing it. He defiles every flower by refusing to live for its sake. There is not a tiny creature in the cosmos at whom his death is not a sneer. When a man hangs himself on a tree, the leaves might fall

off in anger and the birds fly away in fury: for each has received a personal affront. Of course there may be pathetic emotional excuses for the act. There often are for rape, and there almost always are for dynamite. But if it comes to clear ideas and the intelligent meaning of things, then there is much more rational and philosophic truth in the burial at the cross-roads and the stake driven through the body, than in Mr. Archer's suicidal automatic machines. There is a meaning in burying the suicide apart. The man's crime is different from other crimes – for it makes even crimes impossible.[2]

But Chesterton is wrong to condemn all self-killing. As we will see, suicides can hardly be delineated from self-sacrifice in any predetermined way. Some acts of taking one's own life are undoubtedly 'good'. Three examples of what might be called good suicides illustrate this.

Three examples of what might be called 'good' suicides

Mohamed Bouazizi, a Tunisian street vendor, set himself on fire in the middle of the road on 17 December 2010 in Sidi Bouzid after local officials had humiliated him and confiscated his wares. In the weeks immediately after the incident, he became the 'Hero of Tunisia' and 'Person of the Year' in *Time* magazine. His action galvanized many Tunisians who were angry at unemployment, housing problems and widespread corruption. Protests occurred just hours after the event, culminating in the beginnings of what has been termed the 'Arab Spring' whereby President Ben Ali fled Tunisia with his family on 14 January 2011. The events in Tunisia spread to 14 other countries, resulting in the removal of Hosni Mubarak in Egypt and Muammar Gaddafi in Libya.

Al Azhar, the oldest and most prestigious centre of learning in the Sunni Muslim world, issued a fatwa in January of 2011 reaffirming that suicide violates Islam even when it is carried out as a social or political protest. However, prominent and influential Egyptian cleric Yousef al-Qaradawi spoke sympathetically about Bouazizi and others who attempted suicide, saying that they were driven to it by social injustice and that the responsibility for their deaths lay with the rulers of their countries.

Bouazizi was undoubtedly inspired, if perhaps indirectly, by the self-immolation in Saigon in June 1963 of Thich Quang Duc. Quang Duc, a Buddhist monk, protested against repression of Buddhists by the South Vietnamese regime of Ngo Dinh Diem by setting himself on fire before a Buddhist crowd and gathered media. The event was famously witnessed by the bewildered *New York Times* journalist David Halberstam and the photographer Malcolm Browne, who won an award for his picture of Quang Duc. Duc's sacrifice or suicide had a limited purpose but has become a symbol of resistance and, nearly fifty years later, his name is still well known. It is also germane to our discussion in that the suicide was assisted by another monk who poured petrol on Quang Duc before the latter lit the match.[3]

These deaths, undoubtedly self-inflicted, demonstrate the difficulty in defining – much less condemning in the way that Chesterton did – self-killing. What might have been called simply tragic acts were transformed posthumously into heroic martyrdom; Quang Duc inspired many followers, few as successful as he, Bouazizi's face adorned banners in street protests. Yet Bouazizi, according to his mother, set himself alight not to protest against unemployment and corruption but out of the frustration and humiliation he suffered. Some of the less prominent self-immolating suicides who followed in his wake may well have had more political motives but it is Bouazizi who is celebrated as a martyr. The meaning of all of these actions can change after the event.

We might examine one further less well-known and more private act of suicide. In the Academy Award-nominated 2003 film, *Capturing the Friedmans*, one of few noble acts to come to light was that of Arthur Friedman, whose penchant for child pornography appeared to land his youngest son, Jesse, in prison; he committed suicide in his prison cell in order for Jesse, whose life had been ruined by his association with his father's crime, to inherit $250,000 in insurance money. Such a suicide might appear to have been the best course of action at that point. Arthur Friedman had admitted possessing child pornography and to having paedophilic urges; his carelessness or stupidity in buying a pornographic magazine triggered a police raid on his home. Being a maths teacher at a local school, his after-school maths classes, conducted in the basement of their home, became the subject of police investigation. Subsequently, despite the fact that no complaints had been made by children attending before the magazines were found, various accusations were made against Arthur and his youngest son, 19-year-old Jesse, who helped out in the class. If Arthur was innocent of the assaults in the maths lessons (which looks likely, given the lack of physical evidence and the coercive natures of the interviews with the alleged victims), he had destroyed his career and his name but, more importantly, he had triggered the destruction of a large part of the life of his innocent son. If he was guilty (and thus his son was guilty also), he had corrupted his son. Either way, he felt he owed his son and had no way – except through his death – to help his son when he came out of prison. Assuming the facts are correct, his suicide at least speaks of his love for his son and the seriousness with which he took his obligations as a father.[4]

Whatever their opinions on these three deaths, most people will allow that certain kinds of self-inflicted deaths are not only legitimate but laudable but there are many more that are shocking and hurtful to those left behind. We might all agree that there are 'bad' and 'good' self-killings. Though many might regard the death of Arthur Friedman as essentially bad – the product of an unravelling tragedy – we might still admire this final act for its apparent selflessness. Even those who regard it as entirely bad would probably concede that other examples of self-killings are good.

But what about assisted suicide? Can a death that alleviates the suffering of someone close to death be good? Our central question can only be answered by resolving the prior questions involving the definition of suicide. Is there a difference between suicide and self-sacrifice? In what terms do we define the act? If a death is deemed 'good' or at least beneficial, does it matter whether it is suicide or euthanasia?

A collective and general disapproval of suicide – a taboo against it – exists simply because we automatically assume that the existence of others is valuable to us. Just as there is a general rule that taking the life of another is wrong, though there are some instances where it is not, for the same reasons we can say that taking one's own life is wrong unless proved otherwise. However, perhaps unlike killing another, the act of self-killing can be one of true selfless inspiration, of almost unfathomable nobility and courage, having the ability to render us speechless in awe and admiration. It can be the most beautifully human and stunning demonstration of what elevates humans from beasts. Such rare acts remind us of our shared meanings and values, the ability of the individual to rise above his or her self.

Thus, the case against legalizing assisted suicide need not have recourse to a strict 'sanctity of life' criterion to condemn all suicides. Nor do we need to be absolute in our condemnation of all assisted suicides or euthanasia in the very few cases where such acts are applicable and right. The absolute rule that humanists can surely accept without recourse to theological explanations is the value of the existence of others to ourselves.

Defining suicide

Just as the quarrels about definitions of euthanasia, voluntary euthanasia, assisted suicide and assisted dying that we discussed in Chapter 1 provide clues to the nature of the entire discussion, so it is with suicide.

We all know what suicide is but attempts to define it precisely – particularly for our purposes – are contested and no real satisfactory definition exists. What makes suicide distinct from other sorts of death? Is self-sacrifice entirely different than suicide?

According to the *Oxford English Dictionary*, the word 'suicide' is derived from the Latin word 'suicidium' meaning 'to kill oneself' and was first used in 1651. Before the seventeenth century, the English terms for suicide included self-homicide, self-destruction, self-slaughter and self-murder. Recently, a Catholic author stressed the intention of the act: 'Suicide occurs when the intention inherent in the human act (the moral object, purpose, or *finis operis* of the act) is self-destruction.'[5] The *International Encyclopedia of the Social Sciences* defined suicide as 'the human act of self-inflicted, self-intentional cessation.' The problem is that, though we all know what we mean when we say the word, it is very difficult to define it.[6]

We might think of suicide as simply self-killing or self-inflicted death. This is, most agree, too broad as it includes other forms of self-killing – such as driving into a wall accidentally. We might then narrow the definition to reflect the intent on the part of the killer. Suicide thus becomes intentional self-killing. Emile Durkheim defined suicide as any act that brings about the agent's own death, provided only that the agent knew the act would bring about his death. A suicide, he writes, is any 'death resulting directly or indirectly from a positive or negative act of the victim himself, which he knows will produce this result'.[7] This means that any self-destructive act that results in death counts as suicide so long as the agent had knowledge that the act would be self-destructive. The act must be taken specifically with death in mind in order to be suicide. Other literature mentions several factors: death was caused by actions or behaviour of the deceased, that the deceased desired to die and was willing to die, and that the deceased was responsible for his own death.

But must it be the result of an intentional *act* rather than an omission? Just as murder or manslaughter involves the killing of another by an intentional act rather than as a result of a failure to act, so suicide is the result of an intentional action by the suicide. As R. F. Holland noted, we might regard as suicide the act of a man placing his head upon railway tracks. Much as the train actually does the killing, there is little doubt that such an act would be suicide. If a person refuses food with the express intention of killing herself, should we regard that as suicide? Few would argue that these examples do not constitute suicide, despite the fact that death is caused by omission rather than by specific action taken by the suicide.[8]

However, we might venture that suicide must have death of the subject as the purpose behind whatever causes the death to occur. The man places his head on the tracks knowing that this action of his will result in his death. It must be the result of planning and execution. Drinking oneself to death when one has been warned that continued drinking will result in death is different; one does not usually drink with the express purpose of causing death, unlike when one ingests poison. Nor, if we accept this definition, can animals with no ability to rationally plan be said to commit suicide. Suicide is different than 'giving up', such as when a zebra gives up the fight against lions or a starving bear lies down to die. If I, having contemplated suicide previously, fall accidentally into a stream, decide not to swim, and drown as a result, my death, even if on some level it *would* have constituted an action and might be considered suicidal by those who know me, must be counted as an accident in the absence of evidence to show that I intended to die from the outset (evidence which is impossible to obtain). The simple failure to act to save oneself cannot be considered suicide just as the failure to save, say, a drowning man, though thoroughly reprehensible, could not be said to be murder. Letting one's own death occur is not suicide.

Moreover, in order for the act to be suicide, the subject must be conscious of what she is doing. Dying after sticking my finger into a socket without knowing that I will be electrocuted, most people would concede, is not suicide; dying after sticking my finger in a socket knowing that I will be electrocuted is suicide. There must be some connection between conception of the probable immediate results of my action and the action itself.[9]

In other words, suicide is neither resignation to fate nor failure to take action but a purposeful and deliberate endeavour. As anthropologist Jean La Fontaine said, a working definition of suicide is 'a death for which the responsibility is socially attributed to the dead person'. It is a question of moral responsibility; if I take action to end my life, I am responsible for my death. If I drown after accidentally falling in the water – even if I purposefully do nothing to save myself, my death is accidental or 'an act of God' and I cannot be held to be responsible. As we shall see, this distinction is important partially because it makes suicide a specifically *human* act.[10]

Self-sacrifice and suicide

One important issue is how to discriminate between self-sacrifice and suicide, an important subject for Catholic moralists and others who wish to morally forbid suicide but to draw a clear line between suicides and the self-sacrifices of soldiers and martyrs. Immanuel Kant presented this distinction when he asserted that 'he who defends himself and his fellows even unto death is no suicide, but noble and high-minded'. Suicide was, according to Kant, destructive, whereas self-sacrifice was creative. Kant delineated between suicides and justifiable self-killing where honour or virtue might be preserved by such an act. These acts constituted sacrifices occasioned by fate; the suicide does not strike the blow himself but sets out to preserve rather than destroy. Kant felt that these were victims of fate rather than suicides. Whereas suicide is blameable self-contempt, self-sacrifice was noble.[11]

We might allow Socrates' drinking of hemlock to be regarded as something other than suicide; he was forced into the act against his will. But women venerated as martyrs who killed themselves when they were about to be raped by pagans were excused from the crime of suicide by Augustine only because they were acting under divine instruction (which is itself problematic, as we shall see). As Robert F. Martin shows, however, it is nigh-on impossible to discriminate between suicide and self-sacrifice without such divine instruction.[12]

The double-effect pointed to by Thomas Aquinas and, more recently, by Catholic moralists allows that, if an act is morally good (or at least indifferent), and if a bad effect is not willed but simply permitted, is outweighed by the good effect, and is merely a side effect of the primary intention of the good effect, it may be morally permitted. Pope Pius XII issued advice in 1957, in response to a question by anaesthetists, allowing morphine injections that had the double-effect of killing the pain and stopping the breathing of the patient.[13]

Using the double-effect, we might distinguish between the Commanding Officer at a grenade training ground who leaps upon a grenade that has dropped to the ground in order to save his men. Though he clearly caused his own death, the probable primary reason for the action was not to kill himself but to save his men. However, the courageous action of Captain Oates must be regarded, under these criteria, as suicide, though it may also be said that the primary thought behind his action was the safety of his colleagues.[14] But we may introduce more problematic cases, such as the three highlighted at the beginning of the chapter. There was no need for any to kill themselves; they might have accomplished their goals in other ways. Yet Quang Duc gambled that his act of self-immolation would have a dramatic effect, so he might be said to have had a larger purpose than simply self-destruction in mind. The case of Arthur Friedman, too, provides a similar example. If looked at in the light of the commandment 'thou shalt not kill', the most important precept against suicide in Augustinian and Thomist thought, neither Bouazizi's, Quang Duc's nor Friedman's deaths would be justified. If we substitute the hand that killed them for that of another, keeping all other details, all deaths would constitute murder. It would be difficult to draw a clear line, in these cases, between allowable self-sacrifice and destructive self-murder.

Can suicide be assisted?

Thomas Szasz makes the point that, 'strictly speaking, the phrase "assisted suicide" is an oxymoron'. Though Szasz is correct to say that there are profound moral and legal issues for the person who assists the suicide (to be discussed later), for the suicide herself it does not matter who effects the killing so much as that she intends to die and that she actively seeks death. As Peter Windt notes, suicide might be defined to include actions that deliberately get oneself killed. So-called 'suicide by cop' or 'death by cop', whereby someone points a weapon at police officers or the public in order to be shot by the police, thus defined, constitutes suicide, despite the fact that it requires assistance – albeit involuntary assistance. But Quang Duc required a companion to pour petrol over him before he lit the match. The fact of such assistance has little bearing upon how his act was and is regarded. We might also say that Brutus's death, when he asks his servant Strato in Scene V, Act V of Shakespeare's *Julius Caesar*, to 'Hold then my sword, and turn away thy face, while I do run upon it', is suicide. *Contra* Szasz, suicide, so defined, may be assisted and remain suicide.[15]

Iain Brassington notes, in a piece accurately pointing out the contradictions within Kant's objections to suicide, that allowing assisted suicide becomes a logical step (so long as we agree that it is permissible to assist persons pursuing a permissible action) if we are to allow suicide:

> The implications for assisted suicide should be clear: if suicide is not wrong, then there would seem to be no reason why soliciting help for suicide should be wrong. Equally, if suicide is permissible, I think we may suppose that it is also permissible to respond to a call for assistance by assisting. Although there is no reason to suppose that it may be obligatory actually to help someone die, neither is there any basis for a refusal to do so in the wrongness of a proposed suicide, because there is no wrongness.[16]

The problem is that, though we may admit that certain deaths might be a relief or even beneficial, most would agree that the demise of human individuals is generally a bad thing. If it were the case that the only reason why the death of others is generally bad is because individuals generally value their lives and that, therefore, something valuable has been lost, we might only regret the death of others if they valued their lives. We could have no real cause to regret the suicide of a 21-year-old man who felt his life was worthless after the break-up of a relationship because his assessment of his life defines ours. Yet his action, though legal, is widely regarded as wrong. Without knowing the 21-year-old, most would regret such a death and, if asked for assistance before it happened, would provide reasons to live rather than a helpful push off of the proverbial bridge. It is reasonable to assume before it happens that suicide, like death, is generally bad and that deaths beneficial to the subject or those surviving her are the exception. Therefore, we should disagree that suicide is not wrong. It is wrong until proven right rather than vice versa.

But Brassington is correct that, if the original endeavour is good or at least not wrong, it makes sense to conclude that assisting it is at least permissible. However, we must make the following caveat. The suicide must have moral responsibility for the decision and for the action itself. The relationship between the suicide and her assistant is pertinent. The assistant must be acting under the suicide's command; the prime mover of the act must be the suicide. If the relationship is other than that, and particularly where the dominant character in the relationship is the assistant rather than the suicide, it throws into question whether the responsibility lies with the suicide and whether it is a private, personal decision of the suicide herself.

Besides Szasz's objection, there is the objection put forward by assisted-suicide campaigners who prefer not to use the 'pejorative' label of suicide (discussed in Chapter 1). This is behind the attempt by *Dignity in Dying* in Britain and *Compassion in Dying* in the United States to redefine the action they wish to legalize as *assisted dying* rather than *assisted suicide*. They replicate, in some ways, the arguments of theologians who attempt to delineate self-sacrifice (good) from suicide (bad). But there are deep problems with this attempt at re-definition.

As we have noted, no meaningful dividing line according to any criteria so far mentioned can be drawn between assisted suicide and suicide under the criteria legalized in Oregon and Washington and proposed in the UK and suicide broadly undestood. As many have admitted, the 'terminally ill, suffering unbearably' criteria simply elevates certain reasons why suicide takes place above others, either arbitrarily or, worse, because it is assumed that people whose lives are limited either by physical condition or by age lead lives less valuable than others, as we saw in Chapter 2.[17]

First, if we admit that unrelenting pain with no hope of relief from it that ends in certain death is a legitimate reason for the sincere wish to die sooner rather than later, we need also to admit that pain is not the reason why, the evidence shows, individuals request or go through with assisted deaths in Oregon or other areas where assisted suicide is legal. In fact, as we have observed, those requesting assisted suicides share their motivations with suicides accomplished without assistance.[18]

The 'legitimacy' or otherwise of a suicide, as defined by assisted suicide legalization advocates, cannot stand up to scrutiny. The former is only conferred by doctors sanctioning the act by attesting to the imminent demise of the person involved (whether within six or 12 months). But how can a doctor say how much an individual suffers by continuing to exist? In Oregon, a person who takes her life with more than six months to live is said to be a suicide; a person who takes his life with the assistance of a doctor and a terminal prognosis of less than six months is an assisted death. In the case of suicide without official sanction, moral responsibility generally lies solely with the suicide. In the case of an assisted death, moral responsibility for the action is shared. But it is clearly the action of the dying person that causes the death. The difference is that moral responsibility lies partially with the society that condones these suicides.

We must conclude that, so long as the decision to die and the primary moral responsibility for the action lie with the suicide, assisted suicide *is* suicide. Just as no justifiable moral or legal line can be drawn between self-sacrifice and suicide before the act occurs, neither can we draw any morally meaningful distinction between assisted dying and suicide. Euthanasia, of course, differs from suicide in that the moral responsibility for the death lies with the person (usually a doctor) dispatching the patient. But so long as the decision to die is really that of the person who dies, assisted dying must be suicide.

The problem with intent

If we divide those with a liberal stance concerning suicide from those who wish to retain the customary taboo, they clash about the *intent* of the action but tend to agree about its importance. Peter Windt redefines suicide so that acts designed to accomplish something other than self-extinction should not really be counted as suicides. The message in relation to assisted suicide is hard to miss:

> Suppose we became convinced that suicide could be defined, say, as self-caused death, where there is a wish to die on the part of the victim. Such a conviction would lead us to ignore the importance of intention or choice. In that case, we would refuse to count as suicides cases in which persons have no wish to die but intentionally do let themselves die, e.g. persons who have refuse medical treatment because they find the conditions of continued existence (impairment, suffering, etc.) worse than death itself. Such persons intend to die but need not *wish* to do so – they may find death the least undesirable of the choices available to them.[19]

Though the examples are not as clearly suicides as others might be, Windt's last sentences indicate that an assisted suicide or any other who intends to die but does not wish to die should not be counted as suicide. If death is a reluctant choice, the action is not suicide.

But what does it mean to wish to die? How many suicides simply intend to erase themselves from existence (and how would we know about it)? To use such a definition means that the vast majority of persons taking their own life who do so for reasons of honour, fear, humiliation, loneliness or to escape misery are no longer suicides. For all of these people, death is a reluctant choice. How would anyone actually know that the suicide who simply wished to erase himself from the world intended to do so, given that to leave a note would be to leave something of oneself? The act of suicide is loaded with meaning and speaks to everyone aware of it, even if it is to alert them, after the fact, of how miserable was the person who died. Windt wishes, it would appear, to redefine suicide out of existence.

What did the suicide wish to do? For Maurice Van Vyve, such a distinction is key in delineating between morally unacceptable suicide and praiseworthy self-sacrifice: 'To sacrifice oneself is to accomplish one's duty, to be *engagé* to the end, to renounce life for a greater good; to commit suicide is to give it up out of egoism, to give up in the face of one's duty. Diametrically opposed moral attitudes.'[20]

It is difficult to determine what the suicide anticipated, given that the meaning of one's own demise is so personal and subjective as to defy communication to others. It is probable that Arthur Friedman wished to destroy himself because of many conflicting reasons; guilt and self-hatred must have mixed with more noble concern for his son's welfare and determination to provide for him. But we can never know for sure as successful suicides can, of course, never be cross-examined.

There is also a problem with the idea that the suicide actually desired death. If, as a humanist, I see death not as a conduit but as the end of life, my only real understanding of death is a negative of life. Did the suicide have a realistic grasp of such an imponderable and unknowable issue at the moment he decided to die? If it is simply intent, we must accept whatever reasoning the self-killer indicated, if he did indicate a reason, just before the end. Accepting the division between suicide and self-sacrifice, we must *also* regard as self-sacrifice a self-inflicted death with the most noble of intentions but utterly mistaken in the calculation of its effect.

Whereas many who take their lives do not desire death at all but rather to avoid shame, to end suffering (germane to our discussion), to exact revenge on another person, to dramatize hurt and pain or even to draw attention to oneself, other suicides might be 'the enactment of a ritual which for a person in an extreme situation appears inescapable, reasonable, and legitimate'. Or, as Charles W. Wahl noted, an apparently rational suicide might be a 'magical act, actuated to achieve irrational, delusional, illusory ends'. An excellent example of such delusion was the cult, Heaven's Gate, of which 40 members killed themselves to escape the 'recycling' of planet earth and to join a spaceship following the appearance of the Hale-Bopp comet in 1997. The cult members did not intend to die though they swallowed phenobarbital and placed plastic bags over their heads. Though these deaths were nearly universally seen as suicides, the cult members intended to keep living, albeit in an alternative state. Intent, as a way to distinguish self-sacrifice from suicide, is an unreliable concept.

Van Vyve and others who argue for a strict delineation between suicide and self-sacrifice must also answer whether someone who believes himself to be Jesus Christ and sacrifices himself on a cross – surely an act intended to renounce life for the greater good – is really diametrically opposed to someone who sacrifices herself for the sake of her honour. The former act is based on illusions but the latter act, given that the honour is only hers, may be seen as 'egoistical'. Is the former good and the latter bad? So much depends on how history treats the suicide. Moreover, the sacrifice might take place for entirely egoistical reasons, just as warriors fought for their own glory. We can really only conclude, with St Augustine, that self-sacrifice is delineated from suicide by divine instruction or its absence.[21]

All victims? The determinist view of suicide

Many of those proposing to liberalize our views of suicide by redefining the vast majority of them as 'intended deaths' respond – somewhat
understandably – to the assertion by scholars in other fields, especially
those science-oriented fields that deal on a practical level with suicides,
that all voluntary deaths were wrong because the suicide is a victim of
suicide rather than someone who chooses to die.[22]

Such an outlook transforms suicide into a disease and virtually erases
any distinction between suicide and other deaths. Ultimately, the perspective stems from an ostensibly scientific detached viewpoint that
refuses to morally judge suicides and prefers to 'treat' rather than judge
suicides. In other words, if we cannot make a meaningful distinction
between suicide and self-sacrifice, we might pathologize self-sacrifice.
The discipline known as suicidology regards all suicide as the product of
medical problems.

Edwin Sheidman, who did more than anyone else to develop
suicidology, wrote in 1985:

> As I near the end of my career in suicidology, I think I can now
> say what has been on my mind in as few as five words: Suicide is
> caused by psychache (sik-ak; two syllables). Psychache refers to the
> hurt, anguish, soreness, aching, psychological pain in the psyche,
> the mind. It is intrinsically psychological – the pain of excessively
> felt shame, or guilt, or humiliation, or whatever.

To regard suicide as the result of pain implies that this pain is curable
and thus that every suicide is preventable. There can be no rational
suicides or ennobling sacrifices of one's life for a higher cause. All
suicides – and self-sacrifices – are curable medical disorders. An excellent
example of such pathologizing is contained in Sheidman's hopeful volume, *Essays on Self-Destruction*, published in 1967. M. D. Faber discussed
suicides in Shakespeare:

> When an honourable Elizabethan, for example, declared his pref-
> erence of death to dishonour and proceeded to destroy himself in
> the face of a predicament which was sure to compromise his honor,
> his contemporaries were apt to regard his suicide as the product of
> his devotion to honor. Today, however, such a suicide would prob-
> ably call forth responses composed not of words like 'honor' or
> 'reputation' but of words like 'ego' or 'self-concept' or 'rigidity'.[23]

Published at a time when great causes, like the Vietnam War, faced severe questioning, sacrificing oneself for one's country or for one's honour may well have looked delusional. However, as Szasz rightly points out, there are hugely coercive implications to making all suicides products of psychiatric disorders. Our lives, in effect, are no longer our own to sacrifice. Whereas Sheidman's optimistic attempt to 'cure' suicide no doubt has merits in immediately dealing with some of the destructive and hurtful suicides that many of us have experienced in the past, such an approach denies any that there is any moral agency attached to the act. There is no such thing as good or bad deaths; all deaths are bad. No one may make a rational decision to sacrifice her life for others, for a cause, or for any legitimate reason. Courage is the result of 'ego' and 'rigidity' and perhaps should not be regarded as any better than despair. In this perspective, no cause is worth fighting or even risking one's life for and anyone that purports to do so is self-delusional.[24]

There are many aspects that those with a liberal take on suicide and those like Sheidman who deny the legitimacy of any suicide or self-inflicted death have in common. Both deny moral agency to the suicide, the ability of people to make choices between right and wrong, by removing moral responsibility from the act. Sheidman would remove moral agency by defining anyone who takes their life as mentally ill. The liberalizers seek to remove moral agency by reducing suicide from an individual moral decision to a mere choice of medical treatment that is beyond moral judgment.

Is suicide a freedom?

Perhaps in response to the difficulties involved in defining suicide in moral terms, some who argue for legalization of assisted suicide seek to avoid the moral discussion by rephrasing it in individual terms. Margaret Battin has suggested abandoning the troublesome definitional problems:

> If we were to phrase the guiding concern of this inquiry as 'whether suicide is morally permissible'... then much might depend upon reaching a satisfactory definition of suicide. But we can avoid these disputes by describing our inquiry as one concerned with whether it is morally permissible for an individual to choose to die, to determine whether he or she shall die, to acquiesce in death, or to bring about or cause his or her own death.[25]

The simple answer, which can surely be agreed by all except perhaps Sheidman and some in the suicidology camp, is, in at least some circumstances, yes. From there, Battin hopes to establish the right to die as a political principle. But if the right to die is a political principle, assisting *any* suicide is then permissible, so long that it can be established that the suicide intended to die. Assisting religious cult members to die or pushing a 21-year-old off a bridge at his express wish is then permissible. But, as we have seen, intent is particularly difficult to establish after the subject died, returning us to the problem of defining suicide.

One of the problems that emerges again and again in the arguments of assisted-suicide proponents is the clash between Battin's autonomy argument and the attempt to declare causing some deaths moral and causing others immoral. Because most of the arguments utlilized by proponents involve contradicting the sanctity of life arguments put forward by proponents. But there remains a huge gap between Battin's rights-driven view and establishing the moral rightness of causing death, as we discussed in Chapter 2.

The assumption that there is little ethical distinction between killing, letting die and assisting a suicide so long as the person who dies truly wishes to die is based on a moral principle. As we observed in Chapter 2, James Rachels' influential paper argued this point. Rachels used the fact that most would regard both acts as equally morally reprehensible to undermine the distinction between killing and letting die. However, Rachels' example usefully demonstrates the difference between a moral and a political dilemma; whereas the actions of both are perhaps equally morally reprehensible, there is no legal obligation (in most of the English-speaking world) to save a drowning child.[26]

Moreover, the principle can be extended to doctors attending dying patients. But the key question is whether the death, whoever, accomplishes it, is right or wrong. The question of rightness or wrongness involves our collective judgement and clashes with the autonomy argument, where the actor or central subject determines the rightness or wrongness of her death. If autonomy is to be taken seriously, the question of *who* initiates the death again becomes imperative.

Given that few opponents of legalized assisted suicide agree with Rachels' distinction, proponents can leave them to one side. However, we might ask how important consent or the concept of 'ownership' of the life concerned is. Was Armin Miewes' act of murder any less reprehensible, because his victim agreed to be eaten, than other murders? Why do few campaigns for legalizing assisted suicide in the United

States, the UK, Australia, Canada or other places follow the Netherlands model which allows doctors to euthanize patients with or without their agreement? The answers to these questions lie in the huge prominence of autonomy as an argument for legalizing assisted suicide since the early 1970s.[27]

Suicide, autonomy and freedom

As we have seen in Chapter 2, up until recently, autonomy has been the most important weapon in the pro-assisted-suicide camp's armoury. We will now look at autonomy specifically in relation to suicide. Such a perspective evades the difficulty of defining what constitutes suicide by devolving all moral judgement of the act onto the individual concerned. The questions become – does the individual wish to die, is he sane and rational at the time he is wishing it, and does he believe that it is right to take his own life? If we can decide on these questions, it makes the question of what divides self-sacrifice from suicide less important because we defer decisions to individuals. The question becomes one of rights against those who would prevent a suicide.

There are several basic flaws to the freedom/right to die framework for understanding suicide. First, suicide as a possibility precedes, both logically and chronologically, all political rights. As pointed out in earlier chapters, killing oneself is a possibility whatever the law says. The law works by punishing those who transgress the law. A law against suicide, as many observed, particularly in England and Wales before the 1961 Suicide Act removed the penalties from suicide, makes little sense, hardly dissuading the determined suicide and making both those who have made unsuccessful attempts and surviving relatives of successful suicides miserable. Anyone, with determination and a little forward planning, can cause his or her own death. It makes no sense to outlaw suicide but nor should we enshrine suicide as a right. It is a question beyond the reach of law, a fundamental part of the human condition where the law cannot and should not go. It is something any competent human can achieve with or without legitimation in law.

As we have seen in previous chapters, the call for legalization of assisted suicides calls not for freedom but for affirmation, for recognition of the suffering of those who fit the criteria. As Dr Timothy Quill, a longstanding campaigner for a change in the law, has noted:

Our language does not have a term to adequately describe the wish for death when one's personhood is being destroyed by the relentless progression of disease...the consequences of misperceiving the significance for requests for aid-in-dying under such circumstances can be devastating...[28]

Quill is worried here not about legal issues but about the feelings of the dying person. There is, no doubt a fascinating discussion to be had regarding the question of whether one's personhood is destroyed by disease affecting organs other than the brain. However, the point here is that he sidesteps the issue of legality. It is 'misperceiving the significance' that Quill objects to as 'devastating' rather than the threat of jail or disbarment for those assisting. Prosecution in any of the 47 US states that do not permit (or have no relevant legislation on the statute books concerning) assisted suicide is rare; the number of people convicted in Britain under the Suicide Act, fifty years after its passage through Parliament, is zero. It is notable that countries where assisting a suicide is legal maintain organizations designed to promote the 'social acceptance' of assisted suicide. Whatever the philosopher-proponents of assisted suicide say, it is difficult to maintain that the issue is entirely – or even primarily – about freedom.[29]

Before and after the fact: the decision

So, how should we understand suicide? What is its meaning and within what framework shall we better comprehend it? There is one incomprehensible aspect to suicide. The real reasons for such an action being taken can never be known. The individual author of such reasons is gone and we are left with an impenetrable mystery that can, by definition, never be solved. The frustration that sometimes affects those close to a suicide is that the question of 'why?' is unknowable.[30]

Nor do the actual reasons going through the mind of the suicide matter after the fact. The officer jumping on the grenade apparently in order to save his men may have valued his life and others very highly and known precisely what would occur; he may have thought that the grenade was unlikely to go off or that he would survive the blast; he may not have thought at all; he may have had a death wish. What matters is our perception of his action. We who survive the suicides of others assign the meaning to suicide, not those who are dead.

Any decision to take one's life is based on such intensely individual and personal considerations that it would be impossible to create general criteria within which we can judge whether or not it is an appropriate action. As Albert Camus observed: 'An act like this [suicide] is prepared within the silence of the heart, as is a great work of art.' For the act to be considered suicide with no complicating factors, the *decision* must be seen to be made by the individual concerned. In order for moral responsibility to be assigned solely to the suicide, the decision must be made without being influenced by others. If a person asks whether or not she should commit suicide and we agree that her life is not worth living, we must accept some of the responsibility ourselves if she proceeds. Made by someone else (as in the Miewes/Brandes case), the act becomes murder even if the suicide agrees.[31]

We might even say that it is impossible to assign rationality to specific types of suicide (though that does not preclude the possibility of a rational suicide) given that each decision, every weighing of the scales between continued individual existence and self-destruction, is taken for reasons as personal as the life that precedes it. Much discussion, particularly in relation to assisted suicide (largely predating the attempt to re-name assisted suicide 'assisted dying') alleges that suicide can be a rational act and that criteria can be concocted to decide whether someone's suicidal wishes are rational. There are two problems in approving of suicide in certain situations as rational. First, much as we can agree that someone may be in a rational frame of mind when taking the decision, the decision itself is too personal, too private, to be pre-approved as rational, much like the term 'unbearable pain' cannot usefully be defined except by a specific person. Second, the future existence of the would-be suicide cannot be known even by the subject; it is impossible to quantify what is being gambled when suicide is sought.

Nor, by definition, can a suicide be interrogated after the event about motives or the rationality of her decision. Nor can suicide be justified by past example because the effects of one's suicide are unpredictable, given the impossibility that the value of a person's death can be accurately weighed against the value of continued life. Though the decision to kill oneself may be a rational gamble, the considerations are so individual as to prevent communicating them to any but one's closest confidantes; thus, they can hardly be understood as rational because there are no criteria within which we may prejudge the rationality or otherwise of that decision. As Durkheim observed, 'the circumstances are almost infinite in number which are supposed to cause suicide ... The most varied and even the most contradictory events of life may equally serve as pretexts for suicide'.[32]

Such an understanding prevents anyone from advocating suicide as a rational decision in certain circumstances. How might we value the value of an individual's life and balance it against reasons for dying?

We may understand some of what various authors have referred to the individual's 'biographical' (as opposed to 'biological') life.[33] We may understand and perhaps even agree with reasons why the suicide wishes to die. We may have a reasonable prediction of what the future entails for that person. But if we do not know the person intimately, we can have no grasp of the implications of her suicide; if we *do* know her well, we would have to be certain that the benefits of her death will outweigh her continued life and her absence in our lives and the lives of others surrounding her. In other words, we must be sure that the benefits of her death outweigh both her and our loss.

Of course, there are situations where we may morally assent to another's suicidal wishes, even if he is unknown to us; the 'policeman's dilemma'[34] indicates that such instances are possible. But that is hardly a decision for either the policeman or the lorry driver. It is reasonable and rational to prevent needless and un-relievable pain in any living being. If we accept the delineation between 'biographical' and 'biological' life, it is clear in the policeman's dilemma that serving the immediate need of the latter (prevention of several minutes of horrific pain) should trump any musing over the former. But even here, the decision to assist is individual and specific – if not to the subject expressing suicidal wishes, then to the surrounding circumstances. It is impossible to set up rational criteria governing assisting a suicide. Such decisions take place on grounds not of bureaucratic Weberian reasoning but according to very specific and individual circumstances and details.

Even in relatively public suicides such as Quang Duc's, the actual decision was made privately and Quang Duc had to convince other activists to support him in his sacrifice.[35] Certain suicides may appear comparable – two suicides might have perished for the same ostensible reasons of unrequited love, for instance – but it would be mistaken to see the decision to kill oneself as emanating directly from unrequited love. Even individuals, who have a better understanding of how they might react to certain circumstances, often recant the wish, made solemnly at the age of twenty, that they would rather die than endure paralysis. That is not to say that there are no situations where death is a better option than continued existence. It is simply to insist that reasons for deciding to end one's life are as unique as the individual making that decision and cannot be generalized.[36]

Any attempt to make the decision publicly can only underline our inability to communicate such thoughts. Justifying one's reasons before the act can only invite others to appraise one's life, its value, and the aims of the act of suicide. Those others, unless depressed themselves, can only affirm reasons for continued existence. One would have had to live the daily frustrations, anger and perceived futility of Mohamed Bouazizi's existence before we could offer, if able to return to that fateful day in December 2010, an opinion about whether he should set himself alight. Even then it is unlikely that many would agree that his humiliation by the female police officer and his financial problems warranted his suicide. Even if the decision to kill oneself involves someone so close that I can claim some insight into and understanding of his reasons for killing himself, any advice I gave him on suicide would inevitably reflect perspective on my own life. Moreover, should I advocate suicide, I assume at least part of the moral responsibility for the action. Though suicide pacts attract attention, they are rare compared to solitary suicides, reflecting, perhaps, the individual nature of such a decision.[37]

Rather than subjecting the decision of whether or not to continue one's existence to tribunals, as has been suggested by at least one prominent campaigner for assisted suicide, only the individual, after much soul-searching and private reflection, is in the position to make the decision of whether he or she dies or continues to live.[38]

Privacy is important in the decision to die because the individual concerned must shut out the world in contemplating the worth of her existence against the ostensible goods achieved by dying. The choice of whether I live or die must be primarily my own. The sacrifice of Captain Lawrence Oates is celebrated as heroic and brave but his heroism would be diminished if all his colleagues voted that his suicide was the best option. Similarly, some of the nobility of the suicide for his actions is replaced by despair and I assume some responsibility for his death if I agree that his financial situation, wrongful decision or dishonour necessitates him taking his own life. He is in danger of becoming my dupe and I – at least in a moral sense – his murderer. The meaning of a suicide is less if the suicide is in fact a victim.

Suicide as a public act

Whereas the decision to commit suicide must be private, once that decision has been acted upon, the act is entirely social. Unlike a natural death, the suicide is 'man-made', the result of a peculiarly human freedom. The death of an individual does not define him; it normally has little meaning other than the (usually regrettable, sometimes accidental) end to his life. If an individual dies by drowning, we might highlight the death as an indication of the dangers of swimming in a particular lake but it would tell us little of the character of the deceased. If an individual commits suicide (or is murdered) in such a way that it appears as an accident, those surviving her demise will simply understand it as an unfortunate death. If there is no evidence that a death occurred because of the intentional action of the deceased, it is rarely termed suicide, no matter the unknown and unknowable thoughts of the deceased just before her death. To be suicide, an act of suicide must be *understood* as suicide.

Here is where we might reintroduce St Augustine's idea that suicide is self-sacrifice only with a direct, personal command of God (the precedent set by Abraham's imminent sacrifice of his son, Isaac, as God commanded him). St Augustine's (and later Thomas Aquinas's) precept can be easily dismissed by humanists – all suicides are wrong except those that God says are right – but we might apply that to our three examples. It is not God that sanctioned their act but posterity that gave meaning to them, that elevated the effects in the aftermath of their suicides above the sinfulness of the act itself. This is surely the dividing line between self-sacrifice and suicide; it is not the motives with which the self-killer begins but the interpretation of that motive and its posthumous vindication.[39]

Even when the reasons for the suicide are communicated by the suicide herself, posterity – not the suicide herself – determines how the suicide is understood. The perception of those who survive the suicide – not necessarily the reasons for which the act was really taken – is the true meaning of any suicide. The meaning of any suicide is created by the person telling the story of it. For Marx, suicides condemn the society that produces them. Bouazizi's and Quang Duc's suicides all became symbols of much larger issues; the thousands of self-immolators that followed these deaths who specifically designed their deaths to highlight the same or other issues achieved little. The reasoning the suicide had for his act died with the suicide. It is up to others to assign meaning to the act.[40]

Thus, a murder or a suicide is public in the sense that history is public and subject to changing meaning long after the event. For instance, we might look at the suicide of Lucretia. In a story recounted by Ovid, Sextus Tarquinias, son of Tarquin, the king of Rome, raped Lucretia (Lucrece), wife of Collatinus, a member of the court. Lucretia committed suicide to prevent the dishonour of her husband (if the reader takes the word of Ovid and accepts some of Shakespeare's embellishments). Her body, paraded in the Roman Forum by the king's nephew, incited a full-scale revolt against the Tarquins, the banishment of the royal family, and the founding of the Roman Republic.

The observer, if we take monstrous liberties with history and pretend that modern sensibilities reigned, might plead after the rape but before the other events that Collatinus would accept that she was innocent and prefer that she lived. The observer might have pointed out the irrationality of the act; her virtue and innocence were intact and the wrong-doer should take all responsibility for his transgression. The observer could argue that her act was unlikely to have any impact beyond robbing Collatinus and others of her presence. Even immediately after the suicide, it might be simply viewed as an irrational and impassioned act, a tragedy with few redeeming aspects.

Yet the meaning of Lucretia's action changed days or even years after her death. Whereas immediately after the event the act might have been considered rash and irrational, it achieved rationality after the fact. Perhaps we might take a different view, armed with the knowledge that her act helped usher in the Roman Republic, influenced the way Christianity developed its concept of sainthood, became a popular moral tale in the Middle Ages. Just as the world might be considered a better place for the literary suicides of Romeo and Juliet, so it might because of the real act that inspired the art of such figures as Titian, Botticelli, Cranach, Veronese and Rembrandt as well as Chaucer, Dante and Shakespeare. The point is that what may have originally looked irrational might look rational later, and vice versa. The meaning of suicide cannot be assessed before it takes place. Its goodness or badness can only be judged by others.[41]

Suicide as action

In various ways, suicide is perhaps best understood as *action* in the way explicated by the philosopher Hannah Arendt. To define suicide – to set the terms within which it is understandable – we might think of the act of suicide as *action* as described by Arendt. In her celebrated work, *The Human Condition*, she resuscitated the ancient Greek conception of action (*praxis*) to delineate it from labour and work. Though she continually stressed natality – that action is a beginning of something – suicide fits well into her description in its expression of human freedom.[42]

First, the freedom Arendt discusses is not, as she is careful to say, freedom as sovereignty. 'If it were true that sovereignty and freedom are the same, then indeed no man could be free, because sovereignty, the ideal of uncompromising self-sufficiency and mastership [sic], is contradictory to the very condition of plurality. No man can be sovereign because not one man, but men, inhabit the earth.'[43]

Whereas the conception of freedom as sovereignty is useful in pre-venting interference into our lives by the state or by others, the 'freedom' to commit suicide is not a useful conception except when it refers to that specific ability to take unexpected action that is counter to the normal pattern of events or the existing moral paradigm. In that human beings are uniquely able to destroy themselves in order to real-ize specific goals, they enjoy a freedom that cannot be taken away by political means. But it is *not* a freedom to have their acts morally exon-erated; it is freedom to breach the expected rules encapsulated within the existing moral structure. As Bruce Mazlish has observed, the indi-vidual 'sinner' against the prevailing moral system 'still operates within an established system. The sinner transcends known limits; he does not intentionally shift the limits'.[44]

A second characteristic of suicide that it shares with Arendt's concep-tion of action is that it bears the 'burden of irreversibility and unpre-dictability' and in uncontrollable in its repercussions. It is impossible to gauge the impact of a suicide before it occurs. We cannot know what experiences a person who kills herself is missing by shortening her life. We cannot say how her death will affect her family and friends. Whereas Bouazizi's suicide sparked the Arab Spring, other similar actions, such as that of Homa Daradi in Iran,[45] more carefully calculated to bring about protest, have failed to have much impact upon the world. Nor have the many monks' suicides that were inspired by Quang Duc's actions had their intended effect. Whereas suicide might very well be a gamble taken for rational reasons, its consequences remain entirely unpredictable.

As Arendt said of action (in what might have been a description of the Bouazizi affair): '...though it may proceed from nowhere, so to speak, [it] acts into a medium where every action becomes a chain reaction and where every process is the cause of new processes... the smallest act in the most limited circumstances bears the seed of the same bound-lessness, because one deed, and sometimes one word, suffices to change every constellation.'[46]

On a smaller level than Bouazizi's or Quang Duc's deaths, suicides are, so to speak, life-changing events for others. Despite the predictability of Friedman's death (that is, if he died, his son would inherit the insurance money), the eventual outcome was not assured. It would be difficult to advise him to gamble with such high stakes involved. Friedman imag-ined that his son could benefit from the insurance money but his son might have died in prison. His son might have been inspired to take his own life by his father's action. Many events might have intervened to make Friedman's actions appear futile and, in hindsight, irrational. Friedman's action was undoubtedly a gamble that his sacrifice would improve his son's life. We might admit that it was *likely* that Friedman's suicide would have this or that outcome, but it would be very difficult to balance the outcome against what Friedman lost by killing himself. What experiences might he have had? What difference would his continued agency have as opposed to his inability to act upon the world after his death?

Suicide, as Mark Twain once said, is the most sincere form of self-criticism. Arendt spoke of the important relationship between speech and action. Whereas suicide with no one to call it by name is simply death, there is also a relationship between speech and suicide in that suicide, if it appears to be for a particular reason, demonstrates the sincerity of the suicide's intentions and the power of the ostensible reasons behind the suicide. When Romeo and Juliet declared that they could not live without each other, their tragic actions at the end of the play demonstrated that this was the case. Equally, suicide for reasons of despair indicates the suffering felt by a fellow human being. As M. D. Faber noted:

> Because suicide inevitably gives expression to what prompts it, because it is the culmination and radical embodiment of particular emotions, because it is, in short, the anagram of motivation, it becomes, from the literary angle, a metaphor. If patriotism stands behind it then it speaks, on the stage, for patriotism; if despair stands behind it then it is fated to speak for despair, and so on whichever catalyst happens to be at work.[47]

Suicide at least speaks for seriousness of the emotion, for strength of devotion or for the depth of despair behind it. It is one way by which we may confirm the genuineness of the speaker.

So while it is impossible to delineate between sacrifice and suicide or to draw up specific criteria upon which to prejudge suicide, it is entirely possible to judge each individual suicide as being either right or wrong. Unless we deny the existence of any perspectives that we share as a community or society (or perhaps deny the existence of society altogether), we must appraise suicides as good or bad. Such a perspective breaks with the older Christian tradition of condemning suicides regardless of the circumstances (though this has hardly been absolute). Saying that a particular suicide is a bad act does not mean we repeat this

Christian code. It does not condemn the suicide himself but simply that particular action taken by the suicide.

So here is perhaps the most important reason to condemn the legalization of assisted suicide. In attempting to redefine self-destruction in neutral terms, as medical treatment rather than a dramatic act, it robs us of our ability to judge, to come to some collective decision on the rightness or wrongness (or, as with the examples of Bouazizi, Quang Duc and Friedman, both at once) of the suicide. If we cannot judge acts of self-destruction as good or bad, it prevents a moral dialogue between us and threatens to undermine the very basis of our relationship with the world. Human action becomes no more meaningful than a disease.

Forgiveness

Not being able to judge also cuts off the relationship with the deceased because we are not able to forgive. We can usefully employ another Arendtian concept: forgiveness as a counteraction to any action. Forgiveness prevents the person that takes the action, with its boundlessness and irreversibility, from forever being a victim of it. Like action, forgiveness begins anew; it is a new point from which a new pattern of existence with new actions might take place. It is, in some ways, an action, in that it is unexpected and sometimes startling, and in its natality, its quality of rebirth. Forgiveness releases the author from the action. In the context of suicide, my relationship with the deceased may change if I forgive him. In neutralizing the act, it removes any consideration that our relationship was important. If he hurt me by his act, by his rejection of the world, I am not allowed to either condemn it or forgive it.[48]

Suicide is a stark example of the social or political nature – the plurality, in Arendt's terminology – of acts of forgiveness. It is impossible to forgive the suicide if suicide cannot be considered either wrong or right. The forgiveness releases the suicide from the one act but only in memory of the person forgiving. The suicide can live in our collective memories without that one fatal action defining her.

Judgment: the coward's way out

Reducing suicide to a medical treatment option is not only is it a dissipation of suicide's moral responsibility – her ownership of the action – but it is an abnegation of the moral duties of the community. One of the objectionable aspects of the campaign for the legalization of assisted suicide is its determination to remove this entire category of suicide from the public sphere and thus from public judgment, to pretend that no act of self-destruction ever took place.

What is really being asked for? Assistance in the act of suicide means that the person assisting either agrees with the endeavour – based generally on despair – or shrinks from the task of advancing any opinion. Either we can't help you or we won't help you, says the community in response to expressions of despair. If we give the benefit of the doubt to those who call for choice and admit that they are not stating that the lives of those suffering from certain illnesses are not worth living, assisted suicide campaigners call for 'choice' in the abstract. But as G. K. Chesterton noted, to admire mere choice is to refuse to choose. By institutionalizing assisted suicide, the community says either that it has not the authority to condemn or praise the act or, worse, says that it simply is of no concern.[49]

The message sent by institutionalizing assisted suicide is fear of what the future might hold. It is a counsel of despair. The reasons for those who do take their lives in places where the practice is legal are reasonably well-documented. Unbearable suffering does not relate to pain but to mental anguish and fear of the future. Such feelings are understandable and only the most hard-hearted of souls would condemn people in such tragic circumstances who take their own lives. But nor would most people suggest to those suffering from despair that suicide might be the right answer.

Assisted suicide dissuades us from saying that an individual suicide is right or wrong, insisting only that it is right for the suicide. But this is destructive to our ability to assign meaning to particular actions. If we accept that suicide is an action, not to judge it is to regard the reasons why it occurred as utterly unintelligible. To assign an action as good or bad, right or wrong, provides a way of understanding it, of giving it meaning.

Just as noble suicides make the world a better place, the world is made worse by meaningless deaths. We are more disturbed by the cold, administratively determined deaths of Dachau and Belsen or by murders carried out for no understandable reason than we are by the more common crimes of passion, partially because passion renders them understandable. We must categorize suicides as tragic, hostile, courageous or simply mistaken or risk concluding that the existence or non-existence of this other human being simply meant nothing at all.

The taboo-aspect of suicide is misunderstood by those challenging it. The taboo reflected (and reflects) the worth of human life and our shared value we place on it. Much as suicide in general was taboo throughout most of history, individual suicides need not undermine the taboo against suicide but may in fact strengthen it when reasons for such actions are discussed. Suicides feature in many tales told between friends, in folklore and, as we have seen, in literature and art. They have been subject to judgment *because* they were particular and could be understood only in their own contexts. As Peter Steinberger notes, judgment is always of a single object, event, or person: 'Since we are outside the realm of proof and demonstration, to judge something is not to employ a universal theory or principle nor to provide a basis for such a theory or principle; it is merely to make a particular claim about a particular object.'[50]

Conclusion

Suicide may be reprehensible, despicable, and as vile as Chesterton maintained. It may simply be tragic or impulsive. It may also be inspirational, transcendent and the most beautiful and awe-inspiring act. The argument here is that it should never be regarded as neutral or no one else's business, which is what those attempting to legalize assisted suicide argue for.

Whereas Quang Duc's and Friedman's suicides were purposeful and calculated, Bouazizi's suicide was a rash, impulsive gesture, but the frustration and anger he expressed resonated throughout not simply Tunisia nor the Maghreb but right across the Middle East. His action gathered meaning in the weeks and months after he self-immolated. It is a reflection of value with which we hold the lives of others that suicide rightly shocks us. To assent to suicide for a category of people is to diminish the value of the existence of all persons in that category.

Suicide is best understood in moral terms because, by its nature, political and judicial attempts to control it fail. In legal terms it makes sense to establish legally the individual's sovereignty over his own body, allowing a competent adult to refuse treatment. There is great difficulty in determining the rationality of the decision of a person to take one's life because the effects are so unpredictable; nor can we weigh what has been gained by the suicide against what might have been had the suicide not taken place. Instead, we must regard suicide as action that may never be undone and which is always subject to our retrospective judgment.

An arrangement whereby it is removed from our scope of judgment – declaring it a medical treatment no more appropriate to judge than an appendectomy – robs those surviving the suicide of our ability to consider whether the action is right or wrong. Is continued existence in the face of suffering better or worse than suicide? How, if we shrug our shoulders, can we look admiringly on those who suffer for their art, or encourage those facing lives with disability or even convince the lovelorn twenty-year old that life is worth the suffering?

Perhaps worst is that it impugns all of us to grant the suicidal wishes of those who are depressed, who present us with resolveable, human problems (as we have seen, the top reasons for assisted suicides in areas where it is legal involve fears and depressions that might be alleviated). The inevitable depredations of age, disability or even terminal illness do not render persons worthless and their lives pointless.

Thus, what we might call cultural dangers far outweigh the rightness or otherwise of the suicides of the very few who take up this 'option' where assisted suicide is legal. If we agree the emphasis on autonomy upon which many of the pro-assisted-suicide philosophers and ethicists base their arguments, we arrive at an unrestricted freedom of conscience which would, as Hannah Arendt noted, 'spell the doom of every organized community'. If suicide for any purpose at all is allowed, the inherent goodness of the existence of other human beings is removed. There is no shared sense of good or bad, no right or wrong.[51]

Whereas comparisons of advocates of legalized assisted suicide with Nazis is unfair and inaccurate, Arendt was surely correct to note in her observation of the Eichmann trial that it was absence of thought or conscience that creates evil. It is 'the refusal as well as the inability to judge, to imagine before your eyes the others whom your judgment represents and to whom it responds, invite evil to enter and infect the world'. There is a great propensity not to judge, to 'judge not, that ye be judged not'. Behind the unwillingness to judge lies the idea that we are all imperfect beings and simply trying to survive in difficult circumstances. As Arendt noted, such was Eichmann's defence.[52]

5
For Abortion, Against Assisted Suicide

In this chapter, I discuss the parallels drawn between abortion and assisted suicide. There is a widespread presumption that a liberal take on abortion implies support for a change in the law on assisted suicide. Both sides of the discussion on assisted suicide promote this perception. There are, in truth, similarities but there are also profound differences between abortion and assisted suicide. Both suicide and abortion are essentially private matters involving individual choice. However, the question at hand is whether or not to assist the woman seeking an abortion or the person seeking an early death. I argue that society has an interest in assisting women, through providing medical abortions, in order that women are able to play an equal role to men in society. There is no composite societal interest in providing assisted suicides; nor are they necessary.

The similarities between the *anti*-abortion movement and the campaign *for* assisted suicide are in that they both seek to redefine existing norms. Right now we regard murder as the murder of a person rather than simply the termination of a human life. But the pro-life movement wants to extend the parameters of personhood back to the creation of an embryo and to those who, like Terri Schiavo, exist in a permanently vegetative state. The assisted-suicide movement wishes to roll back personhood from those with terminal illnesses. Destroying an embryo is clearly not murdering a person, as taking the life of a terminally ill elderly person without their permission would be. In that they both suggest radical redefinitions of human life, the anti-abortion movement and the assisted suicide movement have, perhaps, more in common than the pro-abortion and pro-assisted suicide movements.

There is a conscious attempt on both sides of the assisted-suicide discussion to draw parallels between the two issues. LIFE, the British organization that opposes abortion and any medical technology that involves the destruction of human embryos, is associated with *Care Not Killing*, one of the larger groups opposing assisted suicide. *Pro-Life Alliance*, another prominent organization consistently opposing attempts to legalize assisted suicide in the UK, focuses on four issues: abortion, euthanasia, human cloning and 'embryo abuse'.[1] In the United States one of the most important organizations opposed to legalizing assisted suicide is the *National Right to Life Committee*. Its website notes: 'Many people outside the pro-life movement do not know that from its beginning in 1973, The National Right to Life Committee has opposed infanticide and euthanasia with the same determination and vigor with which it fights abortion.'[2]

The BBC website carries an article by Mike Willis, chairman of the Pro-Life Alliance, as representative of the opposition. He begins by stating that '[t]he drive for legalised euthanasia shares common roots with the legalisation of abortion in 1967. Promoters of these practices take a utilitarian view of human life rather than viewing all human life as uniquely created and deserving of absolute respect'. Later he predicts that '[t]he elderly will go the same way as the unborn – unwanted, useless bread gobblers – but who will be next?'[3]

Others prominent in the campaign against legalization include the United States Conference of Catholic Bishops and its Canadian equivalent which also campaign against legalized abortion. In the UK, the Archbishop of Canterbury argued against the Independent Commission on Assisted Dying's call for a change in the law by stating that '(t)he default position on abortion has shifted quite clearly over the past 40 years, and to see the default position shifting on the sanctity of life would be a disaster ... We are committed, as Christians, to the belief that every life in every imaginable situation is infinitely precious in the sight of God'. Of the major churches, only the Presbyterian Church appears to be liberal on abortion but not on assisted suicide. The others are either in favour of liberalization on both (such as the Unitarian Church) or opposed to both (the Catholic Church, Church of Jesus Christ of Latter Day Saints, Lutheran faiths. Islam is also opposed to abortion after 120 days and, according to some Islamic scholars, to all abortions) or simply vague on both issues.[4]

Those who fight for abortion rights also often take what they imagine is a liberal view on assisted suicide. The word 'choice' often creeps into discussions about assisted suicide and organizations calling for a change in the law on assisted suicide often refer to themselves as 'pro-choice'. The use of this language consciously evokes that of the abortion controversy, appealing to those who support the right of women to make choices about abortion. The organization formerly known as the Voluntary Euthanasia Society in the United States now calls itself *Compassion and Choices*. The British Voluntary Euthanasia Society now calls itself *Dignity in Dying* with the by-line *Your Life, Your Choice*.[5] British columnist Suzanne Moore noted the parallels in the campaign:

> 'Two, four, six, eight, not the Church and not the State. Women will decide our fate,' we used to chant at abortion rallies. I feel the same way about how I die. Yes, my ideology – and I recognise it as such, unlike some people of faith – involves a notion of autonomy. The claiming of rights over my own reproductive system, and how long this body lives, changes as medicine changes. My invoking of this as a right, more properly a choice that can be legislated for, is in no way a judgment about anyone else's quality of life. [...] As with abortion, the issue is: at what point does extending my right encroach on someone else's? For those against abortion, it will be the rights of the foetus. For those against assisted dying, it is more difficult to understand who is being protected.[6]

Moreover, there are many references to 'back-street suicides' in the literature of the pro-assisted-suicide organizations that deliberately uses the language that could be heard to justify legalizing abortion in the 1967 Abortion Act in the UK. *Dignity in Dying* wishes to make back-street suicides a thing of the past. 'Each year, a number of terminally ill people resort to violent and often botched suicides', states their website, echoing the complaints that prefaced legislation allowing abortion. Joseph Arvay, the lawyer for Gloria Taylor, a Canadian woman dying of multiple sclerosis who sued for her right to an assisted death, warned of an increase of 'back-alley' suicides if assisted suicide is not legalized.[7]

It is not only organizations that make the connection; academics often employ interchangeable arguments and line up on either the pro-choice or pro-life sides. Margaret Somerville, prominent Canadian spokesperson against assisted suicide and author of *Death Talk: The Case Against Euthanasia and Assisted Suicide*, is also prominent in condemning abortions and calling for restrictions on the right to abortion in Canada (Canada, uniquely, has no law restricting women's access to abortion). Wesley J. Smith, who opposes assisted suicide, also opposes abortion.[8] Leon R. Kass, who refers to himself as a humanist, also inveighed against the expansion of abortion in an article opposing legalization of assisted suicide.[9]

Many have the same religious objection to abortion as they do to assisted suicide. If God both gives and takes away life, we must leave decisions at the beginning and the end to Him. We might sum up these views in this way:

1. Human life begins at conception and ends at death
2. Every human life is sacred
3. If every human life is sacred, every human has a right to life
4. We may not remove the right to life simply because someone's existence is a nuisance, either to themselves or to others
5. Therefore, both abortion and assisted suicide are morally wrong.

Opposed to both abortion and assisted suicide, Leon Kass demonstrates the interchangeable nature of the slippery slope argument – the idea that, if we allow a very small number of very limited assisted suicides, there will be an inevitable expansion of their numbers – with the example of abortion.[10] But nearly all opposed to both assisted suicide and abortion employ sanctity of life – that all human life is sacred and therefore we should not presume to end it. The fragile weeks before one is born become the fragile weeks before one dies. The lives of comatose patients, those tired of life and unborn infants must be protected. They are united in their vulnerability. There is some room for manoeuvre with the 'slippery slope' argument; Bonnie Steinbock believes that abortion is 'almost always a morally permissible option' but opposes the legalization of assisted suicide. Steinbock, as we have seen in Chapter 2, does not rely upon the sanctity of life argument but points out that the effects of legalization of assisted suicide are too unpredictable.[11]

The parallel between abortion and assisted suicide is further drawn out by successive court cases in the United States. The right to privacy under the due process clause of the 14th Amendment to the Constitution, it was successfully argued in *Roe v. Wade* (1973), extended to a woman's decision to have an abortion. In *Washington v. Glucksberg*, Glucksberg et al. argued, unsuccessfully, along the same lines that Washington's ban on assisted suicide interfered with the right to privacy guaranteed by the Constitution. Though Glucksberg et al. lost their appeal in the Supreme Court, the parallels between abortion and assisted suicide remain. Many of the legal contributions to the assisted-suicide debate continue to derive from precedents set by abortion in the courts.[12]

Ronald Dworkin's *Life's Dominion*

Many who argue in favour of legalized assisted suicide and draw parallels with abortion do so with compelling arguments. First, they admit the sacredness of human life. As Matthew Previn notes, there is a humanist conception of the sacredness of human life: 'According to this conception of life's sanctity, reverence for life derives not from God, but from the ability to exercise the distinctly human qualities of freedom, rationality, and conscience'. Legal philosopher Ronald Dworkin argues persuasively that foetuses are not persons and do not have rights, demonstrating that not even the most insistent right-to-life activist truly thinks this. Dworkin instead accords the foetus intrinsic value. Dworkin compares what he has termed 'biological life' of a foetus or a person with declining and greatly restricted quality of life and no hope of recovery, with 'biographical life' of a woman whose life would be changed for the worse by bearing a child or the preservation of an important element of a dying person's self, such as their independence.

If someone wishes to sacrifice weeks or even months of his biological life in order to realise his, in the words of Dworkin, critical interests (such as remaining physically able, not being dependent upon machines for survival, or other self-defined goals), then this is a value judgment that others should respect. Dworkin notes that there is a difference between the value of what he is describing and instrumental value – things that must fulfil a purpose, like medicine or money. Dworkin justifies his contention that abortion is a private decision by showing that it is a decision based upon religious beliefs. In the context of the United States (and, many would argue, in any country with respect for diverse religious beliefs) it would be considered intolerable for a state to *require* abortions for seriously deformed foetuses. So it should also the private decision – though one that should be taken very seriously and thought through – when a woman decides to abort her foetus.

Dworkin extends his reasoning to assisted suicide. 'Abortion is a waste of the start of human life. Death intervenes before life in earnest has even begun. Now we turn to decision that people must make about death at the other end of life, after life in earnest has ended. We shall find that the same issues recur, that the mortal questions we ask about the two edges of life have much in common.'[13]

According to Dworkin, there *is* a sacred nature to either a foetus or a dying person's continued existence, but life-plans that do not include motherhood or continued life when the body disintegrates trump this sacred nature. To insist otherwise unjustly imposes Judeo-Christian values on those who might not share these values. Rather using arguing a secular versus religious framework, Dworkin identifies both issues as at bottom 'spiritual', admitting the sacrality of human life.[14]

This is the basis of one of Dworkin's arguments both for abortion and for assisted suicide; we must have tolerance for people's individual choices, for their own values, even if we disagree with them. Dworkin finishes his chapter on assisted suicide with an erudite, powerful and oft-quoted statement: 'Making someone die in a way that others approve, but he finds a horrifying contradiction of his life, is a devastating, odious form of tyranny'.[15]

But Dworkin's framing of the two issues is deceptive. First, he makes an illegitimate comparison between a foetus and a dying person. As an example employed by Michael Sandel, amongst others, illustrates, we do not equate a tray of human fertilized embryos with a person. Suppose a fire broke out in a fertility clinic. One had time to save either a young girl, or a tray of ten human embryos. Would it be wrong to save the girl? According to Michael Sandel, our moral intuition tells us to save the girl; what is more, one ought to do so, and this demonstrates that human embryos do not possess full personhood. Such an example points to the social value we place on existing human beings is not the same to potential human beings. But substitute an elderly, terminally ill person who felt her life had no value but who made no resistance to being saved. Which one should we save?[16]

We might turn the situation around. If someone deliberately smashes the tray of fertilized embryos, is this worse than killing the elderly, terminally ill woman? Our horror at the second act reflects our value of human persons above embryos, even if they do not value their own lives. Moreover, Dworkin's justification of assisted suicide on the basis of tolerance for the decisions of others does not rule out suicide at any point so presumably we must assist the suicide of a 21-year-old lovelorn individual who find continued existence a 'horrifying contradiction of his life'. After supporting the principle, Dworkin is silent on details.

The bases for support for abortion

There are at least two strong bases for support of legalized abortion. The first and more limited principle is bodily autonomy. A woman must be able to make and carry out decisions about her own body. We cannot force a woman to bear a child just as we would not force a woman to have an abortion. If a woman takes action to end her pregnancy, we may not interfere with her. If a pregnant woman decides to forgo medical treatment that might save her foetus or herself and the foetus, she must have the freedom to do so. Unwanted medical treatment is assault.

However, this is not enough to support abortion because, as we shall outline below, abortion must, at the moment, be assisted by a physician. From the fact that a woman may take action herself to stop a pregnancy, we cannot derive the right to demand that a doctor provides an abortion. Someone might reply that, if the woman can find a willing doctor, why shouldn't the arrangement between them be private? The corresponding question regarding assisted suicide is obvious.

The objection, however, is that physicians, when they carry out their medical duties, are not performing private acts but carrying out specific medical procedures approved by their profession but also, as Thomas Szasz points out, ultimately sanctioned by the state. They must be licensed to practise medicine and practising medicine without a licence is a serious crime throughout most of the world.

Doctors may have the ability to technically perform operations on a private basis and it is not illegal for someone who is not a doctor to carry out treatment (though it is illegal to claim one is a doctor when one is not) but doctors are public servants and have a duty to do what it is the public interest. They can and do refuse requests from patients on that basis. On the principle of non-interference and privacy, we would have to let a rational, competent person who found sexual titillation relating to amputation to cut off his own leg. But surgeons would also generally refuse to honour such a request on the basis that they could not say it was in the patient's or the public's interest to do so. In an even more stomach-churning example, we must, under the strict privacy rationale, accept Bernd Jürgen Brandes' wish to be eaten; surely forcing him to continue living and give up his dream of being eaten would be 'making him die in a way that others approve', a 'horrifying contradiction of his life' and 'a devastating, odious form of tyranny'? Would cannibalism be acceptable so long as a licensed doctor did the actual killing?[17]

Differences: abortion is a political issue; suicide is an individual issue

Fortunately, there is another compelling reason for making abortion part of the duties a doctor undertakes – the fact that women cannot attain equality without the right to abortion. This is the stronger of the two bases for legal, medical abortions. In order to control their fertility, women need to have recourse to abortion services. First, contraception must be freely available. Second, women should be able to get hold of self-administered abortions such as the RU486. But finally, if the other two measures fail and a woman does not want to be pregnant, she should be able to demand an abortion as part of medical treatment. The basis to that demand is that society has an interest in ensuring that women play an equal role to men. This, as Ann Furedi, president of the British Pregnancy Advisory Service (BPAS), has argued, is still the best reason for conceiving of abortion as a right: 'Abortion is a necessary back-up to birth control for any society that is committed to equality of opportunity for women. The discourse of women's equality may have changed, but its fundamental prerequisites have not.' We enlist doctors as part of the aim of society to bring equality to women.[18]

Moreover, abortion is most certainly an equal rights issue, while assisted suicide is not. Though some in the pro-choice camp might not agree, the strongest reason for allowing doctors to perform abortion is political. The right to abortion, in tandem with contraception, allows women to participate equally with men in society, freeing them from the consequences of their fertility.

Women as a *class* need abortion rights in order to be equal. It is this second reason that divides the issue of abortion from that of assisted suicide more than any other. There is no equality issue with assisted suicide because there are no rights being abridged or taken away by refusal to grant assisted suicides. Women are less free when and where they are denied abortion rights. No one is less free because we prevent doctors (or others) from assisting suicides (as we will discuss in the next chapter) – an act that can be performed by the suicide herself. Society has a compelling interest in ensuring women are equal to men. Society is richer for the equal participation of women. There is no similar interest in ensuring that individuals with six months or less to live are free to die.

Thus, the way the questions are framed indicates their essential differences. The proposed change in the law is for suicide to become, like abortion, a medical procedure where society assigns doctors a duty (though, like abortion, not mandatory) to terminate life at the patient's request under very particular circumstances. But such a request is and can only be made for overwhelmingly personal reasons. Doctors may have a duty to prevent needless pain and to do what is best for the patient (and may carry out occasional acts of euthanasia on those grounds) but they do not have a duty to accede to the wishes of the patient unless there is a socially and legally approved reason for doing so. Moreover, as we have argued in previous chapters, the reasons why patients request assisted suicide have more to do with despair and hopelessness or other non-physical suffering than with pain. These patients seek a medical treatment for suffering that is not in the main physical. This is perhaps why doctors and hospice workers, and the late Elisabeth Kübler-Ross, the pioneering author of *On Death and Dying*, oppose legalizing assisted suicide.

As we have discussed, there can be no right to suicide; as we discussed in Chapter 4, it makes no sense to recognize suicide as a right. In the Constitution of the United States, the 1961 Suicide Act in the UK, in Canada, Australia, New Zealand and every other European country, including Switzerland, suicide is not a right. Indeed, the parliamentary debate surrounding the 1961 Suicide Act made it explicit that suicide continued to be regarded as a sin, even if it was no longer illegal. Every argument in front of a court of law asserting that suicide is a right and that prevention of an assisted suicide denies that right has rightly failed.

The fact that so much of what used to be called pro-abortion sentiment is now framed as choice emphasizes the confusion between abortion and assisted suicide. The very term is deceptive. If the right to abortion is necessary for women's equality, it should be called that. During the long postwar struggle for African-American rights in the United States, few spoke about the need for choice in voting, or in public accommodation. The stalemate in abortion due to *Roe v. Wade*'s emphasis on privacy (the court allowed that such a right to privacy must be balanced against the state's interests in regulating abortion, protecting prenatal life and women's health) and that in Britain due to the 1967 Abortion Act's privileging of doctors' rather than women's rights to abortion allows a comparison with assisted suicide. But the two are very different.

There is a difference between tolerating the disagreeable actions of an individual and affirming them. Actively participating in – rather than simply tolerating – the private choices of individuals implies that we morally approve of these choices. I approve of the right to abortion because I support equality for women. However, in certain circumstances where I might be concerned, I may not agree with a specific choice of abortion. However, such a decision should remain private and must remain open to women. Though I might morally approve of the *individual* suicide and may even assist if I was convinced that it was the right thing to do, that does not imply that I would support the right to suicide. We should support abortion rights for women not because we wish to indulge the private choices of individuals ('indulge' meaning that both abortion and *assisted* suicide require active assistance) but because we agree control over one's fertility is desirable, because it addresses a real, practical need and because, without it, women cannot play an equal role in society. These are political goals.

Differences: abortion is needed; assisted suicide is not

One of the most obvious differences between abortion and assisted suicide is that abortion addresses a real demand, a practical problem. As we observed in Chapter 2, the demand for assisted suicides is extraordinarily low; in Oregon, the number of assisted suicides is 0.2 per cent of total deaths. Compare the number of women requiring abortion. In England and Wales in 2011, 189,931 abortions were carried out. 17.5 per 1000, or 1.75 per cent, of all women in England and Wales between the ages of 18 and 44 had an abortion in 2011. 3.3 per cent of women aged 20 had an abortion in 2011.[19] In the United States, according to the Guttmacher Institute, there are approximately 1,200,000 abortions performed every year. They estimate that one in every three women has an abortion during her lifetime.[20] Similar statistics emerge from Australia,[21] New Zealand,[22] and Canada.[23]

It is clear that the fact that abortion is legal in the UK, the USA, Canada, New Zealand and Australia addresses a real need, whereas assisted suicide is seldom required in areas where it has been made legal. What most people who support legalization of assisted suicide would like is the prospect of a control over their own demise rather than the reality of it. As Deborah Annetts, past president of *Dignity in Dying*, noted: '[F]or many terminally ill people, assisted dying legislation acts as an insurance policy. Just knowing that the option of a safe, legal peaceful death is there, should people need it, is enough to prolong life.' Just knowing that an abortion is there should they need it is not enough for millions of women each year.[24] Similarly, in the campaign for a change in the law in Massachusetts (the ballot initiative that would have legalized assisted suicide was narrowly defeated in November 2012) some observers implied that legalization of assisted suicide will depress the number of suicides in general by comforting those who might otherwise choose to take their own lives.[25]

The negative side to that assertion is that, should we fail to change the law, we condemn those who might benefit to 'backstreet', 'violent' or 'botched' suicides. *Dignity in Dying* informs us that '[e]ach year, a number of terminally ill people resort to violent and often botched suicides'. The allusion to the situation that existed before legalization of abortion can hardly be missed. *Dignity in Dying* claims that 10 per cent of suicides in the UK are committed by those with terminal or chronic illnesses. 'No one knows how many terminally ill people attempt suicide and fail,' they report. But the report they cite *does* show that two per cent of all suicides in the UK involve a terminal illness.[26] Nor is there any evidence that those in this two per cent would care to fill out the myriad forms and go through the interviews required by the proposed legislation in the UK. As well, *Dignity in Dying* might contemplate the fact that that suicides in Oregon, where legalized assisted suicides (which are not deemed suicides for statistical purposes) ostensibly provide comfort for those who might otherwise consider suicide unaided, 'increased significantly since 2000' after declining in the 1990s. Oregon's suicide rate is now 35 per cent higher than the national average. Notwithstanding, it would be unfair to conclude, without further study, that a more permissive attitude to suicide signalled by DWDA was responsible for such a rise. Instead, it shows the error in concluding that there is a relation to numbers of suicides and legality or otherwise of assisted suicide.[27]

In contrast, there continue to be many unsafe abortions each year, resulting in some 47,000 deaths of women in the world each year. An estimated 8.5m women require medical treatment (though many do not get it) because of unsafe abortions each year. Legalizing abortion in the remaining areas where it is illegal would certainly result in fewer women dying, though many of the deaths occur because of inadequate access to medical facilities. Once the 1967 Act was passed in England and Wales, the rate of death by illegal abortion reduced from 50 per million maternities in 1964–1966 to less than 14 per million maternities in 1973–1975, with the 1967 Abortion Act making most of the difference. Between 1952 and 1954 153 women in England and Wales died of abortion; in 2003–2005 the number was three.[28] In the United States, an estimated 160 to 260 women died each year from illegal abortions while thousands more were seriously injured in the 1950s and 1960s before *Roe v. Wade*.[29] Legalized abortion has made a huge difference to women throughout the world.

Differences: abortion must be available as a medical procedure; suicide can be accomplished without medical assistance

This brings us on to another key practical difference between abortion and assisted suicide. Abortion must be a medical procedure but suicide is an act that needs no assistance. Whereas a patient might be able to accomplish an abortion herself (this is much more a possibility now that the R11486 or 'abortion pill' is widely available) most therapeutic abortions, to be safe, must be performed by physicians. Almost all women would vastly prefer to avoid therapeutic abortions and would much rather accomplish the act themselves. As RU486 is a medicine, it will still need to be prescribed but medical intervention can be limited. Assisted suicide candidates, by contrast, very much wish to involve others in an action they can take without any assistance, medical or otherwise. Suicide, as we have seen in Chapter 2, can be accomplished by anyone, with a little determination. Much as poisons prescribed by doctors make the action easier, there are many means by which someone determined to do so can end his life. As Thomas Szasz has argued 'A person has no need for another to perform a service that he could perform for himself'.[30]

Margaret Battin, arguing against Szasz, claims that suicide is 'complex, grave and technical'. Grave, no doubt, but complex and technical? Most suicides are accomplished without medical assistance. Suicide – completely unaided – remains a possibility for nearly everyone. The sad demise of Tony Nicklinson, the British man who was completely paralyzed from a stroke and pursued an assisted death through the British courts, showed that refusing food, which he did the day his request for an assisted death was refused by the High Court, can bring on death even for those who have locked-in syndrome. It is unfortunate that Nicklinson had to die in a way that he did not want. But it is a method that a determined suicide might use.[31]

Historically different directions

Whereas many compare the emergence of the women's rights movement with the movement for the right to die, the *anti*-abortion movement is far more similar in its origins.

The 'right to life' is as modern a phenomenon as – and in some ways even more modern than – the right to die. Historically, religious opposition to abortion was not based on the idea that life began at conception. Instead, church scholars such as Aquinas took Aristotle's view that a foetus took on a soul after 40 days (with 'quickening' or foetal movement); to abort a foetus before then was indeed a sin but was not considered murder as many who oppose abortion today insist it is. Opposition to abortion tended to reflect religious sentiment that the purpose of sex was procreation. St Augustine rounded upon married women who 'in the fashion of harlots' procured abortions.[32]

In fact, the concept of life beginning at conception dates only from 1869 when in his 1869 bull *Apostolicae Sedis moderationi*, Pope Pius IX rescinded the 1591 declaration that punishments only awaited those who aborted a 'formed' foetus. After Pius IX all abortions were punished by excommunication, though it was the sinfulness of the procurer of the abortion and the frustration of God's plan rather than any right to life that concerned the clerics.[33]

Any conception of a 'right to life' emerged only after the 'rights revolution' that took place in the 1960s in relation to black civil rights. Moreover, the right to life movement followed by some years the introduction of liberalization of abortion in the United States, the UK, Canada, Australia and New Zealand. The Society for the Protection of Unborn Children (SPUC) was formed in January 1967 in opposition to the Medical Termination of Pregnancy Bill (later the Abortion Act of 1967).[34] In Australia the National Right to Life Committee formed in 1970 and Right to Life Australia was founded as Right to Life Victoria in 1973.[35] In New Zealand the Society for the Protection of the Unborn Child, later Voice for Life, was formed in 1970.[36] The term 'pro-life' only emerged in 1973 when American opposition to abortion in the form of the National Right to Life Committee emphasized abortion as the killing of innocents rather than a consequence of sexual permissiveness or of women's rights gone too far.

As Michael A. Cavanaugh argues, though the pro-life movement is seen as a traditionalist bloc 'claiming to oppose secularization and return to customary restrictions', it is actually a 'recent social construction. [...] As a result, the movement's ideology is best approached as the product of – rather than the antidote to – secularizing processes'. The destruction of the churches' authority from the late 1960s meant that a straightforward condemnation of sex for purposes other than procreation was no longer effective; like the assisted-suicide movement, which, as we have heard in Chapter 3, changed its emphasis from euthanasia to autonomy in the early 1970s, the abortion movement changed its emphasis from condemnation of the behaviour of the woman procuring an abortion to stressing the right to life of the foetus.[37]

Again, the issue of bodily autonomy or bodily integrity hardly unites the two issues. At first glance, it may seem that it does. The pro-choice movement called for women to control their own fertility; advocates of assisted suicide called for women (and men) to control the timing of their own deaths. Both might be seen as continuation of civil rights struggles that now centre on the body. But even here, there is a different historical origin. The movement to reform abortion laws was initiated in the medical community. California physicians, confronted by rubella outbreaks in San Francisco in the late 1950s and early 1960s, campaigned successfully, with the help of the newly formed National Organization for Women (NOW), for the California Therapeutic Abortion Act of 1967. NOW campaigned for the abolition of all abortion laws as part of a wide package of reforms aimed at creating women's equality, not on the basis of bodily autonomy.

Moreover, NOW, unlike later 'health feminists', celebrated technological developments that had freed women from second-class citizenship. As we discussed in Chapter 3, the intellectual origins of the right to die came from a profound distrust of technology and suspicion of medical authority. But most women's liberationist groups fought against such conservatism, seeing the liberatory potential of technology. NOW, in fact, identified technological changes as the basis of women's liberation. Rather than seeing as problematic the 'halfway technologies' that allowed people to live longer lives, NOW also looked upon the increased life-span as part of the liberation of women from their biological selves.

> ... With a life span lengthened to nearly 75 years it is no longer either necessary or possible for women to devote the greater part of their lives to child-rearing; yet childbearing and rearing which continues to be a most important part of most women's lives still is used to justify barring women from equal professional and economic participation and advance...

> Today's technology has reduced most of the productive chores which women once performed in the home and in mass-production industries based upon routine unskilled labor. This same technology has virtually eliminated the quality of muscular strength as a criterion for filling most jobs, while intensifying American industry's need for creative intelligence. In view of this new industrial revolution created by automation in the mid-twentieth century, women can and must participate in old and new fields of society in full equality – or become permanent outsiders.

If one were drawing a family tree on which we might locate various rights-based movements, we would certainly locate the black civil rights movement of the 1950s and 1960s as the common ancestor. This movement influenced the women's rights movement or what is often referred to as 'second-wave' feminism. By 1970, the women's rights movement, while pursuing its strategy of pursuing equal rights in the form of the Equal Rights Amendment, also branched off into the health feminism of the Boston Women's Health Book Collective, which in turn influenced abortion-rights activists to pursue the 'choice' of rather than the right to an abortion. Such a perspective undoubtedly influenced, in turn, the alternative health movement and the right-to-die movement.

Anti-abortion and assisted suicide movements share an overly physical conception of human life

One of the themes of this book is that the assisted-suicide controversy reveals the degree of confusion currently existing about what the meaning of human existence is. A life blighted and foreshortened by disease may be eminently worth living and to set down criteria for eligibility for an assisted suicide in strict physical terms – like having six months or less to live or the much vaguer 'suffering unbearably' – devalues the meaning of all lives in those situations. As *Not Dead Yet*, a UK organization that opposes legalizing assisted suicide on the basis that it tells disabled people that they are better off dead, notes: 'We oppose policies that single out individuals for legalized killing based on their medical condition or prognosis'.[38]

However, the pro-life movement also presents an overly physical definition of human existence by comparing a lived life of a fully grown woman with a foetus. If we revisit the example presented by Michael Sandel regarding the fire in the fertility clinic, the pro-life movement would have to save, if they really believe that human life begins at conception, the tray of embryos over the young girl.[39]

Another illustration of the over-physical definition of the pro-life movement was demonstrated by the case of Terri Schiavo. The 41-year-old brain-damaged Florida woman was the subject of a debate that captivated the nation in 2005. US President George W. Bush interrupted his vacation to fly in and sign a bill into law. What was the subject of this emergency legislation? To forbid the removal of a feeding tube from Schiavo, who has been in a persistent vegetative state for some 13 years. The hastily passed legislation asked a federal judge to review the case and to require feeding to resume.

Terri Schiavo lapsed into her vegetative state after a heart attack in 1990, caused possibly by lack of potassium. Her husband Michael, her legal guardian, petitioned to let her die. But her parents spent seven years fighting to keep her alive, saying that she could still lead a fulfilling life. This conflict of opinion has meant that no fewer than 19 judges in six courts studied the case at length, commissioning many medical experts. In each, the court has concurred with Mr Schiavo that she should be allowed to die. The federal judge reviewing the case, rendering his verdict as a result of the emergency legislation, agreed with Mr Schiavo.

Schiavo became a *cause célèbre* with those opposed to abortion. President George W. Bush argued that: 'In cases like this one, where there are serious questions and substantial doubts, our society, our laws, and our courts should have a presumption in favour of life.' What they missed was the implications of the case. Pro-lifers effectively identified human life with the ability to breathe. Although her family produced a video of her apparently responding to their stimuli, doctors analysing the tape have said that this was an accidental nerve response rather than a real response. Had Mrs Schiavo no ability to breathe unaided, there would be little controversy, since she would fall into the established definition of 'persistent vegetative state'.[40]

Human persons cannot be reduced to things that live in test-tubes or the bare existence of Terri Schiavo. Neither should human life be understood in terms of the ability to go to the toilet unaided or in strictly temporal terms. There is no good argument for rolling back the frontiers of life either backwards to conception or forwards from natural death.

Conclusion: postmodern movements

What ties these controversies – about abortion and about assisted suicide – is that within both radical forces attempt to push back the boundaries of human existence. Rather than a traditionally conservative side cleaving to outmoded values and ideas, the pro-life movement wants to fundamentally change our perspective of when human personhood begins and, indeed, *what* it is with its claim that abortion is murder. Assisted-suicide proponents similarly wish to radically redefine some lives – or some parts of some lives – as expendable by pre-approving suicide for those who fulfil certain criteria. Both reduce that which is essentially human and worth fighting to preserve to physical criteria, whether by asserting that the ability to breathe makes one a person or that disease renders one no longer part of the human community. This is not only a step back from prior religious understanding of humanity but from Enlightenment universalism.

Both the assisted-suicide movement and the anti-abortion movements are children of the 1970s and represent a huge break with tradition, despite their attempts to locate themselves in historical tradition. In fact, we might fairly say that both emerged after the fight for equal rights for women lost its way. Both movements are essentially entrepreneurs within a period of moral *interregnum* where many of the assumptions of the past are being questioned. Though appearing on opposite sides of an emotive discussion, these two postmodern trends share far more with each other than they differ.

Together they both emanate from and add to basic confusion about what constitutes human life. When the issue concerned the soul – a concept that humanists should not dismiss out of hand – at least there was recognition that the human implied more than simple biology. Rather than seeing human life as one made up of experiences, acquired tastes and preferences, and social relationships, the pro-life movement identifies humanity as the ability to breathe unaided or with a collection of cells. But if, as is true of most supporters of assisted suicide feel, only suicides in very particular conditions should be assisted, the lives of those fitting the criteria, whether or not they choose assisted suicide, are deemed expendable.

6
The Coercive Implications
of Legalization

> If the term totalitarianism is to have any meaning, it is a system
> where the right to possess and act on private preferences is
> continually tested by officialdom.[1]

Campaigning for a change in the law is often presented as concern for
free choices. In fact, a change in the law will mean less freedom from
state intrusion. In this chapter, I first show that the choice offered with
the legalization of assisted suicide is illusory; analysing recent legislation in Oregon and Washington and recent legislative proposals in the
UK, it is plain that doctors and courts, not patients, have a monopoly
on choice with regard to assisted suicide. Today, proposals for legalization envisage 'professionalization' of assisted suicide administration in
which experts decide on the worthiness of requests for assisted suicide,
a far cry from the autonomy-based arguments – flawed as they were and
still are – of the right-to-die movement in the 1970s and 1980s. When
we ask doctors or judges to decide upon the legitimacy of reasons for
requesting an assisted suicide, we allow them to colonize our most intimate thoughts and influence what should be the most personal decision
ever made. Not only is our privacy threatened, legalizing assisted suicide
would undermine the important freedom to refuse medical treatment.
I end with a robust defence of the classical freedom espoused by those
such as John Stuart Mill and a suggestion that might obviate the need
for assisted suicide.

   A tragic case arose in 2012 in the UK that in some ways crystallizes the
problems inherent in legalizing the right to die, particularly in relation
to issues of autonomy. In June, Mr Justice Peter Jackson, a judge in the
Court of Protection, set up under the Mental Capacity Act of 2005,[2]
declared that a 32-year-old woman from Wales would be force-fed in

her best interests though she had clearly indicated that she wanted the feeding tubes removed.[3]

Ms E (the courts decided that she could not be named) had a history of anorexia and alcohol problems and had not taken any calories since the end of March. With the agreement of her doctors, and the cooperation of her parents, she had put herself on the 'end of life' pathway at a community hospital. There she was receiving palliative care, the purpose of which was to let her die in comfort. No one suggested that what she and the hospital were doing was illegal. In 2011, she had signed two advance directives, indicating she did not want to be kept alive.

A local authority, under a veil of anonymity, suddenly asked the Court of Protection to 'investigate and protect' Ms E, whose death was imminent. The Court of Protection was set up by the Mental Capacity Act 2005 to make decisions for adults who lack capacity. As Barbara Hewson has argued, the Court of Protection is 'staffed almost exclusively by judges with a background in family law. This means that they are used to dealing with disputes concerning children rather than adults. [...] The prevailing mindset is therefore paternalist'.[4]

The judge determined that E's obsessive fear of weight gain and her current condition in which she is now subject to strong sedative medication, meant that currently E lacked the capacity to make the decision to refuse treatment. '[F]or an advance decision relating to life-sustaining treatment to be valid and applicable, there should be clear evidence establishing on the balance of probability that the maker had capacity at the relevant time. Where the evidence of capacity is doubtful or equivocal it is not appropriate to uphold the decision.' The judge noted that his was a 'a very difficult decision' to make because it required 'a balance to be struck between the weight objectively to be given to life on one hand and to personal independence on the other'. 'It does not merely entail bodily intrusion of the most intimate kind, but the overbearing of E's will in a way that she experiences as abusive.' The judge also said E's views 'are entitled to high respect'. He added: 'She is not a child or a very young adult, but an intelligent and articulate woman, and the weight to be given to her view of life is correspondingly greater.' The judge said: 'We only live once – we are born once and we die once. E is a special person whose life is of value. She does not see it that way, but she may in future. It is lawful and in her best interests for her to be force-fed if necessary.'[5]

The decision had basis in existing European law. Justice Jackson referred to the European Convention on Human Rights (EHCR) in justifying his decision: '*All human life is of value and our law contains the strong presumption that all steps will be taken to preserve it, unless the circumstances are exceptional. This principle is reflected in Article 2 EHCR, which provides that everyone's life shall be protected by law. It is the most fundamental of the Convention rights.'*

Of course, such a story is relevant to the right to die, and the two sides of the assisted-suicide debate, predictably, lined up to either support or question the judgement. Dr Peter Saunders, the campaign director of *Care Not Killing*, which lobbies against assisted suicide, welcomed the ruling. 'The judge has made a wise and courageous decision,' he said. 'In so doing he has emphasised that all human life is deserving of profound respect and strong protection, and also that acting in the best interests of people who are lacking capacity does not always mean acceding to their demands.' Dr Evan Harris, the former Liberal Democrat MP and member of the British Medical Association's ethics committee, a prominent supporter of the right to die, was perhaps more reticent when he called it a 'very controversial judgment'.[6]

A closer look at the no-doubt complex and difficult case shows that the judge's reasoning – that the subject of the debate is 32 and has her life in front of her – is the same as the reasoning of assisted-suicide advocates who paternalistically tell those who are not imminently dying that they have their lives ahead of them and, therefore, do not qualify for assisted suicide. This case gives a good indication of the anti-liberty repercussions of allowing the state to rule on who can choose to die and who cannot. Inviting the courts to judge the reasons for wishing to die is an intolerable intrusion into what should be a private affair. Like Justice Jackson's Court of Protection, legalizing assisted suicide inevitably sets up a tribunal of doctors and lawyers – state representatives – to objectively decide whether our lives are worth living or not.

The patronizing implications of indicating, through the many and much-vaunted safeguards promised by assisted suicide advocates, who can have an assisted death and who cannot, has hardly been recognized by either side of the debate. The proponents of assisted suicide can maintain an image as freedom fighters only because the pro-life privilege their view of life against any human freedom. This has obscured the real incursions on our rights and privacies made by the campaign for legalization of assisted suicide.

The most important element here is the apparently objective criteria with which an individual's life might be judged. Just as it diminishes the lives of those who fit the criteria to have them judged as dispensable, it patronizingly tells those who do not fit the criteria – like E or like Tony Nicklinson[7] – that their reasons for wanting to end their lives are wrong.

As I have argued throughout this book, only the individual (and perhaps those who know him intimately) has the perspective necessary to decide whether or not to take his own life.

Perverting autonomy

Why is autonomy in these cases so important? There will no doubt be some, like Dr Peter Saunders, who welcome medical paternalism when it might save human lives. If the state is committed to saving life and erring in favour of life, many opposed to legalization argue, we need not worry about the Nazi-inspired nightmare of involuntary euthanasia. But, as we argued in Chapter 5, the freedom from forced medical treatment is an important hallmark of a civilized society made up of self-determining individuals. As the New York Court of Appeals said in 1914: 'Every human being of adult years and sound mind has a right to determine what should be done with his own body.' It is an important principle that should be defended, even if it means that some individuals make cataclysmically wrong decisions.[8]

Of course, such a principle is often – if not usually – invoked in defences of legalizing assisted suicide. Many support the legalization of assisted suicide from ostensibly libertarian motives. The Adam Smith Institute in the UK, the Libertarian Party in the United States and the quasi-libertarian Liberal Democratic Party of Australia all support legalized assisted suicide. The British philosopher A. C. Grayling defended legalization of assisted suicide by stating: 'A civilised and mature society should allow the few – they will always be a very small minority – who desire this option to be granted the right to take it; the coercive paternalism that denies it is wholly unjustified.'[9]

Again, the proponents mix up coercive paternalism preventing individuals from engaging in potentially dangerous or life-threatening behaviour with the essential act of *assisting* a suicide. As we noted above, the right to request an assisted suicide is already there (just as the right to request just about anything, whether reasonable or unreasonable, should remain) but the problem comes with the response to such a request. It is not coercive paternalism to deny a person a right to assistance with a task they can accomplish unaided. Even if the task is impossible for the person to accomplish unaided, no one is obligated to help that person. As we have observed above, the whole connection between autonomy, rights, and assisted suicide is illusory. In fact, autonomy and the right to privacy are threatened by institutionalizing assisted suicide.

The necessity of privacy at one's deathbed

One of the problems is that regulating the deathbed scene, as legalizing assisted suicide would undoubtedly do, threatens its privacy. *Dignity in Dying* calls for a 'transparent process to check for abuse' in order to safeguard assisted dying. *Compassion and Choices* attempts to assuage some of the criticisms from opponents by observing: 'We believe in transparency and constant improvement of patient safeguards.' But should the deathbed scene be transparent? The relationship between privacy and freedom is captured in Alan Westin's valuable theory of privacy: 'Privacy is the claim of individuals, groups, or institutions to determine for themselves when, how, and to what extent information about them is communicated to others.' Privacy provides individuals and groups in society with a preservation of autonomy, a release from the roles they must play in public, a time for self-evaluation and for protected communication. Privacy also shields the social realm from the raw, impulsive and physical selves that make up our private persons.[10]

The problem is that the argument is driven by pervasive and caustic suspicion of the motives of doctors, family members, or anyone else behind closed doors. Opponents criticize plans for legalization by protesting that abuse is possible and that vulnerable people will be killed against their wills which, as we have seen, has apparently not happened yet. Proponents reply with safeguards and a very tight check upon the procedures. As we outline below, the motivations for those arguing for legalization have shifted from autonomy-based arguments to 'professionalization'. Professionalization means that, as in the case of E, our most intimate reasons for wanting to die will be subject to scrutiny. But also, the deathbed scene becomes one where suspicions are only allayed by total transparency. The 'check for abuse' called for by *Dignity in Dying* is suspicion of all that happens behind closed doors.

Freedom from state intrusion into the deathbed scene is important in several ways. First, the deathbed scene should remain private. Death is not a medical procedure that must be monitored. Funerals may be public events but the approach of death is a time for intimacy, of close friends and family, for emotions, personal goodbyes, forgiveness, humility, reflection and sadness. Once the last will and testament is completed, legal matters should no longer concern the dying person. If a doctor attends, it is simply to make the patient comfortable. Already, there are medical reports to file; if assisted suicide ever became institutionalized, the situation would become formal, all those making up the deathbed would have to justify their relationships with the dying person so that ulterior motives might be crossed off, and the deathbed scene would need to be recorded. Dying would, in short, become a public event. As Hannah Arendt observed, emotions displayed in public risk being shallow, false and perverted. We might also observe that for some time all elements of birth and death have hitherto been private events. The term 'palliative' derives from the Latin term *pallium*, which was a cloak. We hide birth and death from the public glare also to protect the public, to shield others from impenetrable mysteries that will not be resolved.[11]

By thrusting its unwelcome attention into the deathbed scene, legalization will, ironically, jeopardize spontaneous acts of kindness by doctors in the last few hours, days or weeks of life. At the moment, this act of euthanasia is unlikely to come to the attention of authorities unless the doctor, family or others in the medical team choose to report the action. When patients are desperately and hopelessly ill and suffering in their death throes, doctors occasionally take such actions and few will or do report them. According to a study published in 2009, which polled doctors anonymously, around three thousand of these final acts of kindness occur each year in the United Kingdom, more than projected assisted suicides should the act become legal. The composite number in the United States would be around 15,000 deaths per year.[12]

Such acts of kindness are threatened by paperwork and safeguards to protect the vulnerable. Given that death will become part of the business of physicians, they will, for their own protection, be unwilling to lend a hand in cases where the patient has not completed the paperwork properly. There is the assumption that many 'vulnerable' people are being killed today simply because there are no established procedures to control the situation. Doctors, at the moment, perform this occasional but necessary task not as doctors but as human beings, just as if, in warfare, any of us might dispatch a mortally wounded friend because we have the means and opportunity to do so. If we make death a treatment, kindness will be secondary to established procedure, paperwork will have to be kept and the whole thing subject to inspection. Perhaps this is why only one in three doctors approves of the legalization of assisted suicide.[13]

Perhaps most disturbing, however, is the tendency of the state, both in the case surrounding E and in assisted-suicide laws and proposed laws, to pronounce upon the reasoning behind an individual's decision to die. Most proponents of legalization rightly balk at what we might agree is the overreach of the courts in forcing E to live because she is a 'special person whose life is of value'. But legalizing assisted suicide will also involve judgments about the value of someone's life by defining those with less than six (or 12) months to live as not having value and those with more of having value. By no stretch of the imagination can this constitute individual autonomy. As *Times* columnist Matthew Parris has percipiently written, the authority to die, where someone tells you whether you may or may not die, not only works against the interests of E, it can also become something else: 'From Authority to Die, it may be a large practical step to Authority to Live: but not, I believe, quite such a large philosophical step as some may suppose – especially where that prolonged life depends utterly upon substantial state funds which, channelled differently, could save many other lives.'[14]

A new role for medics

Before proceeding it is worth observing that, as we discussed in Chapters 2 and 4, there is no real issue of rights involved in the assisted-suicide discussion. Physicians (or lawyers, who will have to rely on doctors for diagnoses and prognoses) will have the real power rather than the patient, who must effectively beg her doctor. As Thomas Szasz comments, the doctor who performs physician-assisted suicide 'does not merely render a clinical judgment and perform a medical intervention; he also renders a moral judgment and performs a social ritual. He legitimates PAS as *not irrational* and therefore not wrong, exactly as he illegitimates physician-unassisted suicide as irrational and therefore wrong'.[15] In this way, doctors, and not individuals themselves, ultimately make the decisions. As we noted, doctors have taken on an entirely new role, in some ways replacing priests, in granting medical absolution for suicides and redefining their acts as 'assisted dying'.

Bureaucratizing assisted suicide removes all elements of personal compassion from the act. Doctors who assist suicides where it is legal do not act out of compassion (though the individual doctors may know their patients well and perform the act out of personal compassion) but as part of their duties as doctors, as professionals. As Szasz states, 'when killing is defined as a type of healing, as a specialized professional role, then the legal apparatus of the State takes a keen interest in it'.[16]

As we have also noted, the relationship between doctor and patient changes when the doctor is called upon to undertake some task – like assisted suicide – that the patient herself can already accomplish unaided. The doctor has become what was in the past accomplished by priests and what is, in today's parlance, an enabler. The role of the physician in this instance is to sanctify the suicide, to render it, through her cooperation, not a suicide at all but an 'assisted death'.

The specifics of legislation and proposed legislation

The right to die could only exist if *all* requests for suicide were honoured. But very few extend the logic of extending assisted suicide as a right to all who seek it. Every scheme for legalizing assisted suicide places myriad restrictions on the right. Even in Switzerland, where suicide for any reason whatsoever is legal, many restrictions apply.[17]

Most of the legislative proposals in the English-speaking world follow along the lines of Oregon's Death with Dignity Act (DWDA) so it makes sense to start there. Oregon is at one end of the spectrum, essentially legalizing prescribing suicide rather than either assisting suicide or voluntary euthanasia.

Once an Oregon resident has been examined by two physicians and found to be dying of a terminal illness, they may make a 'valid request for medication' which 'shall be . . . signed and dated by the patient and witnessed by at least two individuals who, in the presence of the patient, attest that to the best of their knowledge and belief the patient is capable, acting voluntarily, and is not being coerced to sign the request'. 'No less than fifteen (15) days shall elapse between the patient's initial oral request and the writing of a prescription . . . No less than 48 hours shall elapse between the patient's written request and the writing of a prescription . . .'

On the request form, the patient must sign a paper warning: 'I understand the full import of this request and I expect to die when I take the medication to be prescribed. I further understand that although most deaths occur within three hours, my death may take longer and my physician has counseled me about this possibility. [. . .] I make this request voluntarily and without reservation, and I accept full moral responsibility for my actions.' Both witnesses and doctors must attest to the psychological wellbeing of the patient. However, many doctors may well conclude that any patient making a request for assisted suicide must be depressed and therefore ineligible for assisted suicide. But the DWDA also notes that 'actions taken in accordance with ORS 127.800 to 127.897 shall not, for any purpose, constitute suicide, assisted suicide, mercy killing or homicide, under the law'. Again, it is difficult to call knowingly poisoning oneself anything other than suicide except that the action has the blessing of physicians.[18]

Like Oregon, Washington's Death with Dignity Act privileges the rights of doctors rather than patients. A request must be followed by mandatory counselling that will determine whether or not the patient is competent to make the request and will warn the patient of the potential effects of ingesting the drug, advise that the request may be rescinded at any time. Two doctors must sign the request and ensure that all the criteria listed under the Washington DWDA are met:

> If, in the opinion of the attending physician or the consulting physician, a patient may be suffering from a psychiatric or psychological disorder or depression causing impaired judgment, either physician shall refer the patient for counseling. Medication to end a patient's life in a humane and dignified manner shall not be prescribed until the person performing the counseling determines that the patient is not suffering from a psychiatric or psychological disorder or depression causing impaired judgment.[19]

As Thomas Szasz notes, this might be particularly problematic in that depression, when faced with a prognosis of six months or less to live, is not an unreasonable or irrational response. This surely gives the doctors involved a very wide latitude.

Those imagining that Oregon represents very early legislation and that future legislation will gravitate more around the needs of the patient than doctors will be sorely disappointed by what has been proposed. The recent Report of the Commission on Assisted Dying in the UK gives an indication that the rights of the patient are far from consideration. The language used in the report shows which direction the Commission wants us to go. The world imagined by the Commission is not full of people but 'service users' and 'service providers'; the phrase 'health and social care' appears no fewer than 114 times in the report. This report gives the viewpoint of 'health and social care professionals' – not citizens but doctors, social workers and lawyers dealing with health and social work legislation.

The Commission visited jurisdictions where assisted suicide (the report, to its credit, does not dispute the fact that assisted dying is assisted suicide) is legal. However, it dismisses all of them, preferring 'British gradualism'. It lists a prognosis of 12 months to live, rather than six, as the cut-off point. This report distances itself from justifications for assisted suicide involving autonomy, perhaps recognizing the inherent difficulties with the right to die. Baroness Mary Warnock, a prominent philosopher and advocate of legalization, stated to the

Commission: 'Everybody knows that in a civilised country, subject to the rule of law, one can't always have autonomy. One has to give up some freedoms in order to obey the law ... I don't think the principle of patient autonomy is really a very strong ground [for assisted dying].'[20]

Its recommendations are for professionalization rather than autonomy. Indeed, the term 'safeguards' appears no fewer than 179 times in the report; the term 'autonomy' occurs only 68 times. The report proclaims that we must have 'open discussion' so that 'professional assessment and support' can be assured. Rather than have the patient ingest the poison themselves, the report calls for them to be shepherded by a doctor who watches while the patient kills herself. Why? The Commission is 'concerned to avoid the potentially dangerous ramifications of allowing lethal medication to be kept in an unregulated manner in the community, in a private home, residential care home, hospice or hospital'. The Commission also expressed 'significant concern that assisting suicide remains an amateur activity, and that no prospective safeguards are in place to protect those who seek assistance'. Finally, not only should the doctor make the decision, they 'should have a continuing responsibility for supporting the patient's friends and relatives after his or her death'. The relatives are not even trusted to grieve on their own; instead they must endure more counselling by the representative of the state that facilitated the suicide in the first place. How would a doctor 'support' the relatives and friends? Assisted suicide *in practice* diminishes rather than augments our autonomy.[21]

Paralleling the decision by Justice Peter Jackson, the report downplays the differences between withdrawing treatment and actively ending a life: 'Vulnerability is not just an issue in the context of assisted dying but in all end of life decisions that are made, such as "do not resuscitate" decisions and decisions on withholding or withdrawing treatment (including nutrition and hydration) or administering palliative sedation.' In other words, all decisions by the patient, including the decision to withdraw from treatment, must be scrutinized for signs of vulnerability. Essentially, all Justice Jackson did was define a 32-year-old as 'vulnerable' and decree that she should be force-fed. Who will decide on who is vulnerable? When terms like this are used, there are usually panels of professional advocates who will pronounce on whether an individual is vulnerable or not. If the Commission on Assisted Dying has its way, it will not be the patient who has choice but the doctors and lawyers representing him.

We might look at one more proposal on how to proceed. Lord Joffe, who proposed the Assisted Dying for the Terminally Ill Bill in 2006, made a new proposal that also bears resemblance to the decision by Justice Peter Jackson. Joffe suggested that the medical profession were not happy about assisting suicides: 'Accordingly, what I now propose is to take doctors out of the investigative and decision-making process, which should become the role of a legal body such as the high court or the court of protection or tribunals specifically set up for this purpose.' In effect, the courts would write the prescription and the patient would be able to collect it, after a minimum waiting period, and ingest the poison herself, obviating the need for a doctor.[22]

There are problems with such a solution. First, the court, if it wished to place restrictions on suicide related to disease such as terminal illness, would require medics to examine the patient and provide a prognosis. Second, the courts, as we have seen in the case of E, are even further removed from the patient; at least physicians know their patients and often know their families as well. When there is a chronic illness or condition such as those suffered by E, the doctor is likely to have dealt with the patient over a number of years. The courts are likely to render decisions according to evidence they receive from the experts rather than taking the individual situation of the patient into account.

Doing what's good for you

As the matter-of-fact but significant observation about the vulnerable by the Commission on Assisted Dying should signal, one of the harms done by those advocating assisted suicide is to blur the line between the right to refuse treatment and requesting an assisted suicide. This has been a theme both in literature defending legalization and in that attacking it, where euthanasia, voluntary euthanasia, assisted suicide and suicide are all rolled into one. If, proponents reason, it is reasonable and permissible for doctors to remove life-support machinery at the request of the patient, why is it not similarly permissible to take action to end life? The effect, after all, on the patient will be similar and, so long as the motive is compassionate, what possible delineation could be made? I will argue here that it is essential that we draw a thick line between the *right* to refuse medical treatment and assisting a suicide.

In the midst of the professionalization outlined above, individuals are losing this important right as their motives for refusing medical treatment are constantly scrutinized and judged. We need to insist that in this decision made by a competent adult (and not one judged incompetent only at the time of and in light of their decision) the doctor does not get any say in the matter. Patients should be able to discharge themselves and request an end to treatment even if a judge does feel that they are special and their lives are valuable. The right to bodily integrity and freedom from unwanted force upon the person is the basis for many other rights and should be defended. It is worth citing John Stuart Mill who has hardly been bettered in his exposition of freedom and liberty.

Mill's conception of freedom is a useful basis for understanding the assisted-suicide debate in context of liberty. Representing perhaps the apogee of conceptions of individual freedom, Mill discussed liberty in terms of non-interference. In *On Liberty*, Mill noted:

> Human beings owe to each other help to distinguish the better from the worse, and encouragement to choose the former and avoid the latter. They should be for ever stimulating each other to increased exercise of their higher faculties, and increased direction of their feelings and aims towards wise instead of foolish, elevating instead of degrading, objects and contemplations. But neither one person, nor any number of persons, is warranted in saying to another human creature of ripe years, that he shall not do with his life for his own benefit what he chooses to do with it.

In other words, we do not need to approve of individuals' decisions – or to help them carry out an act with which we may not agree. But neither can we restrain people from making poor decisions. As Mill noted, individuals were capable of idiocy, poor judgment and evil in their conduct. In terms of a man's conduct, however, '[a]ll errors which he is likely to commit against advice and warning, are far outweighed by the evil of allowing others to constrain him to what they deem his good'. By this test both Justice Peter Jackson – if we pay attention to his patronizing assessment that E has her life in front of her – and those who would allow assisted suicides only for those in certain very restricted categories fail. Clearly, both signify that continued life is good for E or for those outside the accepted assisted suicide criteria but depressed enough to ask for assistance to end their lives.

Of course, Justice Jackson questioned the competence of E to make such a decision but, as George Annas and Jill Densberger have argued in regards to competence, '[t]he vagueness of this definition, coupled with the dearth of legal literature on the subject, make competence determinations ripe for arbitrariness and pose a danger to individual liberty.' Such reliance on competence and incompetence has also caused some such as Joel Feinberg to argue: 'Nevertheless, there are some actions that create a powerful presumption that an actor in his right mind would not choose them. [...] The desire to commit suicide must always be presumed to be both nonvoluntary and harmful to others until shown otherwise.' Many in the pro-life camp might also employ the argument that all people facing imminent death are depressed, by definition but, as Sheila McLean observes, such a principle would surely invalidate any wills written by those facing certain and imminent death.[23,24]

As Mill noted, it is permissible to stop someone crossing a bridge that is unsafe if they are not aware of the danger. But when there is 'only a danger of mischief, no one but the person himself can judge of the sufficiency of the motive which may prompt him to incur the risk: in this case, therefore, (unless he is a child, or delirious, or in some state of excitement or absorption incompatible with the full use of the reflecting faculty) he ought, I conceive, to be only warned of the danger; not forcibly prevented from exposing himself to it'.[25]

In fact, in Mill's discussion itself, though he never deals directly with suicide, contained arguments that might (and have been) employed against allowing suicide:

> In this and most other civilized countries, for example, an engagement by which a person should sell himself, or allow himself to be sold, as a slave, would be null and void; neither enforced by law nor by opinion. The ground for thus limiting his power of voluntarily disposing of his own lot in life, is apparent, and is very clearly seen in this extreme case. [...] The principle of freedom cannot require that he should be free not to be free. It is not freedom, to be allowed to alienate his freedom.[26]

There are many interpretations of the particular meaning of this passage for suicide. Mill did not directly address the issue, and he may have simply wished to make an argument against slavery at a time when it was still a live issue.

Mill's argument is entirely compatible with the harm principle and Mill's general dislike of government interference. Feinberg addresses the argument about Mill's position on slavery, noting the assertion that 'the principle of non-exploitation ... isn't aimed at preventing one person from being a slave so much as preventing the other from being a slave-owner' would be 'uncongenial' to Mill. Perhaps, but there is no need to imply that Mill relied on such legal moralism; the principle of non-interference remains intact. The key is that slavery requires that an authority enforces, as a last resort, the contract between two people; making the other parties involved as it necessitates a contract.

We might also think of assisted suicide, in the way it is proposed by advocates of a change in the law, as a contract between a doctor and patient (if we restrict the administration of assisted suicide to medical professionals, as most existing and proposed legislation does). The situation right now is that such a contract is not legal, despite the fact that suicide itself is legal. The legal principle we might embrace is that no one may consent to be killed or that consent on the part of the victim of a killing is no defence. Just as a contact regarding slavery or duelling will not be recognized in law, neither will a presumed contract where one person kills another or aids the suicide of someone who has agreed to be killed or has asked for assistance.

A suggestion

Lest critics see this book as a jeremiad, I have a suggestion that might alleviate some of the worries that so many people have about the end of life as well as increase general freedom of individuals. We have already observed in previous chapters that most of the sentiment in favour of a change in the law seeks not an immediate suicide but assurance that a quick and painless death is available should one need it. Why shouldn't those who feel the need for security of a quick and easy departure have it? A libertarian answer is to make deadly drugs available to the public, albeit with warnings about what ingesting them will do and perhaps even a waiting period.

It is unlikely that many members of the Commission on Assisted Dying, which worried about such poisons being out of sight of a doctor, would agree with the freedom of the public to purchase such deadly drugs. Nor would those deeming themselves pro-life approve with a scheme making it easier to take one's (or someone else's) life. To dismiss such a suggestion, however, is to deny that the difficulty in committing suicide is not in the physical means to do it but with the necessary will and determination to kill oneself.

Against the worry that the suicide rate would go up should drugs be made more easily available, we can observe that anyone with a little planning and determination can eventuate her own death. Each of Dr Kevorkian's patients was capable of accomplishing the act with no help whatever. Just as medical technology can keep people alive longer, if not 'indefinitely' or even to biblical proportions, technology also makes easier anyone's escape from life. There are more ways now of killing oneself than at any time in the past; the internet has made researching suicide more easy than ever. Moreover, studies show that restricting methods of suicide has little effect on the suicide rate. As Ohberg et al., in a study conducted in Finland, note, restriction of a method of suicide reduces its use for suicide, but other methods of suicide tend to replace it. The dangers of impulsive suicides, according a study published in 2001, were less for drugs than for other methods of suicide, according to Keith Hawton et al., who found that impulsive suicide almost never involved drugs. We need not overly worry that the suicide rate will jump in response to legalization.[27]

Such a solution obviates the need for the legalization of assisted suicide whilst assuring all competent adults of equal liberty. The very few who would take the option would not need the blessing nor the assistance of a doctor and for those beset by anxiety about death and the way that they will die, the vial might play a reassuring role just by sitting on a shelf 'just in case'. Suicides would take all moral responsibility for their actions and such a measure would also undermine the trend of restricting ostensibly self-destructive behaviour, like drinking, smoking and eating too much. The drug could eventually be, through the miracle of DNA technology, made specific to the person who purchases it. This is not a solution to all of the problems discussed throughout this book but a simple solution that removes any need for legalized assisted suicide.

Is it permissible to intervene in suicide attempts?

A final question might be addressed. Many with personal experience of suicide may want to know whether the suggestions I have made here imply that it is impermissible to intervene in an attempted suicide of an individual. Some may feel that the principles of autonomy and interference militate against interfering in suicide attempts; others may feel justified only in arguing their point to the suicide rather than physically preventing it from happening.

But in a situation where we might physically prevent a suicidal person from completing that suicide, potential good outweighs the potential harm. Furthermore, though not legally obligated, we are morally compelled to save a life if we are given the chance. We know, empirically, that, typically, 95 per cent of those who attempt suicide live for at least five years after the attempt.[28] We also know that many attempted suicides are a cry for help and that there are many relatively foolproof ways that a determined suicide might succeed. Therefore, it is reasonable to assume that, should we come across an attempted suicide, there is a good chance that the person does not wish to succeed. The possible harm of delaying a determined suicide's death by a few days, should they make a successful attempt later, is outweighed by the potential good done by saving a life. The man teetering on the bridge wants to be convinced, we may fairly assume, that life is worthwhile. Otherwise, why does he teeter? If he really wanted to die, there are many certain ways of accomplishing his goal swiftly and assuredly. Finally, we might look to our own moral worth, which can only be elevated through the act of saving a life; the courage and determination that is required to save a life will not be lessened even if the would-be suicide succeeds the following week.

Though some libertarians might disagree, representatives of the state also have – and should have – the duty to save lives when they have the opportunity to do so. Harking back to Mill, a policeman might warn people about a dilapidated bridge without preventing access to it but, should he come across someone who is about to shoot herself or someone hanging from a noose, he has a professional duty – as well as a personal obligation – to save a life when offered the chance to do so.

A public servant who failed to save a life when given the chance would be suspect professionally just as we would look upon the failure of a member of a community to save someone as morally suspect. It does not breach an individual's rights to be saved from death. Though we certainly interfere with someone 'for their own good', we also do so for the good of the community. We take full responsibility for our actions, gauging that the small harm of assault outweighs a potentially much larger harm of death. Most would risk an assault charge in order to prevent someone from drowning. Moreover, this is an immediate and personal response to a specific situation; it would clearly be wrong to follow someone around, because we felt she was drinking herself to death, preventing her from purchasing or imbibing alcohol. The latter would be wrong because it unreasonably restricts their freedom, whereas if a man teeters near a bridge we might reasonably assume that he does not wish to fall.

Conclusions

Many in the assisted-dying movement and many more observers who vaguely support the legalization of assisted suicide see it as the choice for freedom and against religious zealots who would impose their values on the rest of it. The purpose in this chapter has been to show the ways in which legalization of assisted suicide undermines rather than supports freedom. One has been to show that, though abstractly, we might think of the freedom to request an assisted suicide as simply a liberty that all should have, the concrete expression of existing and even imagined laws drown liberty in safeguards. Not only would such safeguards and regulations breach the privacy of the deathbed, they extend into the deepest and most private recesses of the individual's decision by evaluating the reasons for taking it.

There is little difference between denying E her wish for death because she is special and valuable and denying the wish of a patient with seven months to live; both are predicated on assessments of individual worth by criteria that will mean little to the patient. I have argued that both inappropriately use objective criteria for judging the worth of a life whereas only the individual has a real sense of what might be lost or gained by suicide. By reducing suicide to a medical procedure, we give doctors and judges the ultimate decision. By doing so, we endanger important liberties such as the right to refuse treatment. If suicide is assisted because someone judges it to be in our best interests, why wouldn't they also insist on continued treatment in our best interests?

Finally, I have outlined a suggestion that would prevent the need for assisted suicide and preserve important freedoms as well as emphasizing moral responsibilities for our actions. If deadly drugs are made available to all competent adults, one of the main reasons for supporting legalization of assisted suicide – the fear of losing control of our dying – will disappear. Practically no one will need assistance and the attendant dangers of institutionalizing assisted suicide will be avoided.

Conclusions

What appears to be a simple legislative move affecting a very few persons who are suffering, I have shown, is instead pregnant with meaning and implications far beyond the few directly affected. If the majority looked beyond this immediate goal, it is doubtful that they would support, in such overwhelming numbers, legalization. (In fact, as we have noted, that when they are asked whether they support assisted suicide for those without terminal illnesses, support for legalization fades, in the UK, to less than 15 per cent.) It is changes to our culture that are most concerning about the drift towards legitimating assisted suicide.

First, this book has demonstrated that legalizing assisted suicide is unnecessary. Not only can everyone, with planning and determination, accomplish suicide unassisted, there is very little demand for it where it is legal. Moreover, the ostensible reasons for legalizing assisted suicide – pain and unalleviable physical suffering – are not the reasons why the few that choose the option in areas where it is legal do so. It is still possible that the numbers will slowly gain momentum and that some of the fears of opponents may be realized, but, so far, there is little evidence for such developments. As I have demonstrated, the spectre haunting those proponents of a change in the law of a death drawn out by medical technology, where the patient is devoid of control, is chimerical, a modern nightmare rather than a realistic prospect. Unlike the right to abortion, which serves a real practical need on the part of millions of women, legalizing assisted suicide would make no one freer and would release no one from pain and suffering. We (rightly) tolerate genuinely merciful acts to end life by doctors and, occasionally, family members by not prosecuting them or by refusing to convict them or send them to prison. As I have demonstrated, if the privacy of the deathbed scene is maintained, doctors will occasionally be able to take compassionate decisions to end a patient's suffering in her final hours, days or weeks. Certainly, nothing will be gained by, in the fashion of the day, making the deathbed scene 'transparent' with numerous 'safeguards' that do little other than cast suspicion upon doctor and family member alike.

Historically, such actions have been tolerated because we understood the tragic choices to be made and that no interest would be served by a prosecution. The fact that so many have joined movements dedicated to the freedom of so very few should alert us to the fact that the need is not practical but psychological. The call for doctors to assist suicide (none of the proposed legislation plans to allow those who are not doctors to assist suicides) is, as we have seen, really about *affirming* the rightness of such an act. It is perhaps therapeutic in that the patient is able to enter into a space where his or her action will not be judged.

The campaign for legalized assisted suicide implicitly campaigns for release of individuals from the moral responsibility for their suicides. As Daniel Callahan has hinted, there is a strange process whereby the vicissitudes of life are personalized at the same time as human actions are naturalized. As a plaintiff in a recent case said: 'Please do not call it suicide; that is an insult to my fight against cancer.' Cancer becomes a victimizer rather than a disease, whereas the act of taking one's life becomes dying from a disease rather than suicide.

There is another facet to this confusion. Rather than wishing for death, campaigners for the right to die seek to control the timing of death. They wish to identify the right moment to die and ensure that they do not live past it. But when is the right moment to die? How does one balance up the positives and negatives of continuing to live? There are no answers and nor can there be certitude. The frightening beauty of life is its contingency.

Ideally, I would have liked to include another chapter that analyses the psycho-social reasons for sentiment in favour of assisted suicide but space does not permit. It would be useful to look at why we seem to need such certitude and to examine assisted suicide within the scope of risk. In Shakespeare's *Othello*, we watch as love is destroyed by the fact that Othello cannot be absolutely sure of Desdemona's faithfulness. Love is dynamic and contingent; we always take risks when we love others and can never be entirely certain of their love. Is life not the same? Suicide seems to exist as possibility in the minds of those whose own demises are still far off as a way to inure oneself from the possibilities of the future. As Isaiah Berlin observed: 'The logical culmination of this process of destroying everything through which I can possibly be wounded is suicide... Total liberation in this sense (as Schopenhauer correctly perceived) is conferred only by death.'[1] Some might legitimately point out that, even if it is only a psychic need on the part of the many who feel they need the prospect of an assisted death, a compassionate society should provide it. Assurance of a good death enhances living, they say. If we accept such needs as genuine, the solution I have set out, whereby any competent adult may buy deadly drugs at a pharmacy, obviates the need for doctors and allows those who wish to prevent the ravages of disease a painless death. This alternative serves both the actual need of the few patients who need it and those who feel the need to have a quick and painless escape.

Second, I have located the development of this controversy within its historical context. Here, I have emphasized the radical nature of the 'simple' matter of legalizing assisted suicide. Both the assisted-suicide movement and the pro-life movement wish to roll back the parameters of human life; the former wishes to regard the final six months of peoples' lives as no longer valuable enough to dissuade them from suicide and the latter wants to redefine foetuses and those with no interaction or possibility of interaction with the world as living persons.

The assisted-suicide movement emerged in the 1970s[2] but developed because the assumptions, in the form of taboos, of the sacred nature of life faced pervasive questioning. Some might welcome the questioning of taboos but the taboo against suicide merely reflects the value with which we hold society and its individual members. Much as we might agree that questioning taboos is positive, we should also think hard before jettisoning taboos held by nearly every human society to date like those against suicide and incest.

Third, I have shown that the arguments of both sides have ill-served those who want to clarify the issues. Those who oppose legalizing assisted suicide rely either on a concept that desperately needs a new explication – the sacredness of life – or upon an essentially conservative argument that allowing assisted suicide will lead to more widespread euthanasia. As I have argued, it is not that there is no basis to the slippery slope argument, it is simply that there is little credible evidence of abuse occurring in areas where it is legal.

However, it is only the weakness of the arguments made by those opposing legalization that has given those who would change the law a veneer of rationality, coherence and scientific objectivity. The assisted-suicide movement seems inspired by the fact that it can turn what was once a Christian virtue – compassion – against those who call themselves Christians today. As G. K. Chesterton wrote some time ago: 'When a religious scheme is shattered (as Christianity was shattered at the Reformation), it is not merely the vices that are let loose. The vices are, indeed, let loose, and they wander and do damage. But the virtues are let loose also; and the virtues wander more wildly, and the virtues do more terrible damage. The modern world is full of the old Christian virtues gone mad.'[3]

One aspect of this book that readers may find shocking (as I did when researching it) is how incoherent and contradictory many of the arguments for legalizing assisted suicide are. It is if there is no need for complex arguments or a coherent case; the fact that religious folk are pushing their values on the rest of us and the emotional urgency of the stories advocates are fond of regaling us with are enough. Assisted-suicide campaigners are perhaps best thought of as moral entrepreneurs, colonizers of the moral hinterland, taking advantage of the weakness of the traditional concept of the sacredness of life. They blindly push forward without really knowing where they are headed.

Rather than an extension of liberal, rationalist critiques of the dogmatic elements of religion, the assisted suicide movement is postmodern, rejecting the sacredness of life, the idea that we must treat all human persons as equally valuable, the parameters we use to define human beings, and the classical idea of autonomy as being free from state interference. When, for instance, those calling for legal assisted suicide use the term 'autonomy', they refer to a new type of what has been called 'relational autonomy' that moves away from John Stuart Mill's conception of the responsible, self-reliant individual. Relational autonomy predicates the ability to act effectively on one's own values on a social support structure that allows the subject to gain the self-confidence needed for effective agency. In privileging *assisted* suicide over what relational autonomy might refer to as the 'over-individualistic' view of suicide, proponents are surely part of the postmodern project of redefining autonomy rather than the tradition of John Stuart Mill.[4]

Their central justifications for a change in the law – autonomy and compassion – are contradictory. Who should have the ultimate decision? Proponents will answer that the subject herself should have the decision, fulfilling the autonomy but not the compassion criteria, but that the subject's wishes should only be honoured if they fit certain criteria which we decide and prove to two doctors that they are competent, severely curtailing autonomy. A cooling-off period of fifteen days must be observed and a plethora of regulations must be observed, which surely abnegates compassion, which must be personal and spontaneous.

Suicide is at the heart of the issue which is, I have shown, moral rather than political or legal. Laws are beside the point for a determined suicide; there are no legal impediments to suicide. To be a right, suicide would have to, like abortion, serve some interest within society. Instead, as the framers of the UK's 1961 Suicide Act, which removed criminal sanctions against suicide, intended, suicide became tolerated but not approved of. It remained a sin even if it was legal. It is moral approval or affirmation rather than the right to die that is sought by assisted-suicide campaigners.

And here we come to a **fourth** point – the harms that attend our acceptance of institutionalizing assisted suicide. Legalization would be an important step along a process of institutionalizing assisted suicide as a medical treatment but the damage inflicted may not be immediately perceptible. As I have argued, opponents are wrong to point to collateral casualties as the most important reason for opposing assisted suicide. Instead it is injurious to our culture.

Perhaps the most important transformation would be the change in our relationships with others from a moral to a therapeutic basis. To take a neutral stance towards another human being's suicide is surely to sit dispassionately in the therapist's chair, nodding understandingly but refusing to judge. Such a relationship is cold, dispassionate, professional, administrative, and neutral to the question of whether an individual lives or dies. By implementing this apparently compassionate piece of legislation, we erode the very basis of compassion and sympathy.

Suicide is a decision that can only be taken in the dark recesses of the heart and mind of the individual but it is never of no concern for those who survive the action. In one sense, suicide remains as individual as the life that precedes it and only the individual concerned can gamble her life against the potential gain she feels will occur with her death. A solemn decision to die can only be made by the individual; the advice of others can only reflect the value they see in their own and others' lives. Hamlet's famous soliloquy is just that, not a discussion with other characters or, worse still, a conversation with his physician. It is important for the ability of the individual to have control over her circumstances to be able to have this inner dialogue undisturbed.

However, once the act is taken our attitude may be sorrowful, happy, relieved, angry, condemnatory or admiring, or an admixture of all of these. But we may never be neutral towards the act of suicide. Our sense of moral community, where we identify actions as good or bad, is not simply a Christian construct; humanists should passionately praise the good – such as the heroically selfless suicide of Captain Oates – and just as passionately condemn the actions of those who reject life for poor reasons. That is not to condemn out of hand those who are placed in invidious situations and choose to leave life early – we can treat some suicides as the understandable actions of those in tragic circumstances – but to insist that it is an action that transcends the moral norms. Suicide's power is that it is exceptional; to include it as everyday, acceptable behaviour would reduce its meaning and power.

There is also a real difference between toleration and approval in regard to suicide. Whereas we currently tolerate suicides or mercy killings in tragic situations, we will continue to judge them as right or wrong, something that by treating suicide as a medical treatment choice we will not be able to do. Why should we judge? As Hannah Arendt has argued, 'judging is one, if not the most, important activity in which this sharing-the-world-with-others comes to pass'. Judgement does not dismiss other peoples' beliefs but 'the power of judgement rests on a potential agreement with others'. To place entire categories of people beyond our judgement or to be prevented from judging the morality of suicide is to admit that we no longer inhabit the same moral universe. Suicide involves an individual voluntarily renouncing his own existence but in many cases, as G. K. Chesterton noted, renouncing the world. Of course, such an action requires our judgement upon it.[5]

Legalizing assisted suicide would also reduce the value with which we hold certain members of our society. The misanthropic idea that the mere existence of some people is undesirable to the rest of us haunts the assisted-suicide discussion. Changing the law – much as we can agree that few people will be affected in the short term – opens a Pandora's box. As its justification is suffering, more and more categories will seek recognition of their suffering by demanding assisted suicide for themselves. The categories have a tendency to expand and those who insist that it should only be those with terminal illnesses had better be ready to answer these demands from those who, on good grounds, can demonstrate their own suffering. It is not that large numbers will come forward but that those determined few who do undoubtedly have a good case if we allow that suffering as the basis for requests.[6]

The assisted-suicide discussion did not emerge in a vacuum. It has come at the same time as a discussion about limited resources and how the elderly use far too many of them, particularly health-related resources. Therefore, there are campaigns already afoot to be able to include those above 70, whose lives are apparently not as valuable as the rest of ours. The categories may well expand because of these sorts of pressures.

The 'right to die' sought by proponents of legalization of assisted suicide is not a right or a freedom at all. It is a heavily regulated process that will undoubtedly become more and more regulated with so many safeguards that those who suffer at the end of life will be worse off. Only those with two doctors testifying that the patient has less than six months to live, with checks made for competence and to ensure the decision is not made out of depression or impulse, will have the 'autonomy' that many think legalization will bring.

Compassion will fare no better. The deathbed scene will have to be regulated if it is to be 'transparent'. The actions of relatives and doctors alike may have to be monitored. The time-honoured tradition whereby doctors occasionally bring relief to suffering patients in their last few hours or days will be brought under official control. Physicians who lose paperwork risk five years imprisonment in current Oregon, Washington and proposed British legislation. If we officialize the whole process whereby doctors occasionally dispatch patients in order to prevent needless suffering, we threaten the tolerance with which we viewed and still view these actions. Once bureaucratized, there will be no real space for compassionate deeds; all, in the name of transparency, will have to be accounted for and a paperwork trail established. Doctors may well be increasingly reluctant to go down an unofficial route. Thus, ironically, legalizing assisted suicide may well be worse for the dying. Whereas we might impute the noblest of reasons to those campaigning for a change in the law, the devil is in the details.

Such safeguards and checks, I have demonstrated, destroy our freedoms. The shocking case of E gives an indication of the two-tier world where officials approve or deny requests to die. The decision of whether or not to continue existing will no longer be ours. We will lack moral ownership of and responsibility for our own lives, just like E. We risk being infantilized by the need for evaluation by two doctors of our applicability and competence, complete with a list or reasons why we wish to die. In seeking affirmation, we lose control over our destinies. 'Unapproved' suicides will be implicitly or perhaps explicitly condemned not because of the reasons why they occur but because they have not been approved.

The judgement of the reasons for requesting an assisted suicide also threatens the important freedom to refuse medical treatment. In an unintended conspiracy, both sides of the debate have de-emphasized the important differences between 'active' and 'passive' euthanasia, whether action taken by the patient or her doctor. Making the effect on the patient the centre of their discussions, they have lost sight of the reason why we tolerate self-destructive behaviour and stupid decisions in competent adults; freedom for all. If we must appeal to doctors to commit suicide, why would we not also have to appeal to have our treatment stopped?

I hope that by reframing the issue, by pointing out the various inconsistencies and problems with both sides of the debate, and by alerting the reader to the less obvious implications of legalizing assisted suicide, I have made the reader think again. If I have shown that this is no simple case of religious dogma versus enlightened compassion, I have done my job. If I have awakened some nagging doubts inside the thoughts of those who supported legalization of assisted suicide out of immediate political instinct, this book has served its purpose.

Notes

Introduction

1. See Kevin Yuill, 'The Devaluation of Disabled Peoples Lives' and 'Assisted Dying: Simple, Neat – and Wrong', *spiked-online.com*, 14 March 2012 and 20 August 2012, at: www.spiked-online.com/site/article/12247/ and www. spiked-online.com/site/article/12784 (accessed 25 August 2012).
2. Sunny Dhillon, 'Assisted-suicide Activist Gloria Taylor Says She Fears Death that "Negates" Life', *Globe and Mail*, 16 June 2012. Gloria Taylor died from an infection on 4 October 2012.
3. Keith Fraser, 'Court Upholds Right-to-Die Activist Gloria Taylor's Exemption Allowing Her a Doctor-assisted Death', *The Province*, 10 August 2012.
4. Peter Munro, 'Son's Mercy Killing Splits Family', *Sydney Morning Herald*, 15 January 2012.
5. Whereas many of these polls results are disputed, there is no question that a majority in every country other than New Zealand support legalization of some assisted suicides. For New Zealand opinion, see www.researchnz.com/ pdf/Media%20Releases/RNZ%20Media%20Release%20-%202010-08-19%20 Assisted%20suicide.pdf (accessed 1 July 2012). For Australia, see Marina Kamenev, 'Australia's Dr Death Lobbies for Euthanasia Down Under, *Time*, 17 May 2011. Polls differ on Canadian support of assisted suicide. See 'Reaction to the Striking Down of Canada's Laws on Assisted Suicide', *CBC* community blog, 18 June 2012, at: www.cbc.ca/news/yourcommunity/2012/06/reaction-to-the-striking-down-of-canadas-assisted-suicide-law.html. For US opinion, see *Compassion and Choices* opinion polls page, at: http://compassionand choices.org/document.doc?id=893; and on British opinion, see AP: 'Assisted Dying Poll Shows Support for Change in Law', 2 August 2011.
6. Nicklinson closely fits the criteria issued by the DPP – see www.cps.gov.uk/ news/press_releases/109_10/ (accessed 1 July 2012).
7. Yale Kamisar, 'Some Non-religious Views Against Proposed "Mercy Killing" Legislation', *Minnesota Law Review*, Vol. 42 (1958), pp. 966–1004. Kamisar was responding to Glanville Williams, *The Sanctity of Life and the Criminal Law* (London: Faber and Faber, 1958), especially chapter 8, 'Euthanasia', pp. 277–312.
8. The Parliamentary Under-Secretary of State for Justice, Maria Eagle, was not accurate when she stated, in answer to a question in Parliament on 11 November 2008 (Column 223WH, available at http://www.publications.par liament.uk/pa/cm200708/cmhansrd/cm081111/halltext/81111h0005.htm), that the number of persons sentenced to prison for assisting a suicide was zero. David March was convicted of assisting his wife's suicide in the Crown Court on 19 October 2006. March, whose wife was a multiple sclerosis sufferer and had made previous suicide attempts, had re-tied string around a plastic bag over his wife's head and held her hand until she died in June 2005. He was initially charged with murder but pled guilty to assisting a suicide and received a nine-month suspended sentence. But it is accurate

to say that there have been very few prosecutions under the 1961 law. It is fair to say, as Lord Carlile did, that the present law has a "stern face but an understanding heart". See Bonnie Malkin, "Man who aided MS wife's suicide goes free", The Guardian October 19 2006, available at http://www.theguard ian.com/society/2006/oct/19/health).

9. See the interview with Kübler Ross in Leslie Miller, 'Kübler-Ross, Loving Life, Easing Death', *USA Today*, 30 November 1992, p. 9.

1 Defining the Terms

1. E. J. Emanuel, 'Euthanasia: Historical, Ethical, and Empiric Perspectives', *Archives of Internal Medicine*, 154 (1994), pp. 1890–1901, cited here p. 1892.
2. *Report by the Commission on Assisted Dying* (London: Demos, 2011), 37.
3. Cited in Penney Lewis, *Assisted Dying and Legal Change* (Oxford: Oxford University Press, 2007), p. 5.
4. 'The Right to Kill', *Time*, 18 November 1935. See Peter Singer, *Rethinking Life and Death: The Collapse of Our Traditional Ethics* (Oxford: Oxford University Press, 1995).
5. Cited in Germain Grisez and Joseph M. Boyle, *Life and Death with Liberty and Justice: A Contribution to the Euthanasia Debate* (London: University of Notre Dame Press, 1979), p. 7.
6. Cited in Thomas Q. Martin, 'Euthanasia and Modern Morality: Their Moral Implications', *The Jurist*, Vol. X (January–October, 1950), pp. 437–464, cited p. 460, fn73.
7. Ian Dowbiggin, *A Merciful End: The Euthanasia Movement in Modern America* (Oxford: Oxford University Press, 2003), pp. 118, 140.
8. *Compassion and Choices*, Language Matters Press Kit, at: www.compassion andchoices.org//documents/LMPressKit.2009.pdf (accessed 14 July 2009).
9. *Compassion and Choices*, Language Matters Press Kit, at: www.compassion andchoices.org//documents/LMPressKit.2009.pdf (accessed 14 July 2009), cited in Kathryn L. Tucker, 'The Campaign to Deny Terminally Ill Patients Information and Choices at the End of Life', *Journal of Legal Medicine* (October–December, 2009), pp. 495–514.
10. See www.dignityindying.org.uk/assisted-dying.php.
11. See the proposed Assisted Dying Bill at: www.publications.parliament.uk/pa/ ld200203/ldbills/037/2003037.pdf.
12. Daniel Callahan, *The Troubled Dream of Life: In Search of a Peaceful Death* (Washington, DC: Georgetown University Press, 1993), p. 67.
13. Ray Tallis, 'Should the Law on Assisted Dying Be Changed? Yes', *British Medical Journal* (21 April 2011).
14. For Derek Humphry's perspective, see http://dying.about.com/gi/dynamic/ offsite.htm?zi=1/XJ&sdn=dying&cdn=health&tm=22&f=10&tt=13&bt=0 &bts=0&zu=http per cent3A//assistedsuicide.org/blog/2006/11/22/euphe misms-for-death-dying-suicide-euthanasia-right-to-die-dead/ (accessed June 2 2012). Report of the Commission on Assisted Dying, 5 Jan 2012, at www. demos.co.uk/publications/thecommissiononassisteddying.
15. Agnes van der Heide et al, 'End-of-Life Practices in the Netherlands under the Euthanasia Act', *New England Journal of Medicine*, No. 356 (2007), pp. 1957–1965, cited p. 1957.

16. Rosemary Bennett and David Rose, 'Public Supports Assisted Suicide for Terminally-ill people', *The Times*, 25 July 2009.
17. 'Strong Public Support for Right to Die', Pew Research Center for the People and the Press Survey Report, 5 January 2006. Polls, of course, must be treated with caution but all must admit that a majority now supports the right to die for at least some.
18. Cited in Dominic Lawson, 'Why the Disabled Fear Assisted Suicide', *The Independent*, 14 June 2011.
19. Cited in Ian Dowbiggin, forthcoming, 'From Sander to Schiavo: Morality, Partisan Politics, and America's Culture War over Euthanasia, 1950–2010'.
20. Clive Seale, 'Legalisation of Euthanasia or Physician-assisted Suicide: Survey of Doctor's Attitudes', *Palliative Medicine*, 23 (2009), pp. 205–212.
21. The Montana Supreme Court ruled on 31 December 2009 that state law protects doctors in Montana from prosecution for helping terminally ill patients die, effectively legalizing assisted suicide. But the court, ruling with a narrow majority, did not find that assisted suicide is a right guaranteed under the state's Constitution.
22. See Oregon Death with Dignity (DWDA) Act Annual Reports at: http://public.health.oregon.gov/ProviderPartnerResources/EvaluationResearch/DeathwithDignityAct/Pages/ar-index.aspx and Washington Death with Dignity Act at: www.doh.wa.gov/DWDAa/.
23. Suicide Act 1961, available at the Office of Public Sector Information: www.opsi.gov.uk/RevisedStatutes/Acts/ukpga/1961/cukpga_19610060_en_1.
24. In *Washington v. Glucksberg* (1997), the Supreme Court found that there was no 'right' to assistance in committing suicide.
25. www.nvve.nl/nvve-english/pagina.asp?pagnaam=homepage (accessed 20 September 2011).
26. http://sparta.projectie.com/~uitvrije (accessed 28 May 2012).
27. http://sparta.projectie.com/~uitvrije/. See also reporting on the issue by Radio Netherlands Worldwide at www.rnw.nl/english/article/right-choose (accessed 28 May 2012).
28. Martin Beckford, 'Baroness Warnock: Dementia Sufferers May Have a "Duty to Die"', *Daily Telegraph*, 18 September 2008. As will be explicated in Chapter 4, Warnock is right to suggest that suicide out of duty to others 'is not to be abhorred'. However, the difficulty the author has with her argument is that we should help those who wish to die to do so; it is *our* moral peril, as helpers, which is at issue. See Mary Warnock, 'A Duty to Die?', *OMSORG*, 4/2008, available at: http://fagbokforlaget.no/filarkiv/Mary per cent20Warnock.pdf.
29. For an excellent analysis of this fear, see Phil Mullan, *The Imaginary Time Bomb: Why an Ageing Population Is Not a Social Problem* (London: I B Tauris, 2001).
30. Martin Beckford, '"Dr Death" Calls for Assisted Suicide for Those Who Are Not Terminally Ill', *Daily Telegraph*, 16 August 2010.
31. Monika Ardelt, 'Physician-assisted Death', in Clifton Bryant (ed.), *Handbook of Death and Dying* (London: Sage, 2003), pp. 424–434, cited at p. 427.
32. See Washington and Oregon DWDA Annual Reports available at: http://public.health.oregon.gov/ProviderPartnerResources/EvaluationResearch/DeathwithDignityAct/Documents/year14.pdf (2011) and www.doh.wa.gov/Portals/1/Documents/5300/DWDAA2009.pdf (2009) (accessed 10 July 2012).

33. Cited in J. Pereira, 'Legalizing Euthanasia or Assisted Suicide: The Illusion of Safeguards and Controls', *Current Oncology* (April 2011); Press release by Washington State Department of Health, March 2010, at: http://www.doh. wa.gov/DWDAa/forms/DWDAA_2009.pdf. Henk ten Have, Ruth Chadwick, Eric M. Meslin, *The SAGE Handbook of Health Care Ethics* (London: Sage 2011), p. 208.
34. Neil M. Gorsuch, *The Future of Assisted Suicide and Euthanasia* (Princeton: Princeton University Press, 2006), p. 6. John Keown, *Euthanasia, Ethics and Public Policy: An Argument against Legalization* (Cambridge: Cambridge University Press, 2002), p. 33.
35. Terri Schiavo was a patient diagnosed as being in a persistent vegetative state from 1990 to 2005; her husband petitioned for her to have her feeding tubes removed. Her parents disagreed, resulting in numerous court cases and, ultimately, in Florida and federal government legislation. Her case became politically contentious and President George W. Bush returned early from holiday to speak to Congress on the matter. The courts consistently sided with Michael Schiavo and Terri Schiavo died on 31 March 2005 after having her feeding and hydration tubes removed. See Kevin Yuill, 'In the Wake of Terri Schiavo, the Real Slippery Slope', *Journal of Cancer Pain and Symptom Palliation*, vol. 1, no. 2 (2005), pp. 43–46.
36. Howard Ball, *At Liberty To Die: The Battle for Death with Dignity in America* (New York: NYU Press, 2012), p. 132.

2 An Analysis of the Key Arguments on Both Sides

1. Margaret Somerville, *Death Talk: The Case against Euthanasia and Assisted Suicide* (Montreal and Kingston: McGill-Queen's University Press, 2001), p. 107.
2. Kevin Yuill, 'In the Wake of Terri Schiavo, the Real Slippery Slope', *Journal of Cancer Pain and Symptom Palliation*, vol. 1, no. 2 (2005), pp. 43–46.
3. Nigel Biggar, *Aiming to Kill: The Ethics of Suicide and Euthanasia* (London: Darton, Longman and Todd Ltd., 2004). See also Theo A. Boer, 'Recurring Themes in the Debate about Euthanasia and Assisted Suicide', *Journal of Religious Ethics*, vol. 35, no. 3 (September 2007), pp. 529–555.
4. Arthur J. Dyck, *Life's Worth: The Case against Assisted Suicide* (Cambridge, MA: Center for Bioethics and Human Dignity, 2002).
5. Neil M. Gorsuch, *The Future of Assisted Suicide and Euthanasia* (Princeton: Princeton University Press, 2006).
6. Publications of the Select Committee on Assisted Dying for the Terminally Ill Bill, available at: www.publications.parliament.uk/pa/ld200405/ldselect/ldasdy/86/8606.htm (accessed 30 November 2011).
7. Somerville, *Death Talk*, p. 106.
8. Gorsuch, *The Future of Assisted Suicide*, pp. 26–27.
9. Leo Alexander, 'Medical Science under Dictatorship', *New England Journal of Medicine*, vol. 241, no. 2 (1949), pp. 39–47; Thomas Q. Martin, 'Euthanasia and Modern Morality: Their Moral Implications', *The Jurist* Vol. X (January–October, 1950), pp. 437-464, cited here, pp. 452–453.
10. See Wesley J. Smith, *Forced Exit: The Slippery Slope from Assisted Suicide to Legalized Murder* (New York: Times Books, 1997); John Keown, *Euthanasia,*

Ethics, and Public Policy: An Argument against Legalisation (Cambridge: Cambridge University Press, 2002).

11. New York Task Force New York State Task Force on Life and the Law, *When Death Is Sought: Assisted Suicide and Euthanasia in the Medical Context* (Albany, NY: May 1994), pp. 130, 131–322.

12. The Oregon Death with Dignity Act, a citizens' initiative, was first passed by Oregon voters in November 1994, but not implemented until after a legal injunction was lifted on 27 October 1997. See all reports at: www.ohd. hr.state.or.us/chs/pas/pas. Raymond Tallis, 'Stop Me', Review of Neil Gorsuch, *The Future of Assisted Suicide, Times Literary Supplement*, 26 January 2007.

13. B. Steinbock, 'The Case for Physician-assisted Suicide: Not Yet Proven', *Journal of Medical Ethics*, vol. 31 (2005), pp. 235–241, cited here, p. 237. See also D. A. Pratt and B. Steinbock, 'Death with Dignity or Unlawful Killing: The Ethical and Legal Debate over Physician-assisted Death', *Criminal Law Bulletin* 33 (1997). pp. 226–261; Glanville Williams, *The Sanctity of Life and the Criminal Law* (London: Faber and Faber, 1958), p. 281. Despite Williams' criticisms to what he called the 'wedge principle', these arguments persist. Yale Kamisar penned the first response to Williams' defence of the morality of voluntary euthanasia in 'Some Non-Religious Views against Proposed "Mercy Killing" Legislation', *Minnesota Law Review*, vol. 42 (1958), pp. 966–1004, developed upon the original consequentialist case: 'I see the issue, then, as the need for voluntary euthanasia versus (1) the incidence of mistake and abuse; and (2) the danger that legal machinery initially designed to kill those who are a nuisance to themselves may someday engulf those who are a nuisance to others?' (p. 976). As Steinbock points out, the discussion has hardly advanced beyond these original exchanges. But we are left wondering why this stock defence against legalization continues to be peddled.

14. Saimo Chahal, 'Killing, with Kindness', *The Guardian*, 25 February 2010; Jane Campbell, 'Disabled People Need Help to Live, Not Die', *The Guardian*, 3 June 2010.

15. See, for instance, Diane Coleman, 'Assisted Suicide Laws Create Discriminatory Double Standard for Who Gets Suicide Prevention and Who Gets Suicide Assistance: Not Dead Yet Responds to Autonomy, Inc.', *Disability and Health Journal*, vol. 3 (2010), pp. 39–50.

16. Tony Nicklinson was granted permission to take his case to court early in 2012. See Kevin Yuill, 'The Devaluation of Disabled People's Lives', *Spiked-online.com*, 14 March 2012, at: www.spiked-online.com/site/article/12247.

17. Leon R. Kass, 'Neither for Love nor Money: Why Doctors Must Not Kill', *Public Interest*, 94 (Winter 1989), p. 25.

18. See, for example, Nadine Spiegel, 'Euthanasia and Physician-assisted Suicide: Effect on the Doctor–Patient Relationship', *Penn Bioethics Journal*, vol. 1, no. 1 (Spring 2005), pp. 1–3.

19. See Kathleen M. Foley and Herbert Hendin (eds), *The Case against Assisted Suicide: The Case for the Right to End-of-Life Care* (Baltimore: Johns Hopkins University Press, 2002); 'Introduction: A Medical, Ethical, Legal and Psychosocial Perspective', pp. 1–16, cited here, p. 1. Daniel Callahan, however, observes in the volume: 'Suicide is now understood to be a tragic situation, no longer forbidden by the law but hardly anywhere understood as the

ideal outcome of a life filled with suffering. That delicate balance would be lost and a new message delivered: Suicide is morally, medically, legally, and socially acceptable.' See Daniel Callahan, 'Reason, Self-Determination, and Physician-assisted Suicide', pp. 52–68, cited here, p. 60.

20. See p. 17 above.

21. Peter Singer, *Rethinking Life and Death: The Collapse of Our Traditional Ethics* (Oxford: Oxford University Press, 1995), 196.

22. Margaret Pabst Battin, *Ending Life: Ethics and the Way We Die* (New York: Oxford University Press, 2005), p. 18.

23. *Compassion and Choices* website, at: www.compassionandchoices.org/page. aspx?pid=235 (accessed 1 November 2011).

24. Ronald Dworkin, 'Introduction' to 'Assisted Suicide: The Philosophers' Brief', *New York Review of Books* vol. XLIV, No. 5, 27 March 1997, pp. 41–45, Paul Badham, *Is There a Christian Case for Assisted Dying?* (London: SPCK Publications, 2009).

25. Timothy E. Quill and Jane Greenlaw, 'Physician-assisted Death', in Mary Crowley (ed.), *From Birth to Death and Bench to Clinic: The Hastings Center Bioethics Briefing Book for Journalists, Policymakers, and Campaigns* (Garrison: The Hastings Center, 2008), pp. 137–142, cited here, p. 137.

26. Sheila McLean, *Assisted Dying: Reflections on the Need for Law Reform* (London: Routledge, 2007), pp. 34, 80.

27. Cited in the Report of the Commission on Assisted Dying, 5 January 2012, at www.demos.co.uk/publications/thecommissiononassisteddying, pp. 77–78.

28. Statements are on the respective websites www.dignityindying.org.uk/ and http://blog.compassionandchoices.org/?p=1808 (both accessed 10 November 2011). Emphasis added.

29. 'Experiences of Oregon Nurses and Social Workers with Hospice Patients Who Requested Assistance with Suicide', *New England Journal of Medicine*, vol. 347, no. 8 (22 August 2002), pp. 582–588, cited here, p. 582. However, in the Netherlands physicians report pain as the most important reason why *they* felt the patient's condition was 'unbearable' or 'hopeless'. See Hilde Biuting, 'Reporting of Euthanasia and Physician-assisted Suicide in the Netherlands: Descriptive Study', *BMC Medical Ethics* 2009, vol. 10, no. 18 – available at: www.biomedcentral.com/1472-6939/10/18/.

30. Battin, *Ending Life*, p. 30.

31. Cited in Leslie Miller, 'Kubler-Ross, Loving Life, Easing Death', *USA Today*, 30 November 1992, p. 9.

32. Martha Nussbaum, 'Compassion: The Basic Social Emotion', *Social Philosophy & Policy*, vol. 13, no. 1 (1996), pp. 27–58.

33. See www.guardian.co.uk/uk/2010/jan/20/mother-guilty-murder-disabled-son.

34. Timothy Quill, 'Criteria for Physician-assisted Suicide', in Michael M. Uhlmann (ed.), *Last Rights? Assisted Suicide and Euthanasia Debated* (Washington, DC: Ethics and Public Policy Center, 1998), pp. 326–335, cited here, p. 329.

35. In Rachels' scenario, both Smith and Jones stand to inherit a large amount of money from their respective six-year old cousins, should their cousins die. Smith drowns his young cousin while Jones, intending on the same act, chances upon his young cousin slipping on the bath and concussing himself. Jones then does not interfere with him drowning. Rachels used

the fact that both acts are equally morally reprehensible to undermine the distinction between killing and letting die. James Rachels, 'Active and Passive Euthanasia', *The New England Journal of Medicine*, vol. 292 (1975), pp. 78–80. The article appears in many if not most discussions about assisted suicide published since then. See, for instance, Battin, *Ending Life*, pp. 23–25, McLean, *Assisted Dying*, p. 102, Dworkin, *Life's Dominion*, p. 248. Mary Warnock and Elisabeth Macdonald, *Easeful Death: Is there a Case for Assisted Dying?* (Oxford: Oxford University Press, 2008).

36. Though Dawson spoke against a proposed law allowing voluntary euthanasia, he has been attacked by some opponents of assisted suicide, after his private diary was published in 1995, for hastening the comatose George V's death to ensure that *The Times* broke the news and not the *Standard*. It is possible to see this consideration as commensurate with the royal dignity that Lord Dawson had promised the king and his family. See J. H. R. Ramsay, 'A King, a Doctor, and a Convenient Death', *British Medical Journal*, vol. 308, no. 1445 (28 May 1994). Clive Seale, 'Hastening Death in End-of-Life Care: a Survey of Doctors', *Social Science and Medicine*, vol. 69, no. 11, December 2009, pp. 1659–1666, cited here, p. 1659.

37. *WASHINGTON et al. v. GLUCKSBERG et al.*, No. 96–110 (1997), 724. *VACCO, ATTORNEY GENERAL OF NEW YORK, et al. v. QUILL et al.*, No. 95–1858 (1997). The Supreme Court heard the two cases at the same time and responded to both on 26 June 1997.

38. Cited in McLean, *Assisted Dying*, p. 99.

39. John Stuart Mill illustrates this principle with the example of a bridge: 'If either a public officer or any one else saw a person attempting to cross a bridge which had been ascertained to be unsafe, and there were no time to warn him of his danger, they might seize him and turn him back without any real infringement of his liberty; for liberty consists in doing what one desires, and he does not desire to fall into the river. Nevertheless, when there is not a certainty, but only a danger of mischief, no one but the person himself can judge of the sufficiency of the motive which may prompt him to incur the risk: in this case, therefore (unless he is a child, or delirious, or in some state of excitement or absorption incompatible with the full use of the reflecting faculty) he ought, I conceive, to be only warned of the danger; not forcibly prevented from exposing himself to it.' John Stuart Mill, *On Liberty*, C. L. Ten and Stephen M. Cahn (eds) (Lanham: Rowman and Littlefield, 2005), p. 138.

40. See Timothy M. Quill and Margaret P. Battin, *Physician-assisted Dying: The Case for Palliative Care and Patient Choice* (Baltimore: Johns Hopkins University Press, 2004). Quill first set out his stall in 'Nonabandonment: a Central Obligation for Physicians', *Annals of Internal Medicine*, vol. 122, no. 5, 1 March 1995, pp. 368–374. Quill's original essay was published anonymously in *A Piece of My Mind*, a feature in the 8 January 1988 issue of the *Journal of the American Medical Association (JAMA)*, vol. 259, no. 2.

41. H. Tristram Engelhardt, Jr., 'Aiding the Death of Young Children: Ethical Issues' in Uhlman (ed.), *Last Rights?* pp. 387–398, cited here, p. 389.

42. Despite criticizing the situation in Oregon because doctors did not attend the death and because the deadly drugs prescribed might be misused, and despite its hand-wringing 'concern that assisting suicide remains an amateur activity, and that no prospective safeguards are in place to protect those who

seek assistance', the Commission on Assisted Dying insists that 'any decision to seek an assisted suicide is a genuinely voluntary and autonomous choice'. See *Report of the Commission on Assisted Dying*, pp. 23, 27.

43. Battin, *Ending Life*, p. 20.
44. www.dignityindying.org.uk/ (accessed 2 May 2012).
45. Sheila McLean, *Assisted Dying: Reflections on the Need for Law Reform* (London: Routledge, 2007); Iain Brassington, 'Five Words for Assisted Dying', *Law and Philosophy*, 27 (2008), pp. 415–444, and 'Killing People: What Kant Could Have Said about Suicide and Euthanasia but Did Not', *Journal of Medical Ethics*, vol. 32 (2006), pp. 571–574.
46. McLean, *Assisted Dying*, pp. 3, 21.
47. T. M. Scanlon, John Rawls, Robert Nozick, Ronald Dworkin and Judith Jarvis Thompson, 'Assisted Suicide: The Philosophers' Brief', *New York Review of Books*, 44 (27 March 1997), pp. 41–47.
48. Scanlon et al., 'Assisted Suicide: The Philosophers' Brief', p. 41.
49. Quoted in McLean, *Assisted Dying*, 21.
50. John Harris, 'Euthanasia and the Value of Life', in John Keown (ed.), *Euthanasia Examined: Ethical, Clinical and Legal Perspectives* (Cambridge: Cambridge University Press, 1995), pp. 6–22, cied here p. 10. McLean, *Assisted Dying*, p. 4.
51. David Benatar, 'Assisted Suicide, Voluntary Euthanasia, and the Right to Life', in Jon Yorke (ed.), *The Right to Life and the Value of Life* (Farnham: Ashgate Publishing, 2010), pp. 291–310, cited here, p. 291.
52. See Robert I. Simon, MD, James L. Levenson, MD, and Daniel W. Shuman, JD, 'On Sound and Unsound Mind: The Role of Suicide in Tort and Insurance Litigation', *Journal of the American Academy of Psychiatry and the Law*, vol. 33, no. 2 (2005), pp. 176–182.
53. Cited in Alfred Alvarez, *The Savage God: A Study of Suicide* (London: Weidenfeld and Nicolson, 1971), p. 62. Margaret P. Battin and Ryan Spellecy, arguing against such a conception, call suicide 'complex, grave and technical'. 'Killing oneself is not a simple matter,' they state (Margaret P. Battin and Ryan Spellecy, 'What Kind of Freedom? Szasz's Misleading Perception of Physician-assisted Suicide', in Jeffrey A. Schaler (ed.), *Szasz Under Fire: The Psychiatric Abolitionist Faces His Critics* (Chicago: Open Court, 2004), pp. 277–290. In physical terms at least, Battin is wrong. What is difficult about suicide is the mental strength to carry the task through.
54. John P. Safranek, 'Autonomy and Assisted Suicide: The Execution of Freedom', *Hastings Center Report*, vol. 28, no. 4 (1998), pp. 32–36.
55. McLean, *Assisted Dying*, p. 42.
56. Iain Brassington, 'Five Words for Assisted Dying,' *Law and Philosophy* (2008) 27, pp. 415–444, cited here, p. 439.
57. J. L. Lucas, *Principles of Politics* (Oxford: Oxford University Press, 1966), p. 101.
58. As the Report states, 'it is health and social care professionals who have the knowledge, skills and training structures that would be needed to implement a safeguarded system to permit assisted dying in the UK', *Report by the Commission on Assisted Dying*, p. 27.
59. John Hardwig, 'Is There a Duty to Die?', *Hastings Center Report*, vol. 27, no. 2 (1997), pp 34–42; Daniel Callahan, *Setting Limits: Medical Goals in an Aging Society* (Washington, DC: Georgetown University Press, 1995).

60. Lord Joffe, the Labour peer who proposed the British legislation in the House of Lords, told the Commission on Assisted Dying: 'It's not an objective judgement which the doctor has to make; it is a subjective decision.' He noted, 'It's always a question of what the patient's view is on the matter and the patient's decision', *Report of the Commission on Assisted Dying*, pp. 203, 204.
61. Cited in *Report of the Commission on Assisted Dying*, p. 195.

3   The Origins of the Right-to-Die Movement

1. For a useful critique of medicalization in the British context, see Michael Fitzpatrick, *The Tyranny of Health: Doctors and the Regulation of Lifestyle* (London: Routledge, 2001).
2. Fitzpatrick, *The Tyranny of Health*, p. 6.
3. George Pitcher, *A Time to Live: The Case Against Euthanasia and Assisted Suicide* (Oxford: Monarch Books, 2010).
4. Cited in Ezekiel J. Emanuel, *The Ends of Human Life: Medical Ethics is a Liberal Polity* (Cambridge, MA: Harvard University Press, 1991).
5. *Students' Guide to Aid in Dying: A Brief History of the Aid-In-Dying Movement as Well as Current Efforts for Decriminalization*, at: http://compassionandchoices. org/documents/StudentKit.2009.pdf (accessed 2 April 2011).
6. Mary Warnock and Elisabeth Macdonald, *Easeful Death: Is There a Case for Assisted Dying?* (Oxford: Oxford University Press, 2008), p. ix; Daniel Callahan, *The Troubled Dream of Life: In Search of a Peaceful Death* (Washington, DC: Georgetown University Press, 1993), pp. 66–69.
7. Margaret Pabst Battin and David J. Mayo (eds), *Suicide: The Philosophical Issues* (New York: St. Martin's Press, 1980), p. 2.
8. Sheila McLean, *Assisted Dying: Reflections on the Need for Law Reform* (London: Routledge, 2007), p. 1.
9. Ronald Dworkin, *Life's Dominion: An Argument about Abortion and Euthanasia* (London: HarperCollins, 1995, ©1993), pp. 183, 240.
10. Peter Singer, *Rethinking Life and Death: The Collapse of Our Traditional Ethics* (Oxford: Oxford University Press, 1994), p. 18. 'The Rights and Responsibilities of Christians Regarding Human Death, United Church of Christ, Minutes Ninth General Synod including addresses, St Louis, Missouri, June 22–26, 1973', in J. Gordon Melton (ed.), *The Churches Speak on Euthanasia: Official Statements from Religious Bodies and Ecumenical Organizations* (London: Gale Research Inc., 1991), pp. 36–37.
11. Christel Manning, 'Euthanasia and Its Moral Implications', in Melton (ed.), *The Churches Speak on Euthanasia*, pp. xiii–xxviii, xiv–xv.
12. Arthur J. Dyck, *Life's Worth: The Case Against Assisted Suicide* (Cambridge, MA: Center for Bioethics and Human Dignity, 2002), p. i.
13. Nigel Biggar, *Aiming to Kill: The Ethics of Suicide and Euthanasia* (London: Darton, Longman and Todd Ltd., 2004), p. 14.
14. Cited in Kathleen M. Foley and Herbert Hendin, *The Case Against Assisted Suicide: The Case for the Right to End-of-Life Care* (Baltimore: Johns Hopkins University Press, 2002), p. 1.
15. From the 2001 Reith Lecture given by Tom Kirkwood. Available at: www.bbc. co.uk/radio4/reith2001/lecture1.shtml.

16. A. V. Wolff, 'The Artificial Kidney', *Science*, New Series, vol. 115, no. 2982 (22 February 1952), pp. 193–199, cited here, p. 198.
17. James H. Maxwell, 'The Iron Lung: Halfway Technology or Necessary Step?', *The Milbank Quarterly*, vol. 64, no. 1 (1986), pp. 3–29, cited here, p. 3. L. Thomas, 'The Technology of Medicine', *New England Journal of Medicine*, vol. 285, no. 24 (9 Dec 1971), pp. 1366–1368. For 'good news' stories about life in an iron lung, see 'Iron Lung Does His Breathing for 101 Days', *Milwaukee Sentinel*, 9 December 1931; 'Man in Iron Lung Starts 9600-mile Trip from China', *Los Angeles Times*, 3 June 1937. For a fascinating memoir of a woman who lived over 60 years in an iron lung, see Marsha Mason, *Breath: Life in the Rhythm of an Iron Lung* (Asheboro: Down Home Press, 2003).
18. Perhaps the best is Ian Dowbiggin, *A Merciful End: The Euthanasia Movement in Modern America* (Oxford: Oxford University Press, 2003).
19. Dowbiggin, *A Merciful End*, p. xvi.
20. In the liberal American periodical, *Survey Graphic*, foreign correspondent John Palmer Gavit denounced Hitler's barbaric treatment of the Jews whereas, a few pages later, R. H. Landeman argued for the adoption of German sterilization programs in the United States. See *Survey Graphic* magazine, March 1936.
21. Margaret Sanger, 'A Plan for Peace', *Birth Control Review* (April 1932).
22. Cited in Dowbiggin, *A Merciful End*, p. 72.
23. Ibid., p. 74.
24. See Ellen Herman, *The Romance of American Psychology: Political Culture in the Age of Experts* (London: University of California Press, 1995).
25. Arthur M. Schlesinger, Jr ' "The Vital Center" Reconsidered' *Encounter*, September 1970, pp. 89–93.
26. Margaret Somerville, 'Against Euthanasia', *Arts and Opinion*, vol. 5, no. 4, 2006.
27. Arthur M. Schlesinger, Jr., *The Vital Center: The Politics of Freedom* (Boston: The Riverside Press, 1949), p. 256. See Robert Collins, *More: The Politics of Economic Growth in Postwar America* (Oxford: Oxford University Press, 2000).
28. Hodgson, *In Our Time*, p. 51.
29. Walter A. McDougall, 'Technocracy and Statecraft in the Space Age – Toward the History of a Saltation', *The American Historical Review*, vol. 87, no. 4 (October 1982), pp. 1010–1040, cited here, p. 1011.
30. Cited in Stephen Rousseas and James Farganis, 'The American Scene: Retreat of the Idealists', *The Nation*, 23 March 1963, pp. 240–244.
31. See Fitzpatrick, *The Tyranny of Health*.
32. David Serlin, *Replaceable You: Engineering the Body in Postwar America* (Chicago: University of Chicago Press, 2004), p. 4.
33. Serlin, *Replaceable You*, p. 5.
34. Thomas Szasz, *Ideology and Insanity: Essays on the Psychiatric Dehumanization of Man* (New York: Anchor Books, 1970), p. 5.
35. Ezekiel J. Emanuel, *The Ends of Human Life: Medical Ethics in a Liberal Polity* (London: Harvard University Press, 1991), p. 6. Emphasis is in the original.
36. See Dennis L. Meadows, Donella H. Meadows, Jorgen Randers, William H. Behrens III, *The Limits To Growth: a Report for the Club of Rome's Project on the Predicament of Mankind* (London: Earth Island Ltd., 1972); Fred Hirsch, *Social Limits to Growth* (London: Routledge and Kegan Paul, 1977).

37. Daniel Callahan, 'Limits and Prohibitions', *The Hastings Center Report*, vol. 3, no. 5 (November 1973), pp. 5–7, cited here, p. 5.
38. Ibid.
39. Cited in Meadows et al., *The Limits to Growth*, p. 179.
40. Callahan, 'Limits and Prohibitions', p. 7.
41. Kirkwood, Reith Lecture, 2001. The falsity of such a pessimistic outlook is detailed in Phil Mullan, *The Imaginary Time Bomb: Why an Ageing Population is Not a Social Problem* (London: IB Tauris 2002).
42. Dowbiggin, *A Merciful End*, p. 95.
43. Dowbiggin is the exception. The similarity of arguments heard today and the Williams–Kamisar debate are occasionally astounding. See Glanville Williams, *The Sanctity of Life and the Criminal Law* (London: Faber and Faber, 1958) and Yale Kamisar, 'Some Non-Religious Views against Proposed "Mercy Killing" Legislation', *Minnesota Law Review*, vol. 42 (1958), pp. 966–1004. Kamisar, for instance, may well have suggested the title of Peter Singer's later book, *Unsanctifying Human Life: Essays on Ethics* (ed. by Helga Kuhse [Oxford: Blackwell, 2002]) when he notes that Glanville's book should be entitled 'The Un-Sanctity of Life' (p. 966 fn2). Ezekiel J. Emanuel, 'The History of Euthanasia Debates in the United States and Britain', *Annals of Internal Medicine*, vol. 121 (1994), pp. 793–802.
44. Boston Women's Health Book Collective, *Our Bodies, Ourselves* (New York: Simon and Schuster, 1973), Preface, p. ix. See also Sandra Morgen, *Into Our Own Hands: The Women's Health Movement in the United States, 1969–1990* (New Brunswick: Rutgers University Press, 2002).
45. Barbara Ehrenreich, 'Feminism and the Cultural Revolution in Health', paper given at the Women and Health Conference, 7–8 April 1975. Available at: www.ourbodiesourselves.org/uploads/pdf/women-and-health.pdf (accessed April 22 2010).
46. Callahan, *The Troubled Dream of Life*, p. 67.
47. Carol Downer, 'Women Professionals in the Feminist Health Movement', paper given at the Women and Health Conference, 7–8 April 1975.
48. *Our Bodies, Ourselves*, p. viii. Harold Y. Vanderpool, 'Doctors and the Dying of Patients in American History', in Robert F. Weir (ed.), *Physician-assisted Suicide* (Indianapolis: Indiana University Press, 1997), pp. 33–66, 52–53.
49. Cited in Vanderpool, 'Doctors and the Dying of Patients in American History', p. 53.
50. Dowbiggin, *A Merciful End*, pp. 118, 140.
51. Albert R. Jonsen, 'To Help the Dying Die: A New Duty for Anesthesiologists?', *Anesthesiology*, vol. 73 (February 1993), pp. 225–228, cited here, p. 227.
52. Dowbiggin, *A Merciful End*, pp. 159, 164–165.
53. Nancy Gibbs, 'Ethics: Dr. Death's Suicide', *Time*, 8 June 1990. Available at: www.time.com/time/magazine/article/0,9171,970389-1,00.html#ixzz0lFxF9fvk.
54. Jack Lessenberry, 'Reflections on Dr. Kevorkian', *Metro Times*, 21 October 2009. See also Dowbiggin, *A Merciful End*, pp. 165–167.
55. Deborah Lupton, *The Imperative of Health: Public Health and the Regulated Body* (London: Sage, 1995), p. 4. For a discussion of the definition of a healthy death, see D. C. Smith and M. F. Maher 'Healthy Death', *Counseling and Values*, vol. 36 (1991), pp. 42–48.

4 Considering Suicide

1. Cited in C. S. Evans 'Faith as the Telos of Morality: A Reading of *Fear and Trembling*', *Kierkegaard on Faith and the Self: Collected Essays* (Waco: Baylor University Press, 2006), pp. 209–223, cited here, p. 218. Hannah Arendt presents a theory of action most comprehensively in *The Human Condition* (Chicago: University of Chicago Press, 1998 [©1958]) both in the Introduction (pp. 7–17) and 'Action', pp. 175–243. 'Prepared in the silence of the heart' is Albert Camus' phrase. Cited in Georgia Noon, 'On Suicide', *Journal of the History of Ideas*, vol. 39, no. 3 (July–September, 1978), pp. 371–386, cited here, p. 384.
2. G. K. Chesterton, *Orthodoxy* (London: Unicorn Books, 1939), p. 115.
3. Robert F. Worth, 'How a Single Match Can Ignite a Revolution', *New York Times*, 21 January 2011. Available at: www.nytimes.com/2011/01/23/weekinreview/23worth.html?_r=1&src=twrhp (accessed 2 September 2011).
4. Andrew Jarecki (dir.), *Capturing the Friedmans* (HBO, 2003). See www.imdb.com/title/tt0342172/.
5. Reverend Kevin D. O'Rourke, 'The Catholic Tradition on Forgoing Life Support', *The National Catholic Bioethics Quarterly*, vol. 5, no. 3 (Autumn 2005), pp. 537–553, cited here, p. 540. Cited in Antoon A. Leenaars, 'Edwin S. Shneidman on Suicide', *Suicidology Online*, vol. 1 (2010), pp. 5–18. Accessed 16 June 2011 at www.suicidology-online.com/pdf/SOL-2010-1-5-18.pdf. Also at: Kevin D. O'Rourke, 'The Catholic Tradition on Forgoing Life Support', in M. T. Lysaght and J. J. Kotva Jr. (eds), *On Moral Medicine, Theological Perspectives in Medical Ethics*, Third Edition (Grand Rapids: Wm B. Eerdmans Publishing Co., 2012), p. 1118.
6. Some date the appearance of the term to earlier in the seventeenth century. See, for instance, Michael McDonald, 'The Medicalization of Suicide in England: Laymen, Physicians, and Cultural Change, 1500–1870', *The Milbank Quarterly*, vol. 67, Supplement 1. Framing Disease: The Creation and Negotiation of Explanatory Schemes (1989), pp. 69–91.
7. Cited in Manuel G. Velasquez, 'Defining Suicide', *Issues in Law and Medicine*, vol. 3 (1987–88), pp. 37-52, cited here, p. 42.
8. Cited in Robert F. Martin, 'Suicide and Self-sacrifice', in Margaret Pabst Battin and David J. Mayo (eds), *Suicide: The Philosophical Issues* (New York: St. Martin's Press, 1980), pp. 48–68, cited here, p. 52.
9. There are those who disagree with this precept, especially those who feel it is possible for an animal to commit suicide. See, for instance, Halmuth H. Schaefer, 'Can a Mouse Commit Suicide?', in Edwin S. Sheidman (ed.), *Essays in Self-Destruction* (New York: Science House, Inc., 1967). But the consideration of animal suicides normally seeks to highlight animal cruelty and is not a study of suicide as much as the endowment of animals with human emotions. Medical historian Duncan Wilson says: 'The questioning of animal suicide is essentially people looking at what it means to be human. The people talking about animal suicide today seem to be using it as a way to evoke sympathy for the plight of mistreated and captive animals.' See Duncan Wilson and Edward Ramsden, 'The Nature of Suicide: Science and the Self-Destructive Animal', *Endeavour*, vol. 34, no. 1 (March 2010), pp. 21–24. Duncan Wilson cited in Justin Nobel, 'Do Animals Commit

Suicide?', *Time*, 19 March 2010, available at: www.time.com/time/health/article/0,8599,1973486,00.html#ixzz1Yh74Kf9h (accessed 3 September 2011).

10. Cited in Margaret Pabst Battin, *Suicide: The Ethical Issues* (Englewood Cliffs: Prentice Hall, 1995), 21. See fn7.

11. Kant cited in Martin, 'Suicide and Self-sacrifice', p. 49. Michael J. Seidler, 'Kant and the Stoics on Suicide', *Journal of the History of Ideas*, vol. 44, no. 3 (July–September 1983), pp. 429–453, cited here, pp. 448–449. Allen W. Wood, *Kantian Ethics* (New York: Cambridge University Press, 2008), p. 172.

12. See Martin, 'Suicide and self-Sacrifice'.

13. Recent research questions whether this particular double-effect, of morphine killing the patient as well as the pain, really does take place. See Mary Warnock and Elisabeth Macdonald, *Easeful Death: Is there a Case for Assisted Dying?* (Oxford: Oxford University Press, 2008), p. 111.

14. Captain Lawrence Oates took part in the doomed expedition to the South Pole led by Captain Robert F. Scott in 1911–1912. On the way back from the Pole, the team suffered adverse conditions and Oates, aware that his ill-health was compromising his three companions' chances of survival, chose certain death, famously telling his companions 'I am just going outside and may be some time'.

15. Peter Y. Windt, 'The Concept of Suicide', in Battin and Mayo (eds), *Suicide*, pp. 39–47. Thomas Szasz, *Fatal Freedom: The Ethics and Politics of Suicide* (Syracuse: Syracuse University Press, 2002), p. 64.

16. Iain Brassington, 'Killing People: What Kant Could Have Said about Suicide and Euthanasia but Did Not', *Journal of Medical Ethics*, vol. 32, no. 10 (2006) pp. 571–574.

17. See, for instance, John P. Safranek, 'Autonomy and Assisted Suicide: The Execution of Freedom', *Hastings Center Report*, vol. 28, no. 4 (1998), pp. 32–36; Kumar Amarasekara and Mirko Bagaric, *Euthanasia, Morality and the Law* (New York: Peter Lang, 2002); Bonnie Steinbock, 'The Case for Physician Assisted Suicide: Not (Yet) Proven', *Journal of Medical Ethics*, vol. 31 (2005), pp. 235–241. While these three works oppose legalizing assisted suicide, Iain Brassington and Sheila McLean, who both support it, admit that the six months rule is arbitrary. See Iain Brassington, 'Five Words for Assisted Dying', *Law and Philosophy*, vol. 27, no. 5 (2008), pp. 415–444, and Sheila McLean, *Assisted Dying: Reflections on the Need for Law Reform* (London: Routledge, 2007). As McLean admits (though she words it carefully), 'If it is the case that everyone, and not just those more obviously "in need", can lay claim to the same right to seek assisted dying, so be it' (p. 42).

18. See Chapter 1. Not one report on the reasons why death is sought in these areas has pain as an important motivation. The key reasons listed in the 2010 Oregon Death with Dignity Act report are loss of autonomy (93.8 per cent), decreasing ability to participate in activities that made life enjoyable (93.8 per cent), and loss of dignity (78.5 per cent). All feature loss, which is similar to the motivations of non-assisted suicides. See Warren Breed, 'Suicide and Loss in Social Interaction', in Sheidman (ed.), *Essays in Self-Destruction*, pp. 188–202; David Lester, *Making Sense of Suicide: An In-depth Look at Why People Kill Themselves* (New York: Charles Press, 1997); and Roy F. Baumeister, 'Suicide as Escape from Self', *Psychological Review*, vol. 97, no. 1 (January 1990), pp. 90–113.

19. Windt, 'The Concept of Suicide', pp. 45–46.

20. Cited in Martin, 'Suicide and Self-sacrifice', p. 64.

21. On 26 March 1997, Marshall Applewhite and 39 other members of the Heaven's Gate cult, of which Applewhite was leader, took their own lives. The group timed their suicides according to the comet Hale-Bopp's appearance as they claimed that a spaceship was tailing the comet; see also Charles Wahl, 'Suicide as a Magical Act', in Edwin S. Sheidman and Norman Farberow (eds), *Clues to Suicide* (New York: McGraw Hill, 1957), pp. 23–33, cited here, p. 23.

22. See Battin, *Suicide: The Ethical Issues*. Battin has a useful section discussing just this trend on pages 3–12.

23. M. D. Faber, 'Shakespeare's Suicides' in Edwin S. Sheidman (ed.), *Essays in Self-destruction* (New York: Science House, Inc., 1967), pp. 30–58.

24. Thomas Szasz, *Fatal Freedom: The Ethics and Politics of Suicide* (Syracuse: Syracuse University Press, 1999). This is the main point of Szasz's book.

25. Battin, *Suicide: The Ethical Issues*, p. 21. See also Robert L. Barry, *Breaking the Thread of Life, On Rational Suicide* (New York: Transaction Publishers, 1996), p. 3.

26. See p. 38fn. James Rachels, 'Active and Passive Euthanasia', *The New England Journal of Medicine*, vol. 292 (1975), pp. 78–80. The article appears in many if not most discussions about assisted suicide published since then. See, for instance, Battin, *Ending Life*, pp. 23–25, McLean, *Assisted Dying*, p. 102, Ronald Dworkin, *Life's Dominion, An Argument about Abortion and Euthanasia* (London: Harper Collins, 1995, ©1993), p. 248.

27. Armin Miewes was arrested in 2002 after police saw a video tape of Miewes killing and eating Brandes, who had answered an advertisement on a website for a 'willing victim', ready to be killed and eaten. For an earlier discussion of this issue, see Avery D. Weisman, 'Self-Destruction and Sexual Perversion', in Sheidman (ed.), *Essays in Self-Destruction*, pp. 265–299.

28. Cited in *Dignity in Dying: The Report*, p. 9, at: www.dignityindying.org.uk/includes/spaw2/uploads/files/Dignity per cent20in per cent20Dying per cent20Report.pdf (accessed 2 September 2011).

29. Timothy Quill cited in *Dignity in Dying: The Report*, The figure was cited by Parliamentary Under-Secretary of State for Justice Maria Eagle on 11 November 2008. See: www.publications.parliament.uk/pa/cm200708/cmhansrd/cm081111/halltext/81111h0005.htm#08111147000167 (accessed 2 September 2011). It is difficult to admit, in light of this figure, journalist Polly Toynbee's no-doubt passionately held belief that 'The 1961 Suicide Act is an act of state torture', published in *The Guardian*, 31 July 2009.

30. As H. Rommilly Fedden said, '[t]his most individualistic of all actions disturbs society profoundly. Seeing a man who appears not to care for the things which it prizes, society is compelled to question all it has thought desirable. The things which make its own life worth living, the suicide boldly jettisons. Society is troubled, and its natural and nervous reaction is to condemn the suicide'; cited in Glanville Williams, *The Sanctity of Life and the Criminal Law* (London: Faber and Faber, 1958), p. 240.

31. Cited in Georgia Noon, 'On Suicide,' *Journal of the History of Ideas*, vol. 39, no. 3 (July–September, 1978), pp. 371–386, cited here, p. 384.

32. For discussions of rational suicide, see James L. Werth, *Contemporary Perspectives on Rational Suicide* (London: Brunner/Mazel, 1999), George

P. Smith, 'All's Well that Ends Well: Toward a Policy of Assisted Rational Suicide or Merely Enlightened Self-determination?', *UC Davis Law Review*, vol. 22, no. 2 (1989), pp. 275–419; Margaret Pabst Battin, 'The Concept of the Rational Suicide', in *Ethical Issues in Suicide*, pp. 131–153.

33. For a useful analysis of the distinction made by Dworkin, John Harris and others between the two concepts, see Theo A. Boer, 'Recurring Themes in the Debate about Euthanasia and Assisted Suicide', *Journal of Religious Ethics*, vol. 35, no. 3 (September 2007), pp. 529–555.

34. The policeman's dilemma has been used by many on both sides of the assisted-suicide debate. A lorry driver is trapped in the cab of his burning vehicle after an accident. The police, fire-fighters and ambulance service are at the scene, but it is clear he will burn to death before he can be freed. He is in agony. He begs a policeman (who happens to be armed) to shoot him rather than let him burn. For a discussion of its importance, see, for instance, John Harris, 'Consent and End of Life Decisions', *Journal of Medical Ethics*, vol. 29 (2003), pp. 10–15.

35. Quang Duc asked to burn himself as 'a donation to the struggle'; cited in Michael Biggs, 'Dying Without Killing: Self Immolations, 1963–2002', in Diego Gambetta (ed.), *Making Sense of Suicide Missions* (Oxford: Oxford University Press, 2006), p. 179.

36. It is interesting that many decisions taken publicly appear false. Timothy Leary, the acid guru of the 1960s, pledged to broadcast his own suicide on the internet. However, as *Rolling Stone* writer Mikal Gilmore reported, 'when all is said and done, Leary is not dying outrageously. Rather, he is dying quietly and bravely, surrounded by people he loves and who love him'. In other words, Leary backed away from his publicly declared intention to commit suicide after some private consideration. He did, however, invite a journalist to his bedside to witness the event. See Mikal Gilmour, 'Timothy Leary, 1920–1996', *Rolling Stone*, 11–25 July 1996. Of course, the recent example of Tony Nicklinson's death may have demonstrated the seriousness with which he asked to die.

37. A British study found that 0.6 per cent of suicides involved suicide pacts. See Martin Brown and Brian Barraclough, 'Epidemiology of Suicide Pacts in England and Wales, 1988–1992', *British Medical Journal*, vol. 315 no. 286 (2 August 1997).

38. The author Terry Pratchett has made the case for tribunals to regulate assisted-suicide requests. 'Terry Pratchett: Coroner Tribunals Should Be Set Up for Assisted Suicide Cases', *Daily Telegraph*, 2 August 2009, at: www.telegraph.co.uk/health/healthnews/5960166/Sir-Terry-Pratchett-coroner-tribunals-should-be-set-up-for-assisted-suicide-cases.html (accessed 9 September 2011).

39. For an enlightening discussion of the treatment of suicide by early Christian theologians, see Darrel W. Amundsen, 'Suicide and Early Christian Values', in Baruch A. Brody (ed.), *Suicide and Euthanasia: Historical and Contemporary Themes* (Dordecht: Kluwer, 2010, ©1989), pp. 77–154.

40. As Hannah Arendt observes, 'men never have been and never will be able to undo or even to control reliably any of the processes they start through action'; Arendt, *The Human Condition*, pp. 232–223. Eric A. Plaut and Kevin Anderson, tr., *Marx on Suicide* (Chicago: Northwestern University Press,

1999). For a discussion of how famous suicides inspire others to act, see David P. Phillips, 'The Influence of Suggestion on Suicide: Substantive and Theoretical Implications of the Werther Effect', *American Sociological Review*, vol. 39, no. 3 (June 1974), pp. 340–354.

41. See A. G. Lee, 'Ovid's "Lucretia"', *Greece & Rome*, vol. 22, no. 66 (October 1953), pp. 107–118.

42. Arendt *The Human Condition*. Preceding Arendt, Paul Illich spoke of vitality in similar terms, though he included what Arendt categorized as works (the produce of *homo faber*) within it: 'Vitality is the power of creating beyond oneself without losing oneself. The more power of creating beyond itself a being has the more vitality it has. The world of technical creations is the most conspicuous expression of man's vitality and its infinite superiority over animal vitality. Only man has complete vitality because he alone has complete intentionality'; Paul Illich, *The Courage to Be* (London: Yale University Press, 1952), p. 81.

43. Arendt, *The Human Condition*, p. 234. Adam Smith referred to the ability of human beings to breach the existing social and moral barriers: 'Men have voluntarily thrown away life to acquire after death a renown which they could no longer enjoy. Their imagination, in the meantime, anticipated that fame which was in future times to be bestowed upon them. Those applauses which they were never to hear rung in their ears, the thoughts of that admiration whose effects they were never to feel played about their hearts, banished from their breasts the strongest of all natural fears, and transported them to perform actions which seem almost beyond the reach of human nature'; Adam Smith, 'The Theory of Moral Sentiments', cited in Bruce Mazlish, 'History and Morality,' *The Journal of Philosophy*, vol. 55, no. 6 (13 March 1958), pp. 230–240, cited here, p. 234.

44. Mazlish, 'History and Morality', p. 237.

45. Homa Darabi, an Iranian child psychiatrist, set herself on fire in a crowded Tehran square in 1994. A month earlier, a 16-year-old girl had been shot to death for wearing lipstick, and Darabi – who had lived in the United States and refused to wear the veil – had seen enough. 'Death to tyranny, long live liberty, long live Iran!', she shouted, as flames engulfed her. Yet Iran's official attitudes toward women's rights have scarcely changed. See Worth, 'How a Single Match Can Ignite a Revolution'.

46. Arendt, *The Human Condition*, p. 190.

47. M. D. Faber, 'Shakespeare's Suicides', pp. 35–36.

48. See Arendt, *The Human Condition*, pp. 238–240.

49. Cited in Biggs, 'Dying without Killing', p. 179.

50. Peter J. Steinberger, 'Hannah Arendt on Judgment', *American Journal of Political Science*, vol. 34, no. 3 (August 1990), pp. 803–821, cited here, p. 814.

51. Hannah Arendt, *Responsibility and Judgment*, ed. Jerome Kohn (New York: Schocken Books, 2003), p. 46. A look at the transformation of the term 'dignity' indicates that such a relativization of meanings is in process. Whereas the original term referred to the refusal to let go of one's demeanour and to act in accordance of one's social role in the face of very difficult situations, today it appears to have solely physical attributes and is deemed impossible in certain circumstances.

52. Jerome Kohn, 'Introduction' to Arendt, *Responsibility and Judgment*, p. xxix.

5   For Abortion, Against Assisted Suicide

1. http://prolife.org.uk/about (accessed 25 June 2012).
2. www.nrlc.org/MedEthics/index.html (accessed 25 June 2012).
3. http://news.bbc.co.uk/1/hi/health/background_briefings/euthanasia/331261. stm (accessed 25 June 2012).
4. www.pewforum.org/Abortion/Religious-Groups-Official-Positions-on-Abortion.aspx. Steven D. Aguzzi, 'Suffering Redeemed: A Reformed Argument Against Physician Assisted Suicide and Euthanasia', *Theology Matters*, vol. 17, no. 2 (March/April 2011), pp. 1–9.
5. www.compassionandchoices.org, at: www.dignityindying.org.uk (accessed 25 June 2012).
6. Suzanne Moore, 'My Death Is My Affair: Just Don't Let My Daughter Design My Headstone', *The Guardian*, 17 June 2011.
7. www.dignityindying.org.uk/assisted-dying/law-not-working.html. Keith Fraser, 'Ban on Euthanasia Fosters "Back Alley" Suicides, Lawyer Says', *National Post*, 1 December 2011.
8. 'Margaret Somerville: Focusing on the Fetus Changes the Abortion Debate', *National Post*, 24 January 2012.
9. Leon R. Kass and Nelson Lund, 'Physician-Assisted Suicide, Medical Ethics and the Future of the Medical Profession', *Special Issue: A Symposium on Physician-Assisted Suicide: Duquesne Law Review*, vol. 35 (Fall 1996), pp. 395–425.
10. Kass and Lund, 'Physician-Assisted Suicide', p. 411.
11. See Bonnie Steinbock, 'Why Most Abortions Are Not Wrong', in Bonnie Steinbock, Alex John London and John D. Arras (eds), *Ethical Issues in Modern Medicine: Contemporary Readings in Bioethics* (Boston: McGraw-Hill, 2009), pp. 555–566. For Steinbock's position on assisted suicide, see 'Not Yet Proven', *Journal of Medical Ethics*, vol. 31 (2005), pp. 235–241.
12. For an argument for legalizing assisted suicide that leaned heavily on *Planned Parenthood v. Casey*, see Holley L. Claiborn, 'Assisted Suicide Falls Within Liberty Interests Protected By the Fourteenth Amendment', *Syracuse Journal of Legislation and Policy*, vol. 162 (1995), pp. 162–168. For the Supreme Court Decision on Glucksberg, see http://law2.umkc.edu/faculty/projects/ftrials/conlaw/glucksberg.html (accessed 25 June 2012).
13. Ronald Dworkin, *Life's Dominion, An Argument about Abortion, Euthanasia, and Individual Freedom An Argument about Abortion and Euthanasia* (London: Harper Collins, 1995, ©1993), p. 179.
14. Matthew P. Previn, 'Assisted Suicide and Religion: Conflicting Conceptions of the Sanctity of Human Life', *Georgetown Law Journal*, vol. 84 (1995–96), pp. 589–616, cited here, p. 598. Dworkin, *Life's Dominion*.
15. Dworkin, *Life's Dominion*, p. 217.
16. Though see Gregor Damschen and Dieter Schönecker, 'Saving Seven Embryos or Saving One Child? Michael Sandel on the Moral Status of Human Embryos', *Journal of Philosophical Research*, vol. 32, Issue Supplement (2007), pp. 239–245.
17. Brandes was voluntarily killed and eaten by Armin Miewes after answering an advertisement on a website. See http://news.bbc.co.uk/1/hi/world/europe/3443803.stm (accessed 4 July 2012).

18. Ann Furedi, 'Some Messages Can't Be Massaged', *Conscience: The Newsjournal of Catholic Opinion* (Winter 2006–07).
19. http://mediacentre.dh.gov.uk/2012/05/29/abortion-statistics-england-wales-2011. Scotland's statistics are similar. See www.isdscotland.org/Health-Topics/Sexual-Health/Publications/2011-05-31/2011-05-31-Abortions-Report. pdf (both accessed 2 July 2012).
20. www.guttmacher.org/sections/abortion.php. See also: www.census.gov/compendia/statab/cats/births_deaths_marriages_divorces/family_planning_abortions.html (both accessed 2 July 2012).
21. Annabelle Chan and Leonie C. Sage, 'Estimating Australia's Abortion Rates, 1985–2003', *Medical Journal of Australia*, vol. 182, no. 9 (2005), pp. 447–452.
22. Statistics are available at www.abortion.gen.nz/information/statistics.html (accessed 2 July 2012).
23. See www5.statcan.gc.ca/bsolc/olc-cel/olc-cel?catno=82-223-X&lang=eng (accessed 2 July 2012).
24. See www.dignityindying.org.uk/news/general/n30-assisted-dying-legislation-would-reduce-violent-suicides-new-evidence-12-may-2006.html (accessed 2 July 2012).
25. Ibid. See also http://articles.boston.com/2012-04-29/lifestyle/31478132_1_johnson-palliative-care-hospice-care.
26. See Demos's study at: www.demos.co.uk/files/Suicide_-_web.pdf?1314370102.
27. See www.oregon.gov/DHS/news/2010news/2010-0909a.pdf?ga=t.
28. A. Walker et al, *Reports on Public Health and Medical Subjects No. 97. Report on Confidential Enquiries into Maternal Deaths in England and Wales 1952–1954* (London, 1957). Thomas Clutton-Brook et al., *Saving Mothers' Lives: Reviewing Maternal Deaths to Make Motherhood Safer – 2003-2005* (London, 2007). Available at: www.mdeireland.com/pub/SML07_Report.pdf (accessed 3 July 2012).
29. See Rachel Benson Gold, 'Lessons from Before Roe: Will Past Be Prologue?', *Guttmacher Report on Public Policy*, vol. 6, no.1 (March 2003), at: www.guttmacher.org/pubs/tgr/06/1/gr060108.html (accessed 3 July 2012).
30. Szasz perspicaciously notes that with increasing momentum, the American people and the American government embrace the principle that certain acts prohibited ought to be permitted if prescribed by physicians. Whereas US law prohibits marijuana use, California state law permits it for medical use. Getting around moral objections to drug use, campaigners now claim medical reasons for their drug use. Szasz's point – no doubt correct – is that people tend to cite medical authority to take actions that in the past were simply thought of as bad or immoral. Just as excess promiscuity is less a disease than a moral failing, neither is dying a disease (though it may be precipitated by a disease). Thomas Szasz, *Fatal Freedom: The Ethics and Politics of Suicide* (New York: Syracuse University Press, 2002), p. 64.
31. Margaret P. Battin and Ryan Spellecy, 'What Kind of Freedom? Szasz's Misleading Perception of Physician-assisted Suicide', in Jeffrey A. Schaler (ed.), *Szasz Under Fire: The Psychiatric Abolitionist Faces His Critics*. (Boston: Open Court, 2004), pp. 277–290, cited here, p. 282.
32. Cited in Dworkin, *Life's Dominion*, p. 43.
33. Brian V. Johnstone, 'Early Abortion: Venial or Mortal Sin?', *Irish Theological Quarterly*, vol. 70 (1985), p. 60.

34. See www.spuc.org.uk/about/history (accessed 5 July 2012).
35. www.righttolife.com.au/about.htm (accessed 5 July 2012).
36. www.life.org.nz/abortion/pagefeature1/7-spuc (accessed 5 July 2012).
37. Michael A. Cavanaugh, 'Secularization and the Politics of Traditionalism: The Case of the Right-to-Life Movement', *Sociological Forum*, vol. 1, no. 2 (1986), pp. 251–283, cited here, p. 251.
38. See www.notdeadyetuk.org/notdeadyet-about.html (accessed 6 July 2012).
39. Though see Damschen and Schönecker, 'Saving Seven Embryos or Saving One Child?', pp. 239–245.
40. See Kevin Yuill, 'Private Tragedy as Political Farce,' *Spiked-online.com* (23 March 2005) at: www.spiked-online.com/site/article/1176/.

6 The Coercive Implications of Legalization

1. Frank Furedi, *On Tolerance: The Life Style Wars: A Defence of Moral Independence* (London: Continuum, 2011), p. 146.
2. For a brief discussion of the Mental Capacity Act of 2005, see Kevin Yuill, 'The (In)capacity to Trust', *Spiked-online*, 10 October 2007, available at www.spiked-online.com/site/article/3948 (accessed 9 July 2012).
3. Re E (Medical Treatment Anorexia) [2012] EWHC 1639 (COP).
4. See Barbara Hewson, 'Treating Adults like Children,' *Spiked-online.com*, 20 June 2012, at: www.spiked-online.com/site/article/12559 (accessed 9 July 2012).
5. Editorial, 'Eating Disorders: The Parents' Voices Should Have Been Heeded In The Case of "E"', *The Observer*, 17 June 2012. 'Anorexic Medical Student Should Be Fed Against Her Will, Judge Rules', *Daily Telegraph*, 15 June 2012. Justice Jackson did acknowledge that the right to refuse treatment does exist in English law: *'People with capacity are entitled to make decisions for themselves, including about what they will and will not eat, even if their decision brings about their death. The state, here in the form of the Court of Protection, is only entitled to interfere where a person does not have the capacity to decide for herself.'* See *Local Authority v E [2012]*.
6. Sam Marsden and Martin Beckford, 'Woman Who Wants To Die Must Be Force-fed', *Daily Telegraph*, 15 June 2012.
7. Tony Nicklinson was the British man with 'locked-in syndrome', unable to move independently or to speak after suffering a stroke. He died on 22 August 2012 after refusing food since the British High Court denied his request for an assisted suicide on 12 August. See Introduction to this volume, p. 2.
8. Cited in Ronald B Sklar, 'The 'Capable' Mental Health Patient's Right to Refuse Treatment', *McGill Journal of Law and Health*, vol. 5, no. 2 (2011), pp. 291–293, cited here, p. 291.
9. A. C. Grayling, 'Allowing People To Arrange Their Death Is a Simple Act of Kindness', *The Times*, 31 March 2009.
10. *Dignity in Dying* on-line pamphlet 'A Matter of Facts', p. 14. Available at: www.dignityindying.org.uk/includes/spaw2/uploads/files/A per cent 20matter per cent20of per cent20facts per cent20May per cent202011.pdf (accessed 10 July 2012). *Compassion and Choices* press release: Ganzini study

release comment, available at: www.compassionandchoices.org/sslpage.
aspx?pid=484&nccsm=21&__nccscid=15&__nccsct=Document+Folder&__
nccspID=1223 (accessed 10 July 2012).
11. See Hannah Arendt, *The Human Condition* (London: University of Chicago
Press, ©1958), especially 'Chapter II The Public and the Private Realm'
(pp. 22–78).
12. Clive Seale, 'Hastening Death in End-of-Life Care: A Survey of Doctors',
Social Science and Medicine, vol. 69, no. 11 (2009), pp. 1659–1666.
13. Seale, 'Hastening Death in End-of-Life Care', p. 1659.
14. Matthew Parris, 'Why I'm Opposed To Legalising Assisted Suicide', *The
Times*, 1 August 2009.
15. Thomas Szasz, *Fatal Freedom: The Ethics and Politics of Suicide* (Syracuse:
Syracuse University Press, 2002), p. 73.
16. Szasz, *Fatal Freedom*, p. 75.
17. Ludwig Minelli, who runs the Dignitas Clinic in Switzerland and who has
discussed suicide as a 'marvellous possibility', adds these provisos to requests
to die. 'First, you need to become a member of Dignitas; anyone can join
if they pay an annual fee of 80 Swiss francs … When you are ready to die,
you need to send in copies of your medical records, a letter explaining
why things have become intolerable and £1,860. These files are dispatched
to one of Dignitas's affiliated doctors, who considers on the basis of the
medical history whether or not he would be ready to write a prescription
for the fatal dose.' Only then will Minelli give the green light to would-be
suicides. Amelia Gentleman, 'Inside the Dignitas House', *The Guardian*,
18 November 2009.
18. Oregon Revised Statute, Death with Dignity Act, available at: http://
public.health.oregon.gov/ProviderPartnerResources/EvaluationResearch/
DeathwithDignityAct/Pages/ors.aspx (accessed 8 July 2012).
19. Section 6 New Section, Initiative 1000: The Washington Death with Dignity
Act, available at: https://wei.sos.wa.gov/agency/osos/en/Documents/I1000-
Text per cent20for per cent20web.pdf (accessed 9 July 2012).
20. *Report of the Commission on Assisted Dying* (London: Demos, 2011), p. 77.
21. *Report of the Commission on Assisted Dying*, pp. 31, 32.
22. Joel Joffe, 'A New Proposal for Assisted Suicide', *The Guardian*, 28 July 2010.
23. Daniel E. Lee, 'Physician-Assisted Suicide: A Conservative Critique of
Intervention', *The Hastings Center Report*, vol. 33 (2003), p. 3. George
P. Annas and Joan Densberger, 'Competence to Refuse Medical Treatment:
Competence v. Paternalism', *University of Toledo Law Review*, vol. 15 (1983–84),
pp. 561–596, cited here, p. 562.
24. Sheila McLean, *Assisted Dying: Reflections on the Need for Law Reform* (London:
Routledge, 2007), p. 39.
25. John Stuart Mill, *On Liberty*, Chapter IV: Of the Limits to the Authority of
Society over the Individual, p. 62.
26. John Stuart Mill, *Utilitarianism* and *On Liberty*, ed. Mary Warnock (Oxford:
Blackwell, 2003), p. 170. I have myself argued (wrongly, I now think) that,
whatever Mill's purpose, suicide should not be permitted because the freedom to alienate one's liberty is not concomitant with extending the general
liberty. See Kevin Yuill, 'The Right to Die? No, Thanks', *Spiked-online.com*, 19
May 2006, at: www.spiked-online.com/index.php/site/article/207/.

27. A. Ohberg, J. Lonnqvist, S. Sarna, E. Vuori, et al., 'Trends and Availability of Suicide Methods in Finland: Proposals for Restrictive Measures', *The British Journal of Psychiatry*, vol. 166 (January 1995), pp. 35–43. Keith Hawton et al., 'UK Legislation on Analgesic Packs: Before and after Study of Long Term Effect on Poisonings', *British Medical Journal*, vol. 329 (2004), p. 1076.
28. See D. Owens and A. House, 'Fatal and Non-fatal Repetition of Self-harm, Systematic Review', *British Journal of Psychiatry*, vol. 181 (2002), pp. 193–199.

Conclusions

1. Isaiah Berlin, *Four Essays on Liberty* (Oxford: Oxford University Press, 1979), Chapter III, 'Two Concepts of Liberty', pp. 118–173, cited here, pp. 139–140.
2. See Chapter 5.
3. G. K. Chesterton, *Orthodoxy* (London: Unicorn Books, 1939), p. 50.
4. Anderson and Honneth criticise existing autonomy: 'By articulating a conception of autonomy in terms of, more specifically, a theory of mutual recognition, we aim to pinpoint the individualistic bias in liberal accounts and the concomitant underestimation of our dependence on relationships of respect, care, and esteem.' Joel Anderson and Axel Honneth, 'Autonomy, Vulnerability, Recognition and Justice', in John Christman and Joel Anderson (eds), *Autonomy and the Challenges to Liberalism: New Essays* (New York: Cambridge University Press, 2005), pp. 127–149.
5. Cited in Frank Furedi, *On Tolerance:A Defence of Moral Independence* (London: Continuum, 2011), p. 82.
6. I have shown this process of expanding categories in relation to affirmative action in *Richard Nixon and the Rise of Affirmative Action: The Pursuit of Racial Equality in an Era of Limits* (Lanham: Rowman and Littlefield, 2006).

Bibliographic Essay

The difficulty for those wishing to explore the topic of assisted suicide is that there are so many different facets of and approaches to the problem. What follows is very general advice on the scholarship that the author found most useful. It is organized around particular approaches, from the general to the specific.

Before leaping in, there are a few caveats to keep in mind. Is the issue of assisted suicide a political, legal, philosophical, theological or moral problem? The contention made in the preceding pages is that, though it is chiefly a moral and philosophical issue, it is a legal and political question in that a change in the law will have legal and political ramifications (we have discussed this at length in the penultimate chapter). The answer to this question dictates the approach to most books on the subject, making it difficult for the non-expert to jump in before deciding what sort of a problem it is.

It is also useful to understand the issues within the specific contexts within which they occur. Legal and political issues in particular vary considerably between different countries but there are cultural variations that come into play as well. The issue is different in England than it is in the United States and Australia. Even within the United States, a state like Oregon, with its independent streak, differs from what might be termed more conservative states. Different religious influences also affect how the issue plays out in different locales.

Finally, it is worth noting that, while there are a few carefully neutral volumes presenting both sides of the argument, each individual author generally has a perspective on the question of whether or not the law should allow assisted suicides. There is no neutral ground and readers must prepare to have their deepest beliefs and perceptions challenged – no bad thing.

Empirical sources of information

Often dry and containing all the problems usually accompanying writing by committees, the various reports are still essential and can form a useful introduction to the topic. The Oregon Death with Dignity Act (DWDA) Annual Reports contain no justification and express no opinion but are invaluable for detailed empirical information. They are available for free at http://public.health.oregon.gov/ProviderPartnerResources/Evaluation Research/DeathwithDignityAct/Pages/ar-index.aspx. Washington's DWD, passed in 2008, has similar information at www.doh.wa.gov/YouandYourFamily/Illness andDisease/DeathwithDignityAct.aspx.

The *Report of the Commission on Assisted Dying*, though aimed, it appears, exclusively at medical, legal and social work professionals, and despite the fact that it creates rather than resolves confusions, is incredibly useful. It argues for legalization though some of its witnesses and committee members disagreed. It is both a snapshot of the discussion in Britain in 2012 and a record of the

perspectives of various prominent witnesses it called. It is available here: www.
demos.co.uk/publications/thecommissiononassisteddying. Also fairly recently, a
report to the Tasmanian Parliament makes useful reading, particularly in relation
to Antipodean issues connected with assisted suicide. See: www.parliament.tas.
gov.au/ctee/REPORTS/Dying%20with%20Dignity%20Final%20Report.pdf

In May 1994, the New York State Task Force on Life and the Law published an influential 217-page report titled 'When Death Is Sought: Assisted
Suicide and Euthanasia in the Medical Context' (available at: www.health.ny.gov/
regulations/task_force/reports_publications/when_death_is_sought). The report
advised against legalizing assisted suicide because, amongst other things, depression and the particular vulnerability of those who were poor or from a stigmatized
social group.

In the Netherlands, euthanasia has been tolerated since the 1980s and became
legal in 2002. It is difficult to compare euthanasia there with assisted suicide
in Oregon because the two are both regarded as euthanasia in the Netherlands
(though the criteria set out by the 2002 legislation means that all euthanasia
should be after a voluntary and well-considered request by the patient) is only
reported when there is non-compliance to the criteria by the physician, effectively reducing interference with doctors' end-of-life decisions. The empirical
results of the Dutch experiment have been documented, for instance, in Judith
A. C. Rietjens, Paul J. van der Maas, Bregje D. Onwuteaka-Philipsen, Johannes
J. M. van Delden and Agnes van der Heide, 'Two Decades of Research on Euthanasia from the Netherlands. What Have We Learnt and What Questions Remain?',
Journal of Bioethical Enquiry, vol. 6, no. 3, September 2009, pp. 271–283. Those
wishing to research euthanasia and assisted suicide in Europe can usefully begin
with John Griffiths, Heleen Weyers and Maurice Adams, *Euthanasia in Europe*
(Oxford: Hart Publishing, 2008).

There are of course a plethora of websites that provide information about and
opinions on assisted suicide. *Dignity in Dying* in the UK and *Compassion and
Choices* make up the orthodoxy advocating legalized assisted suicide. *Lifenews*
matches the pro-assisted-suicide sites for stories about people who came back
from situations where they wished to die.

Books dealing directly with assisted suicide

Monographs dealing directly with assisted suicide are not as plentiful as one
might imagine. Those older than a couple of decades tend to lump together
euthanasia and assisted suicide. Hugh Trowell's prescient *The Unfinished Debate
on Euthanasia* (London: SCM Press, 1973) is fascinating for its early rehearsal of
some of the arguments we still hear today, including sections on the case for,
the history of suicide and euthanasia, and legal, ethical, medical and psychological aspects of these issues. Some of the best that favour a change in the law are
Sheila McLean's *Assisted Dying: Reflections on the Need for Law Reform* (London:
Routledge, 1997). McLean comes from a laudably Millian or even libertarian perspective at the issue. Margaret Battin's *Ending Life: Ethics and the Way We Die*
(New York: Oxford University Press, 2005) is more a series of essays than a single
book. Many of them are both fascinating and necessary reading. A useful chapter
to start with, outlining the main arguments for and against, is 'Euthanasia and

Assisted Suicide' (pp. 17–46). Mary Warnock and Elisabeth Macdonald, *Easeful Death: Is There a Case for Assisted Dying?* (Oxford: Oxford University Press, 2008) is thoughtful and fairly well-balanced, though the authors certainly favour legalization. Anglican cleric Paul Badham has produced a very interesting Christian case for legalization in *Is There a Christian Case for Assisted Dying?* (London: SPCK Publishing, 2010).

Perhaps the best of those opposed to legalizing assisted suicide to come out relatively recently is federal judge Neil M. Gorsuch's *The Future of Assisted Suicide and Euthanasia* (Princeton: Princeton University Press, 2006). Despite the legal focus, Gorsuch has much to say about ethics and the book is tightly argued. The discussion goes beneath the surface and he usefully recounts the history of assisted suicide. Gorsuch's emphasis is on intention, and he re-emphasizes the distinction between taking a life and letting someone die. Whereas most today conflate the workings of nature with human causation, Gorsuch reminds us of the key question of moral responsibility for one's actions. Margaret Somerville's *Death Talk: The Case against Euthanasia and Assisted Suicide* (Montreal: McGill-Queens University Press, 2001). Somerville's thoughtful contribution notes the complexity of the issue of assisted suicide. Assisted suicide, she notes, is a technical solution to a spiritual crisis. Arthur J. Dyck, in *Life's Worth: The Case Against Assisted Suicide* (Cambridge, MA: Center for Bioethics and Human Dignity, 2002), discusses the ethical reasons for keeping the law as it stands and usefully critiques the case for legalization. Nigel Biggar, *Aiming to Kill: The Ethics of Suicide and Euthanasia* (London: Darton, Longman and Todd Ltd., 2004), does not so much oppose assisted suicide per se as argue against legal arrangements. Though it is written from a religious perspective, nonbelievers will find this volume useful. Whereas the above are academic volumes, there are also some general cases against by columnists and pundits which are equally valuable, though many more that centre around the author's own experience with a dying relative but have little to say on the broader issues. George Pitcher's *A Time to Live: The Case against Euthanasia and Assisted Suicide* (London: Monarch Books, 2010) is sharply observed and as useful for the secular reader (Pitcher is an Anglican cleric) as for the religious thinkers.

Edited collections of essays

The many for-and-against collections of essays are often a first port of call and usually collate valuable material from the past few decades. Perhaps most valuable is Robert F. Weir's 1986 volume, *Ethical Issues in Death and Dying* (New York: Columbia University Press, 1986), which has a section on euthanasia and one on suicide and includes chapters by James Rachels, Peter Singer, Tristram Engelhardt, Edwin Sheidman, Thomas Szasz and Margaret Battin. Battin edited, with David J. Mayo, *Suicide: The Philosophical Issues* (New York: St Martin's Press, 1980), an often insightful and fascinating discussion at once illuminating the issue and providing a helpful demonstration of how the issue has changed in the forty or so years after it moved into the mainstream.

More specific to the issue of assisted suicide, Michael M. Uhlmann's *Last Rights? Assisted Suicide and Euthanasia Debated* (Washington, DC: Ethics and Public Policy Center, 1998) is a hugely useful edited collection of material relevant to the issue of assisted suicide, containing chapters from Alfred Alvarez and Jack Kevorkian and Pope John Paul II's *Gospel of Life*. In an interesting volume published in 1998, Gerald Dworkin and R. G. Frey argue in favour of legalization whereas Sissela Bok argues against in *Euthanasia and Physician Assisted Suicide: For and Against* (Cambridge: Cambridge University Press). However, rather than a dialogue between philosophers, this books is more of a collection of essays that intersect only occasionally. John Morgan's edited collection, *An Easeful Death? Perspectives on Death, Dying and Euthanasia* (Sydney: Federation Press, 1996) also contains valuable materials. Battin also co-edited, with Rosamond Rhodes and Anita Silvers, *Physician-assisted Suicide: Expanding the Debate* (London: Routledge, 1998), a useful volume that, though most of the chapters are supportive of legalization, asks some excellent questions. Contributions by Leslie Pickering Francis, Battin herself, and Frances S. Kamm stand out and it has appendices containing Supreme Court decisions relating to assisted suicide as well as the famous 'Philosophers' Brief' (discussed below). John Keown (ed.), *Euthanasia Examined: Ethical Clinical and Legal Perspectives* (Cambridge: Cambridge University Press, 1995) is amongst the best volumes and includes a useful (if somewhat heated!) exchange between John Harris and John Finnis. Germain Grisez and Joseph M. Boyle's *Life and Death with Liberty and Justice: A Contribution to the Euthanasia Debate* (London: University of Notre Dame Press, 1979) is an early contribution to a still-emerging debate, perhaps most useful as a historical record of the debate.

Some very valuable books touch upon assisted suicide as part of another question, whether it be death, suicide, law or medical ethics. Medical ethics figures in Jonathan Glover's *Causing Death and Saving Lives: The Moral Problems of Abortion, Infanticide, Suicide, Euthanasia, Capital Punishment, War and Other Life-or-Death Choices* (London: Penguin, 1990) which gives a very well-written, even-handed and careful account of the issue. Peter Singer, who published the hugely influential *Animal Liberation* in 1975, published a book supporting assisted suicide in 1995. *Rethinking Life and Death: The Collapse of our Traditional Ethics* (Oxford: Oxford University Press, 1995) argued that variable value should be placed on human life. The book is very useful for showing the logical ends of assisted suicide.

There is a rich seam of writing on assisted suicide within the relatively recent discipline of bioethics. An interesting blend of medical and philosophical issues, the whole discipline owes its existence in part to the tendency to see what in the past were regarded as philosophical issues as, at bottom, medical. Bioethics came into being in the 1970s. Daniel Callahan, a medical doctor, has written some of the most interesting tracts, borne of long experience at deathbed scenes. Like most others in his profession, he opposes assisted suicide but was also a prime mover in the limits-of-technology discussion referred to in Chapter 3. An excellent place to start is *The Troubled Dream of Life: In Search of a Peaceful Death* (Washington, DC: Georgetown University Press, 1993), where he considers some of the more troublesome aspects of death, including assisted dying.

Ezekiel Emanuel's *The Ends of Human Life: Medical Ethics in a Liberal Polity* (Cambridge, MA: Harvard University Press) is also a clearly written discourse on medical ethics in general but it bears heavily upon the discussion of assisted suicide. Emanuel, almost uniquely in the literature, notes that it is not technological change but the transformation of public values in the past 40 years that provokes today's discussion on assisted suicide. Ian Thompson included a sharply observed chapter entitled 'Is There a Right to Die?', in Ian Thompson (ed.), *Dilemmas of*

Dying: A Study in the Ethics of Terminal Care (Edinburgh: Edinburgh University Press, 1979). He notes that because criminal sanctions have been removed from the act of suicide this does not imply that a would-be suicide is entitled to expect assistance (p. 83).

Other useful tracts written from a bioethical perspective include those by Margaret Pabst Battin. She has written on suicide and assisted suicide for many years and her volumes are constantly challenging and clearly written. To her credit, she addresses every argument against legalization and constantly updates her own arguments. Besides the volume mentioned above, *The Least Worst Death: Essays in Bioethics at the End of Life* (New York: Oxford University Press, 1994) is a collection of carefully considered essays, well worth reading.

Leading bioethical journals such as the *Journal of Medical Ethics*, *Bioethics* and particularly *The Hastings Center Report* often discuss assisted suicide and related issues. Some medical journals such as the *New England Journal of Medicine* and the *British Medical Journal* often contain brief but useful articles on assisted suicide. Many of the authors mentioned above argue their cases in these journals. Providing insightful and challenging arguments against legalization are Bonnie Steinbock's 'The Case for Physician Assisted Suicide: Not Yet Proven', *Journal of Medical Ethics*, vol. 31 (2005), pp. 235–241; John P. Safranek, 'Autonomy and Assisted Suicide: The Execution of Freedom', *Hastings Center Report*, vol. 28, no. 4 (1998): pp. 32–36. Useful arguments in favour of legalization include Ray Tallis, 'Medical Ethics in the Real Mess in the Real World', *Medico-Legal Journal*, vol. 76 Part 3 (2008), pp. 95–112; Iain Brassington, 'Five Words for Assisted Dying', *Law and Philosophy*, vol. 27, no. 5 (2008), pp. 415–444, and 'Killing People: What Kant Could Have Said about Suicide and Euthanasia but Didn't', *Journal of Medical Ethics*, vol. 32, no. 10 (2006), pp. 571–574; and Daniel E. Lee, 'Physician-assisted Suicide: A Conservative Critique of Intervention', *The Hastings Center Report*, vol. 33, no. 1 (Jan–Feb., 2003), pp. 17–19. A European view in relation to euthanasia and palliative care (and, like most palliative care specialists, opposed to legalization) is expressed in Lars Johan Materstvedt et al., 'Euthanasia and Physician-assisted Suicide: A View from an EAPC Ethics Task Force', *Palliative Medicine*, vol. 17 (2003), pp. 97–101.

Bioethics is by no means uncontested and it is worth looking at critical perspectives. Jonathan Baron published *Against Bioethics* (Boston, MA: MIT Press, 2006), though its title is perhaps more provocative than an apt description of its contents. He seeks to change the basis of rather than destroy bioethics. See also David J. Rothman, *Strangers at the Bedside: A History of How Law and Bioethics Transformed Medical Decision Making* (New York: Basic Books, 1991), a critical history of bioethics, and Tod Chambers' *The Fiction of Bioethics: Cases of Literary Texts* (London: Routledge, 1999). Wesley J. Smith's *Culture of Death: The Assault on Medical Ethics in America* (San Francisco: Encounter Books, 2000) is an attack on the control bioethicists have over the medical profession.

Some books and articles deal specifically with the law. Many more discussions in legal journals and amongst legal scholars discuss general principles. Glanville Williams and Yale Kamisar rehearsed many of the discussions heard today over 50 years ago. Williams was a Welsh legal scholar who fired the first salvo in the modern discussion about what was then called voluntary euthanasia with *The Sanctity of Life and the Criminal Law* (London: Faber and Faber, 1958). There, he noted that the 'prohibition imposed by a religious belief should not be applied by law to those who do not share the belief'. Kamisar, a liberal legal scholar credited with authoring the *Miranda* laws in the United States in the 1960s, argued directly against Williams in an oft-cited article, 'Some Non-religious Views against Proposed "Mercy Killing" Legislation', *Minnesota Law Review*, vol. 42 (1958), pp. 966–1004: 'Will we not sweep up, in the process, some who are not really tired of life, but think others are tired of them; some who do not really want to die, but who feel they should not live on, because to do so when there looms the legal alternative of euthanasia is to do a selfish or a cowardly act?' (p. 990). Penney Lewis, in *Assisted Dying and Legal Change* (Oxford: Oxford University Press, 2007), provides an unambiguously legal perspective, emphasizing the specificity of legal changes to existing assisted-suicide laws and arguing against the imposition of universal ethical frameworks on the issue.

In favour of a change in the law but one of the most valuable books this author came across is legal scholar Ronald Dworkin's *Life's Dominion: An Argument about Abortion and Euthanasia* (London: Harper Collins, 1995, ©1993). Dworkin also wrote the famous 'Philosopher's Brief' in which six prominent philosophers supported legalization of assisted suicide, writing a friend-of-the-court brief in the case *State of Washington et al.* v. *Glucksberg et al.* and *Vacco et al.* v. *Quill et al.* (1997) and published in the *New York Review of Books*. Dworkin's book considers both abortion and assisted suicide. With crystal clear prose, he shows that we place intrinsic value upon both human life and potential human life and delineates between critical and experiential interests. He draws the parallel between abortion and assisted suicide: '... if someone thinks that it is morally permissible to terminate a pregnancy when the fetus is seriously abnormal ... then he is also likely to think that it is preferable to end the life of a desperately suffering patient who wants to die or a patient who is in a persistent vegetative state.'

History

There is somewhat of a dearth of histories of the assisted-suicide movement. The standout book is Ian Dowbiggin, *A Merciful End: The Euthanasia Movement in Modern America* (Oxford: Oxford University Press, 2003). Dowbiggin also published a broader history of euthanasia advocates throughout history going back to antiquity in *A Concise History of Euthanasia: Life, Death, God, and Medicine* (Lanham: Rowman and Littlefield, 2005). Ezekiel J. Emanuel wrote a very good introduction to the history of the issue: 'The History of Euthanasia Debates in the United States and Britain', *Annals of Internal Medicine*, vol. 12, no. 10 (1994), pp. 793–802. Shai J. Lavi has some fascinating historical material in his book, *The Modern Art of Dying: A History of Euthanasia in the United States* (Princeton: Princeton University Press, 2007). N. D. A. Kemp provides a comprehensive history of the British Voluntary Euthanasia Movement in *Merciful Release: The History of the British Euthanasia Movement* (Manchester: Manchester University Press, 2002). This book has emphasized the centrality of the issue of suicide within the assisted suicide/assisted dying movements.

Suicide

There is a huge amount of material written from a number of different disciplinary standpoints; it would be difficult if not impossible to cover all the material. Plus, of course, the discourse on suicide must reflect other debates, such as those on autonomy and moral responsibility.

Those who wish to explore this captivating and disturbing subject have 25 centuries of writings to choose from. For a brief but insightful and fairly comprehensive introduction, see Georgia Noon's 'On Suicide', *Journal of the History of Ideas*, vol. 39, no. 3 (Jul–Sep., 1978), pp. 371–386. In terms of the history of suicide, readers will profit from perusing George Minois, *The History of Suicide: Voluntary Death in Western Culture* (London: Johns Hopkins University Press, 1999); S. E. Sprott, *The English Debate on Suicide: From Donne to Hume* (La Salle: Open Court Publishing, 1961), which is especially good on the many precedents set before David Hume's classic essay on suicide (which should not be missed itself), and Michael McDonald, 'The Medicalization of Suicide in England: Laymen, Physicians, and Cultural Change, 1500–1870', *The Milbank Quarterly*, vol. 67, Supplement 1. Baruch A. Brody, (ed.), *Suicide and Euthanasia: Historical and Contemporary Themes* (Dordecht: Kluwer, 2010, ©1989) contains some useful discussions, especially Darrel W. Amundsen, 'Suicide and Early Christian Values', pp. 77–154.

As a reader unfamiliar with many of the autonomy/moral responsibility discussions, I benefited from reading Robert S. Taylor, 'Kantian Personal Autonomy', *Political Theory*, vol. 33, no. 5 (Oct. 2005), pp. 602–628. For Kant's very interesting discussion on suicide, see Michael J. Seidler, 'Kant and the Stoics on Suicide', *Journal of the History of Ideas*, vol. 44, no. 3 (July–Sep., 1983), pp. 429–453. For an interesting introduction to discussions about moral autonomy and moral responsibility, see Gerald Dworkin, *The Theory and Practice of Autonomy* (Cambridge: Cambridge University Press, 1988), and Ben Colburn's recent publication, *Autonomy and Liberalism* (London: Routledge, 2010). Charles Foster's attack on the use of autonomy, particularly in relation to medical ethics, is germane to the assisted-suicide discussion. See *Choosing Life, Choosing Death: The Tyranny of Autonomy in Medical Ethics and Law* (Oxford: Hart Publishing, 2009). Similarly, Onora O'Neill's well observed *Autonomy and Trust in Bioethics* (Cambridge: Cambridge University Press, 2002) indicates that trust has been denigrated and autonomy inappropriately privileged. As she notes, the prevailing view of autonomy as independence has less to do with Kant and Mill and reflects 20th-century conceptions. Allen W. Wood, in *Kant's Ethical Thought* (Cambridge: Cambridge University Press, 1999), defends Kant against modern attacks. Iain Brassington's aforementioned 'Killing People' contains some useful criticisms of Kant in relation to suicide.

Other valuable readings on suicide must include Emile Durkheim's *Le Suicide: A Study in Sociology* (London: Routledge and Kegan Paul, 1952), a pioneering sociological account valuable both in its analysis and as a snapshot of thinking about suicide at the turn of the last century. Sidney Hook, 'The Ethics of Suicide', *International Journal of Ethics*, vol. 37, no. 2 (Jan. 1927), pp. 173–188, is similarly both insightful and a demonstration of what has and has not changed in thinking about suicide over the past 85 years. Edwin Sheidman's hugely useful edited collection, *Essays in Self-destruction* (New York: Science House, Inc., 1967), was published on the cusp of change in thinking about suicide and contains imaginative and experimental approaches to the problem. Battin and Mayo's *Suicide: The Philosophical Issues*, mentioned above, reflects the return of suicide from the medical and sociological realms into philosophic consideration. It contains very useful material, particularly the essays by Peter Y. Windt and Robert F. Martin, and also indicates how the issue has evolved since it was written.

Most insightful for its unique perspective on suicide is Thomas S. Szasz's *Fatal Freedom: The Ethics and Politics of Suicide* (Syracuse: Syracuse University Press, 1999). In a characteristically brilliant but flawed book, Szasz argues against medicalization and in favour of personal responsibility for one's actions. See also Battin and Ryan Spellecy's reply to some (certainly not all) of Szasz's points in 'What Kind of Freedom? Szasz's Misleading Perception of Physician-assisted Suicide', in Jeffrey A. Schaler (ed.), *Szasz Under Fire: The Psychiatric Abolitionist Faces His Critics* (New York: Open Court, 2004), pp. 277–290.

Other valuable books

Less easy to categorize but extremely valuable for anyone wanting to understand the issue of assisted suicide and amongst the most influential for this book, some of the following books may appear peripheral to the main topic but it would be a mistake to overlook them. Martha Nussbaum's 'Compassion: The Basic Social Emotion', *Social Philosophy and Policy*, vol. 13, no. 1 (Dec. 1996), pp. 27–58, was very important for analysing what compassion, so often a reason given for legalizing assisted suicide, comprises.

An argument in this book is that part of the inclination towards reconsidering suicide that has taken place since the 1970s expressed a crisis in meaning. Those wishing to wade into such deep waters should read Paul Tillich's *Courage to Be* (New Haven Yale University Press, 1952). Published by a noted Christian existentialist, this 'theologian's theologian' might appear tangential to an atheistic perspective but it is not. His discussion of the conception of dread, continuing from Kierkegaard, Nietzsche and Heidegger, and his tackling meaninglessness with his emphasis on existence itself as a creative enterprise, is vital. Leaving the best to last, the insights provided by Hannah Arendt have been at the core of this study. Her theory of action – scattered across several publications – is amongst several fascinating and inspirational observations, of central importance to this book. Written just after Tillich's book was published, Arendt discussed what it means to be human in *The Human Condition* (London: University of Chicago Press, ©1958). In delineating between public and private spheres, between labour, work and action, she provides a framework for understanding the meaning of humanity at a time when it is under heavy questioning.

Index

CPSIA information can be obtained
at www.ICGtesting.com
Printed in the USA
FFOW02n0229210415
12809FF

9 781137 487469